D1631922

http://www.ikbsesk.com
Maisha Ec.

http://www.ikbsta.mu

PROBLEMS AND POLICIES IN SMALL ECONOMIES

Problems and Policies in Small Economies

Edited by B. Jalan

CROOM HELM
London & Canberra

ST. MARTIN'S PRESS
New York

© 1982 Commonwealth Secretariat
Croom Helm Ltd, 2-10 St John's Road, London SW11

British Library Cataloguing in Publication Data

Problems and policies in small economies.
   1. States, Small   2. Economic policy - Congresses
   I. Jalan, B.
   338.9   HD82

   ISBN 0-7099-1410-5

First published in the United States of America in 1982
All rights reserved. For information write:
St. Martin's Press, Inc., 175 Fifth Avenue, New York, N.Y. 10010

Library of Congress Cataloging in Publication Data
Main entry under title:

Problems and policies in small economies.

   1. States, Small—Economic conditions—Addresses,
essays, lectures. I. Jalan, Bimal.
HC59.P6735   1982   338.9   81-21291   AACR2
ISBN 0-312-64741-7

Printed and bound in Great Britain by
Biddles Ltd, Guildford and King's Lynn

Contents

Foreword

The papers contained in this volume were prepared for a conference on problems and policies in small economies, held at Marlborough House in June, 1981. The conference was attended by 21 distinguished development economists representing a mix of geographical, professional and occupational experience, and by staff members of the Secretariat.

The Commonwealth has a special interest in the issues of economic development in small states. A large number of its members are small in geographical area, population and income, and assisting them to overcome some of the problems associated with small size has been a major focus of the technical assistance activities of the Secretariat. However, as the programme of assistance to small member countries has grown, and as the experience in dealing with their special problems has increased, the Secretariat has also become conscious of the need to know more about the economic development processes in small countries. Relatively little economic research has been done on the problems of small economies, and there is also lack of adequate statistical information and sustained empirical work on the past development experience. Our purpose in convening a conference of development economists was to provide an opportunity for discussion at the professional level of issues that are important for the future development of these economies. It was our hope that such a discussion would also increase professional interest in the special problems of small economies and lead to the evolution of analytical tools of practical use to policy-makers.

The papers printed here cover many issues; they range from papers on conceptual and theoretical issues to issues of practical interest and application. Naturally they do not attempt to cover the field. I hope that these papers will be of interest to all those who are concerned with the economic problems and policies in small economies. They represent, of course, the personal views of the authors, and not necessarily those of the Secretariat or Commonwealth Governments.

I express my deep appreciation to the participants at the Marlborough House conference, and to the authors who so readily agreed to prepare the papers for this conference.

Shridath S. Ramphal
Commonwealth Secretary-General

Introduction

Bimal Jalan*

Of 133 developing countries for which data are available, 78 countries have populations of below five million and as many as 49 countries have populations of less than a million. Given the large number of relatively small countries, it is not surprising that, in recent years, a certain amount of attention has been focused on the special problems of these countries.[1] In the United Nations as well as in the Commonwealth, there are now programmes for providing special assistance to small states, islands, land-locked and the least developed countries. Some of these categories overlap. For example, most islands are small with an average population of a little over one million (excluding Indonesia and the Philippines). Most land-locked countries are also least developed, and most of the least developed countries (included in the UN list of such countries) are either small or land-locked or both. A striking common characteristic among these groups of countries which are believed to be 'disadvantaged' is that they are generally small. Interestingly, however, the converse is not true. While most disadvantaged countries tend to be small, there is a fairly impressive number of small countries which seem to do very well. The average per capita income of 78 countries with populations of less than five million is considerably higher than the average per capita income of all developing countries taken together ($1,593 per capita and $464 per capita respectively).[2] A number of these countries have also shown high growth rates and high levels of industrialisation. Singapore and Hong Kong are outstanding examples of small countries that have achieved remarkable economic success.

There has been a certain amount of academic activity in studying the problems and prospects of small states. Thus, as early as 1957, the International Economic Association convened a conference of economists to consider the economic consequences of the size of nations.[3] This conference was, however, mainly

---

*A number of colleagues have given me invaluable support at various stages of the research project on small economies. They are too numerous to name individually; however, I would like specifically to thank Ian Thomas, Jackson Karunasekera and Rosemary Minto for their help in editing this volume.

concerned with the issue of size and efficiency irrespective of the levels of income of different countries; in particular, it focused on the problems of small European economies which were already at an advanced stage of development. The number of independent developing countries at that time was relatively small and the issue of size in relation to development received only scant attention.

A large number of small developing countries, particularly in the Caribbean and the South Pacific, became independent in the late 1950s and 1960s, and it soon became evident that the problems of these small developing countries, and particularly their dependent relationships with the erstwhile metropolitan powers, deserved specific consideration. In 1972, another important conference was convened, in Barbados, by the Institute of Development Studies of the University of Sussex.[4] The Barbados conference was devoted to the consideration of development issues, and its main focus was on the implications of economic dependence on the future growth prospects of small Caribbean states. More recently, in 1979, the Development Studies Centre of the Australian National University convened a conference of academics and representatives of South Pacific countries to consider issues of economic development in the island states of the Pacific and Indian Oceans.[5] The scope of this conference was much wider than previous conferences and considerable attention was given to demographic, administrative, political and social issues.

In addition to the papers presented at these conferences, there have been a number of other studies on the problems of small states. Among earlier studies, mention may be made of the work of William Demas (1965) on Caribbean economies. Demas paid some attention to the development of what he called a 'relevant analytical framework', without which a rational choice in the field of economic policy could not be made. An important point made by Demas was that the economic structure of small states was different from that of large countries, and that new analytical tools and concepts were necessary to consider their economic problems. The study by Demas was followed by a volume of papers, published by the Institute of Commonwealth Studies in the University of London, on small territories within the Commonwealth. These papers dealt with the political, economic, administrative and sociological aspects of dependent and independent small countries, and their main preoccupation was the question of the viability of small countries as independent decision-making units.[6] More recently, World Development (1980) devoted a special issue to analysing the characteristics and special problems of island states.

As a result of these and other studies, a body of literature on the problems and issues of small economies is now available. These studies have helped to enhance our understanding of the structural characteristics of small countries and also the problems that they face in promoting their economic development. There are, however, some important gaps. The 'relevant analytical framework', to which Demas referred, is still lacking, and we do not have a plausible or a consistent theory of 'size' as an independent factor in development. Is there a critical minimum economic size of nations?

Is smallness a constraint or a positive factor in development? How is a small state to be differentiated from a large state? Does smallness refer to land, population, market size, or levels of development? These and many other questions remain unanswered.

Another important gap is the lack of adequate decision-making tools for application in small economies. For example, much of the planning literature is concerned with problems of closed multi-sector economies rather than the open, and often one commodity, economies of small states. The trade policy literature has centred around the export promotion/import substitution debate in large economies where these alternative opportunities are in fact available. The literature on project evaluation and social cost-benefit analysis is silent on the special problems of and the applicability of various methods of social cost-benefit analysis in small countries. Finally, while there has been considerable discussion of the structural characteristics of small states and the problems they face, there has been little or no discussion of the policies that these countries should adopt for managing their affairs in areas such as industrial development, exports, foreign investment, transport, tourism, etc.

The papers contained in this volume are an attempt to start a debate on some of the issues that have not been adequately considered in the literature. The focus is on the analytical and policy issues. These papers were prepared for discussion at a conference of development economists, and the constraints of time necessarily limited the scope of the agenda.[7] Sociological, demographic, administrative and political issues were not specifically considered, not because they were considered less important but because economists qua economists perhaps have little to say on political, administrative or sociological issues.

The following is a brief account of the main issues raised in the papers, with some selective references to the conference discussions. It is not a comprehensive account of the discussions, and the participants at the conference are in no way, individually or collectively, responsible for the views expressed here.

EFFECTS OF SIZE ON DEVELOPMENT

An important issue which is at the heart of the case for special consideration of the problems and policies in small countries is whether there are any identifiable characteristics or consequences that are associated with size per se. Most of the economic discussion of the consequences of size has been at the level of the firm and not of the nation, although implicitly it has been assumed that small size is likely to constitute a disadvantage. Thus, in his contribution to the International Economic Association conference, Kuznets argued "small countries are under a greater handicap than large in the task of economic growth"[8]. Intuitively, the· assertion seems valid, but there is no systematic theory which can explain why size should have a negative effect on economic growth.

In their paper, Bhaduri et al., provide a theoretical model

which attempts to examine the constraints imposed by small size on the potential for growth of labour productivity in manufacturing. On the basis of certain simplifying assumptions, they demonstrate that even with moderate increasing returns to scale, a small size of population or employment may act as the fundamental bottleneck in sustaining growth in labour productivity in a small country. This limitation imposes a double disadvantage: a small country may not be able to sustain an international competitive position, and its domestic market is unlikely to grow rapidly due to a continuous adverse terms of trade effect. Under these circumstances, it is likely that only sectors, like services, that are not generally subject to increasing returns can provide a long-term escape route for small economies which are not very favourably placed in terms of natural resources or land:man ratios.

There was an interesting discussion at the conference on whether or not economies of scale in the manufacturing sector, taken as a whole, were significant. It was pointed out that we do not know enough about dynamic economies of scale, but that it was likely that the importance of this factor in relation to the manufacturing sector as a whole was exaggerated. Once the assumption of a closed economy was relaxed, opportunities for productivity growth in particular lines of manufacturing, even for small countries, were substantial. It was also not necessary to assume that small countries necessarily had small plants. Empirical evidence relating to the progress achieved by countries like Hong Kong and Singapore showed that even small countries could achieve substantial economies of scale and growth in productivity.

In particular areas, however, small countries are likely to suffer from disadvantages in developing an indigenous manufacturing capacity, e.g. in capital-intensive manufacturing, in the development of technology, and in the marketing of products abroad. The paper by Lall and Ghosh examines the disadvantages arising out of a limited ability to generate technology and to market manufactured products. They point out that the growth of indigenous technological capability can be seriously hampered because of the lack of a domestic industrial and marketing base which can absorb and utilise new technology efficiently. The absorption of technology typically requires a period of learning and of making mistakes, of innovating and adapting technology to indigenous requirements. Small economies, without an advantage of location or established historical links with foreign enterprises, may find themselves in the difficult situation where they cannot enter world markets because they do not have the experience, and they cannot acquire the experience because they are too small to have import substitution activities. Similarly, any new entrant in the world market is likely to face severe handicaps arising out of strong product differentiation, brand-name preferences, high cost of advertising, and high cost of after-sales service facilities. These handicaps can become formidable for smaller economies which have little past experience, and which are unable to recover some of these costs from sales in the domestic market.

Small economies are also likely to face diseconomies of scale in

4

developing an indigenous banking sector. Fry refers to the strong negative correlation between economic size and dominance of foreign banks in a sample of eleven small economies studied by him. This reflects the high costs of banking and financial intermediation. While a branch of a foreign bank, which can share head office services, may be financially viable, a new domestic bank is unlikely to remain solvent without direct government subsidies. Small size also has the effect of restricting competition in banking, and the range of services provided by banks is likely to be narrower than that available in larger countries. Helleiner refers to certain scale diseconomies in financial management. He points out that the unit costs of information and management systems are likely to be high. In view of the small volume of operations, small economies are likely to face higher charges for exchange cover, earn lower returns on their reserves, and pay more for their borrowings.

So much for the economies of scale. As pointed out by Lloyd and Sundrum, an important characteristic of small populations is just that, i.e. human resources and skills are likely to be scarce. A small population and a small labour force mean that there is a small pool of human potential skills, and facilities for the development of human resources may be highly limited compared with larger developing countries. An example of this is the absence of higher education facilities in many small countries. Irrespective of size, government and economic administration require a certain minimum number of skilled personnel. The small size of population, and the alternative demands for skilled manpower, may constitute an important constraint on the development potential.

Lloyd and Sundrum also deal with the consequences of what they have referred to as the 'concentration phenomenon' on the growth prospects of small economies. An important characteristic of small countries is the concentration of national output in a few industries and a few commodities. Concentration of output means that there is less averaging or pooling of different price trends for individual staple export commodities, and there is likely to be a greater variation over time in the growth rates of small countries.[9] Similarly, when relative prices change permanently, the limited production possibilities of small countries reduce the ability of the economy to adjust to shocks which have reduced the profitability of leading sectors. This characteristic may explain why small economies are generally less able to adjust to external shocks than larger economies.

An important consequence of small size is the vulnerability of smaller economies to fluctuations in commodity trade and capital inflows. As pointed out by Helleiner, the costs of instability can be quite high. These may include costs associated with social disruption caused by wide fluctucations in the distribution of income or with distortions in investment patterns due to greater uncertainty, and costs of 'stop-go' economic and investment policies. The major burden of the reduction in incomes, when terms of trade deteriorate or export markets decline, is likely to fall on the lower income groups, which are most vulnerable to fluctuations in the level of economic activity.[10] While small economies are more exposed and subject to greater fluctuations, their ability to tackle the problems created by external instability is less.

This is an impressive catalogue of disadvantages. Are there any compensating advantages which might explain why several small countries have done so well, and why levels of per capita income in small countries are higher on average than in larger countries? Blazic-Metzner and Hughes have referred to the advantage that a small economy may have in adopting what they call 'appropriate policies'. They point out that small economies are likely to be more open, more competitive, and more flexible in their responses to changing external environment. Small countries are also likely to show greater socio-cultural homogeneity, and a more equitable distribution of income which reduces the potential for social conflicts.

There was some discussion of whether the characteristics of 'openness' had a positive influence on growth. It was likely that given a favourable combination of other factors, e.g. location and skills, openness of the economy could have a substantial positive effect on growth performance. However, openness per se was seldom a sufficient condition for growth, as was borne out by the experience of many backward areas in advanced countries. It was also important to recognise that considerations of external economic policy could not be divorced from internal political and social structures.

THE DEFINITION OF SMALL ECONOMIES

A number of papers deal with this issue. As pointed out in a paper contributed by me, because of the lack of a uniform definition, most writers on small economies have been compelled to use arbitrary cut-off points in terms of population to distinguish small from large countries. The use of different definitions has created difficulties in testing the validity of propositions regarding the structure and processes of development in these economies, and the conclusions of different writers on some important questions (e.g. the effects of size on the level of industrialisation) seem to be ambiguous. The paper proposes a simple classification of countries by size, based on a composite index of population, area and total GNP (as proxy for capital stock). The underlying hypothesis is that differences in economic structure and economic performance among developing countries due to the size factor are likely to be due to differences in the 'resource base' of countries.

However, Lloyd and Sundrum have questioned the validity of combining separate indices of size on the ground that there is no logical basis for assigning weights to different factors. They point out that, with few exceptions, small economies chosen on the basis of the combined index are countries with populations of less than five million as there is a high correlation between population and the other measures of size. They, therefore, suggest that, from a statistical point of view, it may be sufficient to classify countries by population size alone and that a dividing line of five million

6

population may be reasonable for distinguishing between small and other countries. Bhaduri et al., while avoiding a statistical definition of smallness, put forward the hypothesis that there is a critical minimum size of economies in terms of employment (or population) and investment (or income level) below which it is not possible to maintain a positive rate of growth in labour productivity in manufacturing. The notion of the critical minimum size could be used to identify small countries. Lall and Ghosh reject surface area as a significant factor in classification, and suggest that it may be more meaningful to rely on population size and incomes (or together, simply GNP) for defining small economies.

These alternative approaches were discussed at the conference, and several conclusions seemed to command broad agreement. First, for a systematic examination of the problems and policies in small economies, it was necessary to define the concept of smallness in a way which was likely to command general acceptance. In view of the difficulties involved in adopting a sharp and unique definition of small countries, it was also necessary to rely on a rough classification of countries by size. The data provided in the papers broadly supported the use of a working definition of five million population for studying the problems of small countries. Second, within the group of small economies defined in this manner, there was a need to distinguish between very small or 'micro-states' and other small economies. The problems of the micro-states, with very small populations and other resources, were likely to be different and required separate consideration. Third, it was emphasised that generalisations regarding the problems and potential of small economies as a group should be avoided as far as possible because differences among countries within the group could sometimes be as marked as intra-group differences. Fourth, the relative size of countries was likely to affect the development options available to them; however, it should be clearly recognised that, in determining the success or otherwise of development efforts, factors other than size were likely to be significant. It was also pointed out that, in some regions, the inter-linkages between different countries within the region were so important that problems of individual countries could not be studied without reference to the economy of the whole region.

GROWTH EXPERIENCE AND SECTORAL ISSUES

An interesting empirical question is whether the characteristics associated with smallness have in fact affected the growth experience of small economies in the past. The paper by Blazic-Metzner and Hughes provides some interesting data on this question. Their data show that during the period 1965-78, countries with populations of more than five million grew faster as a group than did those with populations of five million or less. However, the very small countries (those with populations of less than one million) experienced a higher rate of growth. The growth experience of small and large countries in different regions has also been mixed.

In South Europe and East Asia throughout the sixties and seventies, and in the Middle East and North Africa during 1965-73, small countries grew more rapidly than large countries. On the other hand, in the Caribbean in both periods and in Africa, south of the Sahara, during 1965-73, they grew more slowly than the large countries. The unavailability of data for a number of small countries may have introduced a bias in the results, but there is little evidence that large countries tend to perform better than small countries or that size is an important factor in explaining differential growth performance among countries. In explaining growth performance, Blazic-Metzner and Hughes have given primary importance to human resource development, 'the appropriateness of policy framework' and its administration, rather than to the size of the economy or its resource endowment.

Thomas examines the industrialisation experience of small economies. The data presented by him show striking differences in industrial experience. These differences are as wide as those among larger developing countries, and generalisations regarding prospects for industrialisation in the small economies as a group, would seem to be unwarranted. In particular, the Chenery-type statistical analysis, linking the proportion of GDP coming from the manufacturing sector to particular levels of per capita income and relative sizes of the economy, was subject to considerable limitations. Interestingly, however, the data support the hypothesis advanced by Lloyd and Sundrum regarding the importance of the concentration phenomenon in the production structures of small countries. The degree of concentration by product groups is indeed higher in small countries than in large countries, and the smallness of the market seems to be an important determinant of the composition of output rather than its rate of growth. The paper by Thomas also refers to the results of regression analysis on the relationship between manufacturing output and a number of explanatory variables, e.g. size, location, skills, long-term capital inflows and direct foreign investment. Because of non-availability of direct information on many of these variables and other methodological limitations, these results are not conclusive and point to the need for further research.[11]

On agriculture, Persaud makes a distinction between economies of scale at the level of the farm and at the level of the sector as a whole. Small economies do not necessarily have smaller farms. Where the land:labour ratio is low, land could be farmed more intensively. At the sector level, however, there is substantial scope for scale economies. In the course of development, especially where the land:labour ratio is low, the existing rigidities in the farm size structure, and in particular in plantation agriculture, could prevent transformation of this sector in line with changing domestic and international conditions. The consequence is that adjustment to appropriate high value crops could be retarded, and a small economy could be stuck with the export of low value crops which have poor demand prospects while food imports increase steeply. In the Commonwealth Caribbean, for example, while traditional exports of sugar and bananas are not expanding, imports of food are increasing and have become a substantial drain on foreign exchange resources. Not only has the agricultural sector become less significant as a net contributor to foreign earnings, there has also been a decline in the capacity of agriculture to absorb labour. Persaud points out that some of the structural problems have been further compounded by policies, such as price control for farm products, which have worsened the terms of trade for agricultural producers.

During the discussion of the agricultural issues, it was recognised that transformation and reform of the agricultural sector were likely to be more difficult in small countries. These countries may also face disadvantages in respect of the provision of public services for agriculture (e.g. research and infrastructure), marketing and procurement of inputs. However, the size of the economy as a whole was not a dominant constraint in achieving increases in agricultural output. Some of the disadvantages could be offset by regional co-operation and/or crop specialisation, and higher productivity could also be achieved through more intensive farming. There were also substantial opportunities for exporting seasonal and high-value food products from small countries to markets in developed countries.

Chen-Young's paper on tourism highlights the importance of this sector in many small economies. The data for Jamaica, for example, show that, in the past, the industry yielded significant benefits to the economy in terms of employment and foreign exchange earnings. However, there are also some costs associated with heavy reliance on tourism. Since the industry is heavily dependent on transnational corporations, foreign airlines and foreign tour operators, earnings from this sector are subject to substantial fluctuations, depending on the attitudes of foreign enterprises to the economic and political situation prevailing in the country. It is a capital-intensive industry, and substantial under-utilisation may result from sudden changes in the flow of tourists. There are also certain costs associated with the accentuation of 'dualism' in the society. However, it has to be recognised that for many small economies there is no alternative to the development of tourism, and the only question for them is to adopt policies which might improve the economic benefits and reduce the social costs.

Bennathan considers the 'retarding effect' of economies of scale in transport, and the policies for attenuating or overcoming this effect.[12] Although smallness by itself is not an important factor in transport, small size usually occurs along with one or more of the several factors of importance to the transport sector, e.g. economies of scale, inability to affect external prices, export concentration, high export shares of neighbouring countries, land-lock and also the relatively short internal distance for movement of people and goods. Bennathan points out that the most obvious policy for reducing the transport disadvantage is to increase demand for services and minimise excess capacity through sharing transport facilities and services with other countries. For land-locked countries, which may suffer from a weak bargaining position in relation to transit countries, the answer may be to promote joint ventures with joint control, which establishes a common interest and reduces the rigidities of intergovernmental dealings. In regard to ocean transport also, regional lines, working independently, may be in a better position than national lines to minimise excess capacity and provide competition against monopolistic or discriminating pricing policies of conference services.

During the discussion, it was generally agreed that solutions to some of the transport problems could only be found in regional co-operation and in joint ventures. There was value in negotiating as a region with outside interests in respect of both shipping and air traffic rights. There was also a compelling case for greater international assistance to overcome the transport problems of small and remote countries. The question of providing direct subsidies for transport was a complicated one and the answers depended on a number of factors, e.g. the period over which the subsidies were required, and the alternative uses of resources spent on subsidies.

PLANS AND PROJECTS

The paper by Dudley Seers examines the current state of planning in developing countries and outlines some alternative planning strategies for the eighties with particular reference to small countries. The case for taking a long-term view of development problems and for 'planning' the structural adjustment of the economy has become stronger rather than weaker because of increased external uncertainties to which developing countries are now subject. But there is a danger that unless correct lessons are drawn from past experience, planning would come to be regarded as being irrelevant to current problems. Among the reasons for the relative lack of success in planning are: the statistical and technical weaknesses, too much concentration on the production and publication of the plan rather than its implementation, lack of effective political commitment, and the remoteness of the planning office from the administrative mechanism. Seers emphasises the need to give a new orientation to planning, with a view to bringing it closer to the actual decision-making process and policy formulation in developing countries.

Seers points out that while the development options for small countries may be fewer, the opportunities for successful planning are likely to be greater because, in his words, "the planning office is less likely to remain forgotten, in political limbo". He also points out that while 'oil shocks' and the deterioration in the terms of trade of other commodities have undermined many existing development plans, they have also opened new horizons for planning offices. In this situation, the main role of planning is seen as being that of analysing and assessing the long-term implications of policies for adjustment to the balance of payments problems currently faced by oil-importing developing countries. Apart from the need to tackle the immediate foreign exchange problem, there is also an urgent need to plan basic structural changes to take account of the new energy situation. In particular, the planning exercises in the eighties would need to pay considerable attention to distributional aspects, in view of the relationship between income and oil intensity of different patterns of consumption.

Andrew Coulson's paper on project evaluation is an attempt to develop some relatively simple rules for social cost-benefit analysis in small economies. Coulson points out that both the UNIDO and the OECD systems of shadow pricing are complex and particularly unsuitable for small economies. Assuming that estimates of the costs and benefits of projects at domestic prices exist, the system of social cost-benefit analysis suggested in Coulson's paper involves making 'adjustments' in the official exchange rate, the market wage rate, and the discount rate used for calculation of the present net value of the project at market prices. These adjustments can be made on the basis of judgements and 'rules of thumb' rather than precise calculations of shadow prices or the social discount rate. In addition to these adjustments, it is suggested that an attempt should be made to quantify the linkage and other indirect effects of projects on the economy, since these are likely to be particularly important in respect of large projects in small economies.

A rational method of project evaluation would seem to be particularly necessary in a small country where one large project could have important economy-wide effects. During the discussion, some doubts were, however, expressed on whether the rough and ready procedures suggested in Coulson's paper were appropriate. A fear was expressed that since the margins of adjustment over market prices were to be based on judgement, almost any project could be justified by choosing the appropriate levels of so-called 'shadow' prices. As a result, it was possible that the short-cut methods could lead to the selection of projects which were neither financially viable nor socially beneficial. The problem of data availability could be over-stated as, in most cases, sufficient data were available to estimate a range within which a particular variable was likely to fall. Such estimates could be used to establish at least a weak ordering of projects, and identify those variables to which a project was particularly sensitive. Greater effort could then be devoted to a more precise calculation of only those variables.

DEVELOPMENT POLICY

Most papers raise one or more issues of development policy, and much of the discussion at the conference also centred around these issues. In regard to the agricultural sector, Persaud argues that there is now an urgent need for policies which would give a much higher priority to production of food crops, and to a more intensive application of new technology in agriculture. A new agricultural strategy is likely to call for a move away from large plantations to smaller-sized family farms. Apart from increasing output in the agricultural sector, he points out that the new agricultural strategy could also have a favourable impact on the structure of demand for manufactured products and the employment of labour. Bhadhuri et al., have highlighted the importance of developing the services sector in a small economy. In their view, this sector neither has the disadvantage of the industrial sector dominated by scale effects, nor does it have the limitation of given land:man ratios which typically characterise the labour productivity of agriculture. In these circumstances, the services sector can provide an important route for sustained economic growth in a small economy. This point has also been made by Seers.

Lall and Ghosh examine the options available to small economies in overcoming the constraints to industrialisation imposed by the lack of technical and marketing skills. They emphasise the importance of exports in the industrial development of small economies, and suggest that the acquisition of the necessary technological skills and the ability to penetrate foreign markets may well depend on foreign collaboration. Unfortunately, in dealing with multinationals, a small economy may be at a certain disadvantage as compared with a large developing economy. These disadvantages may arise because of the inability of small countries to 'unpackage' foreign investment, the need to offer greater inducements, the limited local supply capabilities and the lack of indigenous R & D infrastructure. However, many of these disadvantages are likely to diminish as the manufacturing base develops. A number of small countries, particularly Singapore, have been able to adopt policies for dealing with foreign enterprises and have achieved remarkable success in generating local industry, local employment, and higher incomes. While the success achieved by Singapore cannot easily be replicated in other countries which may not have the same locational and other advantages, there may be lessons to be learnt from its experience, and that of Hong Kong, in working out a suitable strategy for exports of manufactured products.

Fry considers some aspects of an appropriate policy framework for the development of the banking sector. In view of the small size of the financial markets, the banking sector in small countries is generally dominated by a few banks and the promotion of a competitive environment for financial services is difficult. Fry proposes a positive real interest rate policy through measures such as the enforcement of minimum and flexible deposit rates, or the issue of indexed negotiable certificates of deposit. There is also a case for multi-purpose rather than specialised banks. In order to develop the domestic banking sector, an alternative to setting up new banks may be to reserve the field of savings intermediation, i.e. finance companies, savings and loan associations and savings banks, for domestic enterprises. These savings institutions could, in due course, be put on an equal footing with commercial banks, as is now happening in the United States.

A dominant characteristic of small countries is their great dependence on trade and capital inflows. Helleiner examines the implications of this dependence on macro-economic management against the background of current developments in the world economy. Like many other oil-importing developing countries, small countries are also faced with the difficult problem of adjustment to a sharp deterioration in their balance of payments. Policy options available to these economies include further deflation and reduction in aggregate domestic demand, restructuring of production and consumption directed towards improvement in the external balance, larger foreign exchange borrowings, and running down external reserves where possible. The possibilities of restructuring production as well as borrowing abroad are likely to be severely constrained in small economies in the short and medium term because of limited opportunities for import substitution or further export promotion, and already high stocks of foreign debt. In the present situation, therefore, Helleiner argues that there is a special need for balance of payments financing for small economies. Among international policies that could be devised to meet the special problems of these countries are: increasing their access to low-conditionality financing facilities, making aid commitments over a longer term, denominating their borrowings and contracts in terms of SDRs or other currency baskets, and pooling information on exchange and financial markets.

As regards an appropriate exchange rate policy, Helleiner points out that small economies are unlikely to be able to float their exchange rates freely and in any case such a policy may lead to more volatile exchange rates and consequently greater internal price and cost disturbances. If greater stability in the exchange rate were the desired objective, an SDR-linked rate would be appropriate. Judicious management of exchange rates on the basis of an independent basket of currencies is another possibility, which has the advantage of greater flexibility, but may involve higher management costs. In a regime of flexible exchange rates, it is important for small economies consciously to use the exchange instrument in order to reduce external instability while at the same time maintaining the competitiveness of their exports.

The discussion at the conference revealed that it was difficult to make generalisations in respect of appropriate policies which would be relevant to all small economies. The policies for development of different sectors depended on the particular circumstances of each country. Nevertheless, the problems and constraints in a large number of small economies were common enough to permit at least a few broad conclusions in regard to development policies. First, it was likely to be more difficult for a small economy to insulate itself from developments in the world markets and the external economic environment. It was important to devise a policy framework which would minimise the costs associated with external dependence, and maximise the advantages available from external trade and capital inflows. In achieving this objective, regional co-operation, despite difficulties that had arisen in the operation of integration schemes, could play an important part. Many of the constraints imposed by small size could be partially eliminated if development policies were to be pursued in a regional context. Second, while options for a small country were more limited, this enhanced rather than reduced the importance of devising appropriate macro-economic policies. When the external environment was subject to sharp fluctuations, the impact of these developments could be minimised only through conscious and deliberate policy choices. Third, there was a need for greater international assistance, particularly technical assistance, for small economies. The ability of small economies to cope with the problems associated with external fluctuations was limited, and international schemes to assist small countries could be devised at relatively low costs to donors and international agencies. Finally, there was a need for substantial further research and analysis on problems and policies for small economies. The statistical information base was particularly weak, and little was known about the effects of alternative policies in a small economy.

NOTES

1. The phrases 'small countries', 'small economies' and 'small states' have been used inter-changeably in this paper as well as in the others in this volume.

2. If the two most populous countries (viz. India and China) and the oil exporting small countries (viz. Kuwait, Qatar, UAE, Libya, Brunei, Trinidad and Tobago and Gabon) are excluded from the sample, the per capita income figures for small and all developing countries would be $1,021 and $720 respectively. (The World Bank, 1980.)

3. For proceedings of this conference, see Robinson (1960).

4. For papers presented at this conference, see Selwyn (1975).

5. See Shand (1980).

6. See Benedict (1967).

7. Some of the papers contained in this volume are revised versions which have taken account of the points of view expressed at the Marlborough House conference held in June 1981.

8. For a detailed discussion, see Kuznets (1960).

9. For countries with populations of five million or less, the drop in growth rates during the period 1973-78 over growth rates registered during the period 1965-73 was substantially higher than for countries with populations of more than five million. See Blazic-Metzner and Hughes, 'Growth Experience of Small Economies', in this volume, Table 1.

10. For an analysis of the impact of economic fluctuation on poverty, see Arndt et al. (1980); and Sen (1981).

11. A separate note, prepared by B. Banerjee, gives selected results of the regression analysis of a number of variables in respect of small economies. This statistical exercise was undertaken as part of the Secretariat's research work on small economies.

12. In addition to Esra Bennathan's paper, the conference also considered a note, by Q.S. Siddiqi and F.D.C. Wijesinghe, on the transport problems of small islands. This note, which presented some preliminary findings of a Commonwealth Secretariat study on this subject, was prepared only for the purpose of discussion and is not reproduced in this volume.

REFERENCES

Arndt, H.W., et al., 1980, "World Economic Crisis: A Commonwealth Perspective", Commonwealth Secretariat, London.

Benedict, Burton, ed., 1967, "Problems of Smaller Territories", London: Athlone Press.

Demas, William G., 1965, "The Economics of Development in Small Countries with Special Reference to the Caribbean", Montreal: McGill University Press.

Dommen, Edward, ed., 1980, 'Islands'. In "World Development", in a special issue, Vol.8, No.12.

Kuznets, S., 1960, 'Economic Growth of Small Nations'. In E.A.G. Robinson, ed., "Economic Consequences of the Size of Nations", London: Macmillan.

Robinson, E.A.G., ed., op.cit.

Selwyn, Percy, ed., 1975, "Development Policy in Small Countries", London: Croom Helm.

Sen, A.K., 1981, "Poverty and Famines: an Essay on Entitlement and Deprivation", Oxford: Oxford University Press.

Shand, R.T., ed., 1980, "The Island States of the Pacific and Indian Oceans: Anatomy of Development", Canberra: The Australian National University.

The World Bank, 1980, "World Bank Atlas", Washinghton D.C.

1. Characteristics of Small Economies

P. J. Lloyd and R. M. Sundrum

Out of 190 developed and less developed countries for which data are routinely collected and published in international reports, about 100 countries have populations of less than five million and as many as 55 have less than a million. The Commonwealth Secretariat (1979) has compiled some data for 59 less-developed countries (LDCs) with populations of less than five million (and per capita incomes below $2,000); the average population of these countries is only 1.5 million. In terms of population these are very small countries - micro-states - smaller even than medium-sized cities in other countries. Singly, they have not attracted the research attention of many scholars. Therefore, the study of each of them is the lonely work of individual scholars. Yet there are so many of them; the total population of the countries in the Commonwealth Secretariat list adds up to 90 million. This is a considerable number of people living in a condition of underdevelopment. If they all lived in a single country, it would be the fifth largest of the less-developed countries and would have merited more attention than they do at present. The fact that this large total population is distributed among so many countries gives it a much greater political significance in this era of nation states. But even collectively, these small countries have not attracted much interest among economists and other social scientists concerned with development issues.

Country size is of interest because it may be a major or at least a significant determinant of inter-country differences in economic performance. Economic peformance concerns mainly the time path of real income per capita in an economy, that is, the trend rate of growth of per capita income and the fluctuations around the trend. Therefore this paper is concerned with the characteristics of small countries which help to explain their economic performance. Smallness is only one of many characteristics of these countries.

17

SMALLNESS: DEFINING CHARACTERISTICS

The first group of characteristics are those which may be used to define the set of small countries.

The definition of a set of small countries which is implied by all discussion of the special economic aspects of these countries requires three separate steps. It requires a choice of measure of country size, a decision to partition the set of all countries into a sub-set of those which are 'small' and one or more complementary sub-sets, and the choice of the level which demarcates those which are small from other countries. We shall concentrate on the first and third of these assumptions. The second is less obvious. The usual assumption implied in the discussions of smallness is that it is meaningful to partition the set of countries into the two complementary sets of 'small' and 'large' countries but we should at least consider the possibility that the characteristics of countries which are associated with the size of countries may make it more meaningful to partition countries into more than two subsets,[1] say, three; for example, 'large', 'small' and 'micro'.

There are many measures of size. First, there is population. This is the criterion which has been widely used, for example, in the selection made by the Commonwealth Secretariat in their compilation of statistical data. The size of population is very important as a measure of the number of consumers and as a measure of the labour force. Therefore, whatever index of size we adopt, it will have to give considerable weight to population size. The question is whether it needs to be supplemented by any other measure of size to identify the group of countries whose development prospects are seriously affected one way or another by their smallness.

The second measure of size that we have to consider is geographical size measured by the area within national boundaries. Area is the obvious proxy for natural resource endowment. If natural resources of arable land, exploitable minerals and rainfall were randomly distributed on the land areas of the globe, then in general, countries which are small in area would have a smaller variety of endowments. Some would be well endowed with large quantities of fertile land or a valuable mineral and some would be poorly endowed, lacking large quantities of even a single resource, and few would be well endowed with several resources.

Because of our concern with the population measure, we can most conveniently examine the relationship between the population and the geographical measure if we introduce the geographical measure in the form of population density figures. The average density of the 59 small LDCs identified in the Commonwealth Secretariat list is 9.2 persons per square kilometre on the basis of 1977 population estimates. The figures for other countries are shown in Table I for comparison.

The high average density of the large LDCs is, of course, due to the two giants, India and China, with densities of 168 and 80 respectively. There is a tendency for densities to increase with size of population, both among developed and less developed countries

TABLE 1

POPULATION DENSITY BY SIZE OF COUNTRY

Groups of Countries	Average Density (1977 figures)
Developed Countries	
Large (Pop. > 15 million)	20.8
Medium/Small (Pop. < 15 million)	10.3
Less Developed Countries	
Large (Pop. > 15 million)	52.5
Medium (Pop. 5 to 15 milion)	14.9
Small (Pop. < 5 million)	9.2

Sources: Commonwealth Secretariat (1979) and UN publications.

TABLE 2

POPULATION DENSITY OF SMALL LESS DEVELOPED COUNTRIES
(1977)

Density (persons per sq. km.)	Number of Small Countries
Less than 10	17
10 - 19	5
20 - 29	5
30 - 49	7
50 - 99	5
100 - 199	12
200 - 599	7
600 and over	1
	59

Source: Commonwealth Secretariat (1979).

but this is not a systematic relationship. The small LDCs are by no means homogeneous in this respect. The distribution of these countries by density is shown in Table 2. Although there are many small countries with low densities, there are also a considerable number of small countries with densities as high as any in the world.

For most economic activities, it is appropriate to omit mountainous, heavily forested, desert and other uninhabitable areas of land; then a more pertinent index of geographical size is area of habitable, or cultivable land. We find that the small economies in our list have an average density of 170 persons per square kilometre of arable and cropped land. The corresponding figure for all LDCs (for which data are available) is about 190. Thus the difference between large and small countries is less marked when the density is expressed in terms of arable land, but again there is great diversity among the small countries, as shown in Table 3.

The third measure of size that has been proposed is income. The average per capita income of the small LDCs in our list was US$ 453 (in 1977). Their average income is higher than that of the poorer large LDCs, which account for 70 per cent of the LDC population. As will be noted below, the figures for the small countries probably underestimate their actual position more than for other countries. But here again, we see that there is a wide range among the small countries, as shown in Table 4.

Thus we see that there is no systematic relationship between population size and other measures of size. The ranking of countries and the partitioning of the set of all countries into the two groups of 'small' and 'large' will differ acccording to the criterion adopted. This raises the question whether the three measures of size cannot somehow be combined into a composite index of size. There are some standard statistical methods available for constructing such a composite index.

One statistical method is to calculate the principal component of the various measures of size. Our attempts to derive such an index, however, proved unsuccessful. The reason is quite obvious. This approach is most valuable when the various individual indicators are highly correlated among themselves, which is not true in the present case. Further, this method assumes simple linear relationships. Above all, there is no economic theory underlying the mechanical application of such statistical methods. A second statistical method is discriminant function analysis. Since our objective is to study how size affects economic performance, it is more appropriate to consider income or the rate of growth of income as the variable influenced by size, rather than as an indicator of size itself. In discriminant function analysis all countries are divided into two groups according to their economic performance, and a linear combination of various measures of size derived which discriminates most strongly between the two groups in the sense of maximising the between-group-variance. This method was also tried but the results were not satisfactory.

Another possibility is to construct an economic index of size in terms of aggregate primary resources. Area and population are

20

TABLE 3

POPULATION DENSITY RELATIVE TO ARABLE LAND
IN SMALL LESS DEVELOPED COUNTRIES
(1977)

Density per sq. km. of Arable Land	Number of Countries
Less than 100	5
100 - 199	10
200 - 299	9
300 - 499	17
500 - 999	11
1,000 and over	5
	57

Source: Commonwealth Secretariat (1979).

TABLE 4

DISTRIBUTION OF SMALL LDCs BY PER CAPITA INCOME
(1977)

Per Capita Income (US$)	Number of Countries
0 - 99	2
100 - 199	8
200 - 299	9
300 - 499	14
500 - 999	17
1,000 - 2,000	9
	59

Source: Commonwealth Secretariat (1979).

indicators of the quantity of land and labour resources respectively. One should also include resources of mineral deposits under the ground and marine resources which are important for some small countries. The natural weights to aggregate these resources are price weights. However, when the resource products are tradeable, as with mineral and agricultural outputs, the weights are given by the world economy and will vary over time. When the prices are determined within the small countries they depend on the productivity of factor use which then needs to be explained.

We believe population is the most serviceable measure of country size for two reasons. In another paper in this volume, Jalan has constructed an equal-weighted index with three components - population, area and GNP. The use of this method leads to an interesting consequence. When the smallest LDCs are chosen by this index, we find that they are also, with few exceptions, the countries with populations of less than five million. The reason is that, for such a group, there is a high correlation between population and the other measures of size, as shown in Table 5. This suggests that, for the group as a whole, it may be sufficient from a statistical point of view to classify countries by population size alone, the diversity in the other measures of size being averaged out in the process.

The second reason for preferring the population measure of size is that it has the advantage from an economic point of view that it relates to the human resource constraint of economic growth. This is the most significant advantage of population as a criterion. We consider this below.

TABLE 5   CORRELATION OF MEASURES OF SIZE

	Number of Countries with Population (in millions) of:		
	Less than 5	5 and over	Total
(a) Area of Arable Land: (000 sq. km.)			
Less than 15	61	0	61
15 and over	10	40	50
	71	40	111
(b) GNP (US$ billion):			
Less than 2.5	62	11	73
2.5 and over	9	29	38
	71	40	111

Source: Bimal Jalan, in the present volume (Table A.1.)

22

CONSEQUENCES OF SIZE: PREDICTED CHARACTERISTICS

The second set of characteristics are those which follow as a consequence of size, defined in some prior sense. To deal with these, it is necessary to consider underlying relationships. So far we have been considering the characteristics of small countries from a purely statistical point of view.

There are a number of ways in which we can proceed. The first is simply to take the position that small countries are faithful replicas on a miniature scale of large countries, and hence that the theoretical framework which has been intensively studied for the analysis of, and strategy for, development in the large countries can be applied directly to the small ones. This approach amounts to assuming that the various economic variables we are interested in vary proportionately with some measure of size which has to be discovered. This approach will not survive even the most cursory acquaintance with the facts. Small countries are not just smaller versions of large countries.

To come closer to the real world, a second possible approach is to assume that there is a systematic relationship of economic variables to the size variable which is not necessarily one of proportionality and to use the actual observations to reveal the functional form of this relationship; as it were, to let the data speak for themselves.

This is, of course, the happy hunting ground of the statistical economist, one who hopes to discover the secrets of the universe by playing about with the computer. There are a number of statistical pitfalls in applying this approach - the naive assumption of homogeneity, the problems of 'double clustering' of developed and less developed countries (Keyfitz, 1975), multicollinearity, the assumption of a smooth function which rules out vital turning points, threshold levels, etc.

The statistical method has been most fully worked out for our present problem by Chenery and Syrquin (1975). They regress a number of variables on linear and quadratic forms of the logarithms of two variables, population and per capita income. They get high R^2 and significant t values for many equations but because of the income term, these are mostly due to inter-class correlation rather than intra-class correlation; that is, they reflect the difference between developed and less developed countries rather than the variations within each of these groups. Therefore, the statistical relationships become much less impressive when computed for each of these groups. Even so, they find that in most cases there is a significant difference between the regressions fitted separately to large and to small countries (defined in population terms). Therefore, in all countries the relationships between these economic variables and size are much more complex than implied by the simple functional forms assumed in these regressions. Taking the equations found for the small countries, the relationships are not very useful to us because they tend to explain many variables in terms of per capita income, while per capita income in turn depends on these variables and our objective is precisely to explain how these relationships operate through the size of countries.

It may be more useful to consider the economics of the relationships more directly. Elementary economic theory teaches us about the different ways in which size effects operate in the economy through the laws of diminishing and increasing returns. The way the law of diminishing returns operates in agriculture has been traditionally explained by the relationship between population and area of arable land. For this relationship, the most useful combination of the two indicators is in the form of a ratio, namely, the density figure. It has therefore been a persistent theme of development economics that there is a negative relationship between income levels and population densities, i.e. the larger the population on a given area, the lower the income. This is obviously false as a general rule, for there are many rich countries with a high density and many poor countries with a low density. Such cases occur because the effects of density are so strongly overlaid by the effects of the level of development, especially of the extent of industrialisation. Some rich countries are able to cope with high population densities because of their high level of industrialisation, while some countries with a low density are poor because of their low level of development. Also, within the agricultural sector, the level of income depends not only on two of the aggregate factors of production - land and labour - but on all three - land, labour and capital.

We next consider how far the operation of the law of increasing returns might help us to define a meaningful measure of size. This law is particularly applicable to manufacturing industry in which economies of scale are more important. Some economists believe there is a minimum size below which it is not profitable for small countries to establish many industries.

We are sceptical that economies of scale can be closely related to country size. In the first place economies of scale of the standard type are a function of the scale of output of commodities. The magnitude of such economies varies from commodity to commodity. Moreover, the extent to which a country can exploit such economies of scale in any industry depends on the extent of the market. The extent of the domestic market depends on the size of the population and the level of per capita income. It might seem at first sight that the best combination of the two measures of size (per capita income and population) to serve as a measure of the size of the market is their product, namely the national income figure, but this is not necessarily the case. The domestic demand functions for a commodity express the demand per capita as a function of income per capita, given the distribution of incomes and prices, viz. $x = f(y)$ where $x = X/P$. Hence, $X = P.f(y)$. Two countries may have the same national income, one with a large population and a low income per capita and the other with a small population and a high income per capita. Then their demands for a product will not necessarily be the same.

The simplest illustration is to consider two countries 1 and 2 with populations P_1 and P_2 and per capita incomes y_1 and y_2, such that

$$P_1 y_1 = P_2 y_2 \qquad\qquad y_2 > y_1 \qquad (1)$$

Let the per capita demand for a product be x_1 and x_2, determined by the income elasticity of demand

$$E = \big[(x_2/x_1) - 1\big] \ / \ \big[(y_2/y_1) - 1\big] \qquad (2)$$

Then if the extent of the market is given by

$$X_i = P_i x_i \qquad\qquad (i = 1,2)$$

it follows, in view of equation (1), that

$$\big[(X_2/X_1) - 1\big] \ = \ \big[E - 1\big]\big[1-(y_1/y_2)\big] \qquad (3)$$

The two countries will not have the same demand for the product unless $E=1$. If $E > 1$, as is generally the case for industrial products, the demand will be greater in the country with the higher per capita income.

But, of course, to follow these approaches to the study of the economic effects of size is to take a totally autarkic view of the problems of small countries. With international trade, it is the global demand rather than domestic demand which determines total sales and unit costs. Many of the other relationships between size and the various economic variables considered above will also be materially affected by international trade.

Almost all commentaries on small economies emphasise their trade with other nations. Some writers emphasise the benefits of international trade, and some the costs of a high dependence on other countries in some form such as the vulnerability to changes in prices of export staples or in market access. We briefly consider the issues involved.

A common starting point is the observation that small countries tend to have high levels of international trade. This is usually expressed as high levels of export or import trade in relation to national output or national expenditure. The first of these ratios measures approximately the proportion of national output which is exported and the second the proportion of national expenditure on consumer and investment goods which is supplied by other countries.[2]

No matter which measure one takes, empirical studies[3] have observed statistically significant relationships between national income or output on the one hand and levels of international trade on the other. Indeed, a feature of these results is that the statistical fit between trade involvement and the size of economies as measured by national income is considerably better than the fit between levels of per capita income or rates of growth of per capita income on the one hand and national income on the other, as Selwyn (1975) observed in his summary of the Barbados Conference.

Thus country size may be related to other characteristics of countries, such as trade ratios or commodity concentration of exports. Moreover, since the relationship is imperfect, small countries, as defined in terms of population or some other defining characteristic, will have a distribution of high and low values in terms of these predicted characteristics. These values will overlap with those of large countries for the same characteristic. If one is really interested in these characteristics one should consider them directly for countries with the chosen levels of the characteristic since it does not correspond to the definition in terms of country size.

The above results established that trade is quantitatively important in the disposition of national output and expenditure. It is more important to know what the levels of national output and expenditure would have been in the absence of international trade. That is, how large are the gains from trade in terms of the increases in real incomes for these trading countries? There is an old line of reasoning which derives from the late classical economists which asserts that small nations have higher gains from trade.[4] There are two strands to this argument. The first strand is the narrow resource base property of smallness. It was Frank Graham who first constructed a multi-country, multi-commodity model of international trade which shows that the precise advantage of smallness lies in the ability of small countries to specialise exclusively in the production of one or a few commodities in which they have a greater comparative advantage. Possessing a small productive capacity in relation to world demand for these commodities, they can specialise without depressing world prices. Their gains are typically greater because of the greater differences between the product transformation ratios at which they could produce commodities themselves and the world relative price ratios at which they can buy them.

The second strand of argument is that small countries cannot exploit the economies of scale as fully as large countries.[5] This strand emphasises the role of scale in capital-intensive rather than resource-intensive industries. We have already considered the limitations of national income as a measure of size for this purpose. The real significance of size in this context is perhaps that the aggregate productive capacity of the country as proxied by its national income must limit the range of goods requiring a large scale of output for efficient production which can be produced.

While it is not possible to test the hypothesis that small countries generally gain more from international trade, we accept this proposition as it is eminently plausible and seems to fit the circumstances of many of the countries with a population less than five million. Some small countries have high per capita incomes as a result of specialising in the production of endowed natural resources; for example, Nauru and Bahrain.

To us, an important characteristic of the economies of these small countries is what we shall call the <u>concentration phenomenon</u>. This is the phenomenon that the <u>national output is concentrated in a few industries</u>. It is the result of the constraint of size in terms of the production possibilities which shrinks the dimensions as well as the quantities producible of all commodities. Those industries requiring essential inputs of natural raw materials cannot exist and those requiring large scale will not be established for any set of world prices. If an internationally comparable set of input-output transaction matrices existed for all the countries we are considering, this feature would show up in the large number of empty rows and columns and the large number of empty cells for non-essential intermediate products used in the production of those outputs which are not zero. The concentration of international exports, which has received much more attention, is a secondary consequence of this prior effect of national size.[6]

In extreme cases, there is only one major production activity. This has been recognised popularly in the description of 'guano' economies or 'petroleum' economies or 'sugar' economies or 'tourist' economies. One might construct a typology in terms of the leading sector of small countries.

<u>This</u> concentration of production is itself a barrier to <u>international trade;</u> that is, the size effect feeds back upon itself. Countries which are small in population and national output do not have the range of industries to provide the services of engineering and design which aid the design and development of internationally marketable commodities, or of firms and banks to market these commodities. This is a form of economies of scale which is a function of the aggregate size of the nation rather than the size of the output of individual industries. Some writers have drawn attention to this factor (Selwyn, 1975 and Robinson, 1960) but its importance seems greater to us than the attention it has hitherto received.

The concentration of economic production activities has numerous consequences. Considerable attention has been devoted to the possibility that concentration of exports increases the <u>instability</u> <u>of export receipts</u>. However, a number of studies have shown that there is no or at best only a weak positive correlation between export concentration and export instability. When the instability of export receipts varies considerably among individual commodities, the instability of aggregate exports depends on this dispersion itself, the extent to which the country concentrates on commodities which are relatively <u>more</u> or less stable and the inter-commodity covariances terms.[7,8]

It is preferable to consider instabilty of the capacity to import rather than that of total exports since the former is more closely related to the growth performance of an economy. One might use the income terms of trade; that is, the index of exports divided by the index of import prices. This is affected by changes in the relative prices of exports to imports. However, instability in this measure is also only loosely related to export concentration.[9]

There is a more direct effect of size on the growth rates of national output (and exports). For virtually all small countries, the prices of the commodities they trade are determined on world markets which are not affected by the quantities which they trade; that is, they are dependent economies in the descriptive sense of being price-takers. Over an interval of time the prices of these export commodities relative to the price of the bundle of commodities which they import will change. The growth of the real income of the economy will, as a first approximation, be equal to the weighted average of the changes in relative prices of the commodities which the country produces.[10] The relevant prices here are the prices of the commodities produced relative to an index of the prices consumed, but these relative price swings will be largely determined by the swings in the commodity terms of trade for the commodities which are traded internationally. Concentration of output will mean that there is less averaging or pooling of these different price trends for individual staple export commodities. Thus one would expect a greater variation over time in the growth rates of small countries. When 'prices are good' the growth rates of a small country will be high but when they are not good they will be low. And for a cross-section of these countries one would expect over the same time interval that there would be a great cross-country variation. Indeed, one can immediately name countries whose growth rates have been largely determined by the fortunes of the major export commodity; for example, Fiji and its growth dependence on sugar exports. Again we are not able to test this hypothesis systematically for our set of countries because of the lack of reliable data of growth over long periods.

This instability-of-growth hypothesis is reinforced by a second role of the concentration characteristic. When relative prices change permanently the relative profitability of producing different goods also changes, and this induces producers to increase the quantities produced of commodities which have become more profitable. The limited production possibilities of small countries reduce the ability of the economy to adjust to shocks which have reduced the profitability of leading sectors.

This hypothesis predicts that, over a period of time, some small countries will have growth rates significantly higher than average and some will have rates which are significantly lower than average.[11]

So far, we have been considering the relationship between size and the usual economic variables. Our discussion suggests that there is a great deal of diversity among countries and that there is no reliable relationship between these variables and any convenient measure of size. But perhaps there are other variables which depend on size and which may be even more significant, because with respect to these variables there may be a threshold of size which can be used to demarcate small countries from others. The most important of these are human resources. Human resources are essential to develop a country's natural endowments to the optimum extent and to minimise the economic costs of shortcomings. Compared with human resources, the economic importance of natural resources has generally been overrated, as Theodore Schultz (1980) pointed out in his Nobel lecture. We believe that this applies in particular to small countries with poor resource endowments. When smallness is defined in terms of a total population of less than five million, there is an upper bound on the size of the labour force of about 2.5 million and for most of the countries in our set the labour force is much less than one million. A small labour force means that there is a small pool of human potential skills in terms of the variety of innate capabilities available, though it is difficult to separate this endowment factor from the lack of accumulated human capital since all of these countries are developing and have much lower levels of training and education per member of the labour force than those of more developed countries.

One indicator of this handicap of smallness is the absence of tertiary education facilities in most of these small countries. To examine this feature we calculated the number of small countries which do not have a university. Here we are not interested in a local university as a symbol of nationhood or development or even as a mode of training. Rather we are considering a university as a local resource which can make available technical advice and the skills of consultants to local producers; for example, in the agriculture sector these include plant and animal disease control and the development of new varieties. Similarly, the presence of scientific research organisations and other tertiary training facilities provide a variety of economically valuable though usually uncosted services. The 1977-78 Yearbook of the International Association of Universities showed that about one-third of the small countries in our list did not have a university. These limited human resource development facilities, by comparison with those in large developing countries as well as in developed countries, is one characteristic common to all countries in our set.

More broadly, the same argument applies to skilled manpower. The ability to acquire a high level of expertise in any branch of human activity is a rare event, and the frequency of such events may be restricted by the fact that small populations offer too small a sample for realising such rare events. On the other hand, the need to operate an independent political state imposes heavy demands on highly skilled and trained personnel to man the central governments, political representation abroad, sophisticated banking and other institutions, etc. Therefore, small countries suffer a handicap in these respects due to their smallness.

Finally, we have to consider one consequence of a small population which applies to the subset of countries in which the population lives in a small area, namely their compactness. This makes for greater homogeneity as well as greater speed and efficiency of communication among the people of small countries. For example, it is possible that this compactness is the main reason for the oft-noted fact that these countries have generally exhibited a faster decline of fertility in recent times, because the small family norm, once introduced, spreads faster.

OTHER CHARACTERISTICS OF SMALL COUNTRIES

When we examine the small countries on our list in more detail, especially their location, it becomes apparent that there are some characteristics other than smallness which distinguish them from other countries. An examination of this list shows that 35 of the 59 countries listed are either land-locked (10) or are islands (25), that is, are 'sea-locked'. Most of the remaining countries are located in Africa away from easy economic contact with developed countries. This suggests that the problems of the small countries should be studied, not only with respect to their small size, but also with respect to their relative remoteness.

The main point to note is that the production and trade pattern of small countries is not only a matter of their size. If we take note of the fact that the small countries are also remote countries, we have also to consider whether the amount of trade that small countries are involved in is sufficient to compensate for their size.

Land-locked countries have been considered extensively by UNCTAD and others and island countries have been examined as a group (Selwyn, 1980) but they are usually considered separately. Land-locked countries and islands which are remote both have relatively high transport costs. Sea transport is a cheaper form of international transport. However, sea transport requires good harbours and a minimum level of port facilities, either or both of which are absent in many small countries. These locational factors make many small countries isolated and remote. Remoteness increases transport costs often to prohibitive levels.

Empirical studies show that transport costs account for more of the total barriers to trade than do tariffs and measured non-tariff barriers. They also show that international transport costs expressed as a percentage of f.o.b. prices do not decline systematically with the degree of product fabrication, though they vary considerably from product to product (Waters, 1970 and Yeats, 1979). The best conception of these transport cost effects is that they shrink further the production and trade possibilities of those small countries which are already limited by their small resource endowments and market size, and especially the possibilities of more highly processed manufacturing.

Remoteness also acts as a barrier to the transmission of information relating to new technologies, new products and new market opportunities. One consequence for the small countries, especially of the Pacific region, is the persistence of traditional modes of production and of a subsistence economy. The remoteness of many small countries is surely a central characteristic of these countries, which must be seriously considered in any discussion of their viability.

IMPLICATIONS FOR THE ISSUE OF VIABILITY

The handicaps of smallness in terms of endowments of natural and human resources and the restriction on the movements of labour and capital between independent countries raise the question of whether small countries are viable. This question was specifically considered at the Barbados Conference. Selwyn (1975, p.12) noted that "the notion of viability proved extremely slippery." He concluded that "viability has no meaning except in relation to the purposes of the citizens of a country, and in the last resort any national unit which can maintain its separate existence is ipso facto viable." Such a position, however, evades the real issue. For we must distinguish political viability in terms of the continued survival of a state from economic viability in terms of a state which is able to attain certain objectives of growth and development while retaining effective control of its own economy, i.e. both the availability of options to achieve those objectives and the freedom to choose among them. Secondly, there are degrees of freedom. For example, in a customs union, each member foregoes independent action on instruments of policy which are normally the sole prerogative of sovereign states. Thus, tariffs and other controls on third party countries must be decided jointly by all members, export subsidies are prohibited, and there is considerable harmonisation of taxes and exchange rate movements.

With respect to the small countries, the question at issue is whether national sovereignty should be interpreted in the same way as it is for large countries. It is to answer this question that we must examine the implications of independent nationhood for small countries in more detail.[12]

Such autonomy has both advantages and disadvantages. On the plus side is the advantage that small countries can make their policies taking account of the welfare of their own citizens. Further, the fact that each small country is an independent nation gives it a political weight in the current state of international rivalries among major powers and in consequence the small developing countries have attracted aid in per capita terms much greater than the large developing countries. On the minus side, growth opportunities are more limited as we have noted and small countries have to devote a larger part of their resources to the apparatus of a national government; as pointed out above, this may constitute a considerable burden on their economies.

In order to focus on the problems of smallness it is useful to consider other characteristics which differentiate small countries from small regions within large countries. The differentiating characteristic of small countries, of course, is that they are politically independent. Hence, small countries make their own economic policies, while small regions within large countries tend to have their policies made for them from distant capitals. We have taken the independent political status of the small countries as part of our datum. It may be noted, however, that the existence of such small entities as independent countries under modern political conditions is not entirely fortuitous. It is highly likely that it is closely related to the characteristic of many small countries identified above, namely their remoteness.

Certainly some of the concerns expressed by small regions within large countries are the same as those expressed by small countries in the world economy. There is, for example, much discussion of the domination of small regions by central governments of the countries of which they are a part. And there is a parallel between the gains of interregional and international trade which was first developed systematically by Ohlin (1933). Both trade among regions and trade among nations lead to specialisation of production. Interregional trade differs from international trade in that the movement of labour and capital between regions within one country is usually completely unrestricted. This increases the tendency towards the equalisation of real incomes among regions. Yet, the parallel may still carry over since the factor-price-equalisation theorem of international trade theory asserts that, under certain conditions, free trade in commodities alone will lead to the equalisation among countries of real factor incomes.

In fact, however, markets within countries and especially developing countries do not function as efficiently as the neoclassical model assumes, so that small regions within countries are not fully integrated with other regions by commodity trade. Markets among countries are highly restricted by tariff and non-tariff barriers which limit the gains from trade and the consequent narrowing of real income differentials among nations. In the case of small regions within countries, there is a movement of factors which supplements the trade in commodities as a way of integrating the small regions in the national economies. There is much less comparable movement of factors between small countries and other countries, with a few notable exceptions.

There is another interesting parallel between small countries and small regions. In the literature on economic growth there has been a recognition that, largely because of regional differences in output mix, the growth rates of different regions within a country will differ markedly. This has been borne out by empirical studies (Williamson, 1965). By contrast with the differences over time and among countries, differences among regions are reduced by the freedom of members of the national labour force and of owners of capital and other resources to move from regions which are lagging to regions which are growing relatively rapidly.

In a sense, it is now widely recognised that not all less-developed countries are economically viable without assistance and therefore have had to be assisted by aid from the developed countries who have accepted an international responsibility to do so. The flow of such aid between sovereign states is one of the historically distinguishing features of the second half of the twentieth century. The real issue before us is then to consider the actual pattern of aid flows to the small countries of the world and how to improve the flow of such aid, taking account of their principal characteristics, both of size and of remoteness.

Aid may supplement the resources of small countries and increase the opportunities for growth of production. It has been observed that the level of international aid per capita is high for small countries (de Vries, 1975; Fisk, 1981). This has been attributed to the political motivation of aid-giving. A small country is an independent nation with a voice in international affairs and a vote in the General Assembly of the UN and other international bodies. What matters here for donor countries which wish to win and keep friends is the government of these countries, not their peoples at large. For example, it has been suggested that India would have got more aid if it were split into several small nations (Pearson Commission, 1969). However, these high levels of aid may also reflect the economic limitations of smallness.

Aid comes in many forms but the international statistics of aid are confined to capital transfers. These statistics, therefore, understate the aid flows. It is possible that they are also biased in that the understatement is relatively great for some groups of countries, including perhaps the group of small countries. One other form of aid is trade preferences. The Generalised Systems of Preferences which have been introduced by the developed countries are, for each commodity, offered to all developing countries both small and large alike with few exceptions. But there are other bilateral and multilateral non-reciprocal preference schemes. One well-known scheme is the Lome Convention which gives substantial trade preferences to the group of Caribbean, African and Pacific countries covered by this scheme. It appears that other bilateral or multilateral groupings have increased in recent years and the extent of these preferences may be considerably greater than is commonly realised. For example, in the case of Australia, the Australian System of Trade Preferences is a generalised system of preferences but this is supplemented by three Agreements which give preferences on selected commodities to particular groups of countries, viz. the 1967 Agreement on Trade and Commercial Relations with Papua New Guinea, preferences to the Declared Preference Countries, and the South Pacific Regional Trade and Economic Co-operation Agreement which came into effect on 1 January 1981.

These Australian trade preferences illustrate a feature of trade preferences which holds universally. Before 1975, New Guinea was administered by Australia as a UN Trust Territory and Papua was a Territory of Australia and before that a British Protectorate. The Declared Preference Countries include 15 small countries and, since all DPCs are former British colonies or protectorates, these preferences are a remnant of the former British Imperial Preference system. The South Pacific countries comprise the Cook Islands, Kiribati, Niue, Solomon Islands, Tonga, Tuvalu and Western Samoa, all of which are former British colonies or protectorates or territories administered by New Zealand. Similarly, almost all of the Lome Convention countries are former colonies or territories of France or the United Kingdom or other European metropolitan powers. In this respect the trade preferences resemble aid flows in which the same former metropolitan countries are generally over-represented as aid donors to the small countries relative to the levels of their aid distributed globally.

Another particular form of international aid is worthy of mention, namely, aid in the form of free or subsidised services of professional and scientific manpower. We noted above that small countries cannot provide a wide range of such services themselves.

To some extent these services can be and have been provided by groups of countries which pool these resources available in a region of neighbouring countries; for example, the South Pacific Forum. However, many such services and especially the more highly trained and specialised personnel must be obtained from larger countries. The Commonwealth Secretariat itself has been performing a useful function in organising international aid and co-operation in this field.

Other aid is granted to some small countries in a diversity of unrecorded forms such as tertiary and secondary education, diplomatic representation and other government services, and defence agreements. As an example, several of the small countries in the Pacific receive very large amounts of aid from New Zealand, Australia, the United Kingdom and multilateral sources. In discussing the small countries of the South Pacific, Fisk (1981, p.11) observes "Pacific developing countries with limited resources that are adequate to sustain the population well above minimum subsistence levels, but not at their present level of income.... are already well on the way to permanent dependence on aid and/or migration if they have not already reached there. In this category, I include Western Samoa, Tonga, Niue and the Cook Islands." Castle (1980) reached the same pessimistic conclusion for these countries. For these poorly endowed small island economies both authors argued that the only alternatives to permanent aid dependence on some large donor country were either a sharp reduction in their present levels of consumption per capita or emigration.

Emigration is an option that is not available to most small countries. All high income developed countries have strict controls on the entry of migrants from all foreign territories. The levels of permanent immigration are low with the exception of a handful of developed countries, notably the United States, United Kingdom, Canada and Australia, and preferences are given mainly to refugees and skilled workers. Unless preference is given to applicants from small countries, emigration is not a feasible option for them. In any case large-scale emigration can have very harmful effects on the sex and age and skill structure of a country and on the morale of the remaining population.

Of course not all small countries are heavily dependent on aid or other preferences relating to trade or emigration. However, it seems to us that the remoteness of the land-locked and 'sea-locked' small countries severely constrains their growth opportunities. Some of these 'locked' countries are also arid desert lands or infertile islands with poor prospects for the agricultural sector. In the absence of a fortuitous abundant supply of some valuable mineral or the development of marine resources within the 200 mile exclusive economic zone - which may be possible for some of them - their prospects of avoiding recourse to aid in some form as an integral part of their current levels of consumption seem poor.

Even for those small countries which are better endowed, the concentration phenomenon constrains severely their long-run growth opportunities. Such countries may enjoy average or above average rates of growth while the prices of their major export commodities relative to their imports are favourable, but sustained growth is tenuous.

FINAL COMMENTS

For the set of countries which have been designated as small we have observed that there is a considerable diversity in terms of quantities and the nature of their resource endowments. These countries are a heterogeneous group. It may not be possible to evolve a general theory of a 'small country' for the purposes of analysing the growth options of specific countries.

The aspect of smallness which may best characterise these countries is the concentration of output. While this is economically significant, it may be necessary to consider other characteristics of these countries as a group, such as their remoteness and their limited human resources.

NOTES

1. A.K. Sen suggested to us that this partitioning may be incomplete. That is, one might meaningfully discuss the special features or problems of some countries which are 'small' and some which are 'large', in some sense, leaving an intermediate group which are neither small nor large.

2. Strictly speaking one should separate out the import content of the gross value of exports in the first case and the intermediate input content of imports in the second in order to obtain estimates of the proportion of value added from exports and the proportion of the absorption of final goods and services which comes from abroad. Moreover, a non-zero balance of trade may cause these two measures to diverge. However, these adjustments are small.

3. See, for example, Chenery and Taylor (1968), Chenery and Syrquin (1975) and Kuznets (1971).

4. See Lloyd (1968), chapter VI, for references.

5. See, for example, proceedings of the 1957 IEA conference, in Robinson (1960).

6. For example, Erb and Schiavo-Campo (1969). The paper by Ian Thomas in this volume confirms empirically this hypothesis.

7. If one uses the variance around the trend as the measure of instability, instability of aggregate exports decomposes. into the terms

$$V^2 = \Sigma w_i^2 V_i^2 + 2\Sigma w_i w_j V_{ij}$$

$$i \neq j$$

where w_1 is the share of commodity i and V_i^2 and V_{ij} are the variances and covariances.

8. This literature is reviewed by McBean and Nguyen (1980).

9. This is discussed by Lloyd and Procter (1981).

10. Formally, we have national expenditure defined as

$$Y = \Sigma_i Y_i = \Sigma_i p_i z_i$$

where p_i is the relative price and z_i is the quantity produced of commodity i. Hence, over some time interval,

$$G = \Delta Y/Y = \Sigma_i w_i G_i \qquad\qquad G_i = \Delta Y_i/Y_i$$

$$= \Sigma_i w_i \left[(\Delta p_i/p_i) + (\Delta z_i/z_i) + (\Delta p_i/p_i)(\Delta z_i/z_i) \right]$$

$$\simeq \Sigma_i w_i (\Delta p_i/p_i)$$

if the price effects dominate the quantity effects. This is usually so. Unlike the expression for export instability in footnote 7, this expression is the simple weighted average of commodity terms. Hence the growth effects of smallness are more directly related to the concentration of production than are the instability effects.

11. The evidence in the Blazic-Metzner and Hughes' paper in this volume confirms this prediction.

12. Regions within large independent countries have very limited say in determining the policies that govern their lives, policies which are made by their national governments on the basis of many considerations other than the welfare of each small region. Hence, we believe that the move towards greater decentralisation of planning and policy-making that is being discussed for the large countries is a step in the right direction.

REFERENCES

Castle, L.V., 1980, 'The Economic Context'. In R.G. Ward and Andrew Proctor, eds.,"South Pacific Agriculture Choices and Constraints", Asian Development Bank.

Chenery, H.B. and Syrquin, M., 1975, "Patterns of Development", London: Oxford University Press.

_____ and Taylor, L., 1968, 'Development Patterns: Among Countries and Over Time'. In "The Review of Economics and Statistics", Vol.1, No.4.

Commonwealth Secretariat, 1979, "Basic Statistical Data on Selected Countries (with population of less than 5 million)", London.

Erb,G.F. and Schiavo-Campo, S., 1969, 'Export Instability, Level of Development and Economic Size of Less Developed Countries'. In "Bulletin of Oxford University Institute of Economics and Statistics", Vol.31, No.4.

Fisk, E.K., 1962, 'Planning in a Primitive Economy: Special Problems of Papua New Guinea'. In "Economic Record", Vol. 38

_____, 1981, 'Development and the South Pacific in the 1980s', mimeo., Australian National University.

Keyfitz, N., 1975, 'How do we Know the Facts of Demography?' In "Population and Development Review", Vol.1.

Kuznets, Simon, 1971, "Economic Growth of Nations", Cambridge, Mass: Harvard University Press.

Lloyd, P.J., 1968, "International Trade of Small Nations", Durham, N.C: Duke University Press.

_____ and Procter, R., 1981, 'Commodity Decomposition of Export-Import Instability: New Zealand', mimeo., Australian National University.

MacBean, A.I. and Nguyen, D.T., 1980, 'Commodity Concentration and Export Earnings Instability: a Mathematical Analysis'. In "Economic Journal", Vol.90.

Ohlin, B., 1933, "Interregional and International Trade", Cambridge, Mass: Harvard University Press.

Pearson Commission, 1969, "Partners in Development", New York: Praeger.

Robinson, E.A.G., ed., 1960, "The Economic Consequences of the Size of Nations", London: Macmillan.

_____, 1969, "Location Theory and Regional Economics in Backward Areas in Advanced Countries", London: Macmillan.

Schultz, T.W., 1980, 'Nobel Lecture: The Economics of Being Poor'. In "Journal of Political Economy", Vol. 88.

Selwyn, P., ed., 1975, "Development Policy in Small Countries", London: Croom Helm.

United Nations Conference on Trade and Development, 1979, "Handbook of International Trade and Development Statistics", New York: United Nations.   .

de Vries, B.A., 1975, 'Development Aid to Small Countries'. In Selwyn, op.cit.

Waters, W.G., 1970, 'Transportation Costs, Tariffs and the

Pattern of Industrial Protection'. In "American Economic Review", Vol.60.

Williamson, J.G., 1965, 'Regional Inequality and the Process of National Development'. In "Economic Development and Cultural Change", Vol.13, Supplement.

The World Bank, 1979, "World Economic and Social Indicators", Washington, D.C.

Yeats, A.J., 1979, "Trade Barriers Facing Developing Countries", London: Macmillan.

2. Classification of Economies by Size

Bimal Jalan*

Most large countries contain smaller political or administrative sub-divisions within them, and much of the economic activity takes place at the level of firms, farms or individuals. In that sense, a large economy may be considered to be, in effect, a conglomeration of smaller decision-making units. Similarly, a small economy, independent or otherwise, may be considered to be no different from a small region or a district within a large economy. The question, therefore, arises whether the size of the aggregate or of the nation as a whole is particularly·relevant in understanding and analysing the behaviour of the economy or of the economic entities within it.

It is probably true that if a country were fully integrated with a larger trading block, with no restrictions on the movement of goods or factors of production, and were satisfied with the results of such integration, the problems of such a country could be analysed as part of the problems of the larger region. These assumptions are, however, seldom fulfilled in practice. The movement of factors of production and goods among nations is not free of restrictions, and what is more important, many small countries are not entirely satisfied with the consequences of their dependence on certain metropolitan or erstwhile colonial powers. In their search for a better economic future, the governments of the small, and indeed the larger, developing countries are attempting to exercise a measure of control over the allocation of resources, and the distribution of the gains from the use of these resources. The smaller countries, however, face totally different options from those available to the larger developing countries. For example, the economic structure of most small countries is characterised by a much greater dependence on foreign trade and foreign investment. In its quest for a measure of national self-reliance, a large country has the option of establishing domestic industries, encouraging domestic skills, and promoting domestic investment as a matter of deliberate policy. These options are seldom open to a small country and, even when they are available, the problems that arise in the implementation of these policies are likely to be of a totally different magnitude from those in large countries.

*The author is grateful to J. Karunasekera for his help in preparing this paper.

Svennilson argued, in his contribution to the International Economic Association conference in 1957, that the concept of a nation is important for purposes of economic analysis as the boundary of an independent nation represents a point of discontinuity. The boundaries of a nation represent a change in the degree of mobility of almost all the factors of production and, above all, a discontinuity in the mobility of goods. To some extent, these discontinuities are the result of real differences in language, education and skill, but in a great part, they arise from the exercise of political authority for purposes of regulating trade, industry and the movement of factors of production. An important manifestation of the economic discontinuity, for example, is the notion of 'national' currencies and the neêd for countries to balance international payments.[1]

For these reasons, it is unrealistic to consider problems of economic policy in developing countries independently of size. If the hypothesis is correct that economic structures and the processes of development are likely to be different in small countries from those in large countries, it also becomes necessary to define the basis for distinguishing between the two groups. The question of classification of countries according to size has been discussed in the literature, but with no conclusive results. It is generally agreed that the neoclassical definition of 'smallness' in international trade (i.e. countries which are price-takers and have no influence on the terms of trade) is not particularly helpful, as on this definition most developing countries will fall into this category. This definition also does not make a distinction between the size of the total economy and the control that an economy may exercise on the price of a particular product or commodity. It has also been rightly emphasised by some writers that the definition of a small or large economy is dependent on the issues that are being examined. Thus, E.A.G. Robinson, in his introduction to the International Economic Association conference volume, pointed out that "for some purposes, it is relevant and significant to discuss the relation of the number of persons comprising the population to the average productivity per head of that population. For some purposes - ability to provide a market for an optimum plant for some industry, for example - one is concerned, not with numbers but with expenditure, and it is relevant to discuss the size of the total home market for the country....."[2]

Percy Selwyn, in his introduction to the Barbados conference volume, reached a similar conclusion, "if we are concerned with constraints resulting from a narrow range of resources, we may identify size with physical area. If we are concerned with manpower limitations of the small clientele for public and other services, we will measure size in terms of population......" He went on to suggest that "this ambiguity may however be less important than it may appear; many of the countries with which we were concerned were in fact small on any measure".[3] Bhaduri, et al., in their contribution to this volume, suggest that in fact it may not be possible to find a statistically satisfactory index of smallness because (a) various relevant characteristics of smallness, e.g. population, geographical size and natural resource base, may not be positively correlated; and (b) an ordering of countries in terms of the relevant indices of smallness is unlikely to remain invariant over time.

From a theoretical point of view, these views may be correct, but they are not very helpful for purposes of analysing the problems and policy issues in small countries as a group. It is interesting that, in the absence of a satisfactory definition, most writers on small economies have been compelled to use arbitrary cut-off points to distinguish the economies that they were dealing with from those that they were not. Kuznets (1960) used a cut-off point of ten million as in his view this figure provided "a rough decision made with an eye to the distribution of nations by size as it exists today and has existed over the last 50-75 years". Demas (1965) defined small countries to be those that had populations of five million or less and with usable land area of 10 to 20 thousand square miles or less. Chenery and Syrquin (1975) used a cut-off point of 15 million population.

The use of arbitrary and different cut-off points has created enormous difficulties in testing the validity of propositions advanced by various writers regarding the development process in small economies. This is part of the reason why a certain amount of confusion prevails on the question of the importance of size in explaining the historical behaviour of economic variables, e.g. growth of manufacturing or national income, in developing countries.[4] It is clear that if the study on small economies has to proceed in a systematic way, there should be generally agreed criteria for defining what we mean by small. The conceptual problems that arise in classifying countries according to size are not intrinsically different from those that arise in classifying countries according to levels of development or standards of living. Yet by practice and usage, there is now a generally acceptable basis for distinguishing between developed and developing countries. A similar approach is needed for classifying countries by size.

There are a number of alternative methodologies that may be adopted for this purpose. One possible approach is to establish a theoretical link between, say, prospects for productivity growth in manufacturing and the absolute size of investment/employment in an economy, and argue that there is a critical minimum size of population and investment below which growth in productivity is not possible. If this minimum size could be statistically computed, countries with population/income below this critical minimum could be classified as small. This procedure has been suggested by Bhaduri et al., and has some intellectual appeal. The difficulty, however, is that the restrictive assumptions of their model (e.g. the assumption of the constancy of the investment/output ratio, and the constancy of the investment elasticities of the productivity ratios) and the lack of data relating to the crucial variables make it statistically impractical to establish the critical values of employment/income.

An alternative possibility is to examine the historical behaviour of certain variables which, on a priori grounds, are likely to be affected by size (e.g. growth of manufacturing or the ratio of foreign trade), and then divide countries into different groups according to certain values of these variables. Thus, if it could be assumed that economic performance is likely to be affected by size, all developing countries could be divided into two groups according to their performance and a linear combination of various measures of size, which discriminates most strongly between two groups, could be derived. From an economic point of view, this approach may also have a certain attractiveness. However, statistical exercises carried out in the Commonwealth Secretariat along these lines did not lead to any meaningful results. There is also the question whether there is a degree of circularity in this approach as we would have pre-determined the likely consequences of size as a factor in development.

A practical, even if somewhat less exciting, approach is to take a simpler route and measure size in terms of a few physical and economic indicators which may be considered relevant for economic analysis. A number of writers have considered the question of criteria that might be used to define the size of nations.[5] The most commonly used criterion is that of population as many important economic consequences of size seem to flow from the limited size of the populations of small countries. Other criteria that have also received some attention are national income, per capita income, total land area, arable land area, and natural resource base. For an analysis of a specific problem or a development issue, the use of each of these criteria is justifiable. However, for a general classification of countries according to size, we need to be more selective and choose those criteria which may be taken as representing different dimensions of a country's development potential. A feasible approach from this viewpoint is to take those factors into account which, taken together, define the aggregate production potential of the country. If one assumes that the production possibility frontier for a country will be determined by the size of the labour force, the total capital stock and the total available arable land, the three indicators that could be used to define the size of a country are population (as proxy for labour force), total national income (as proxy for capital stock), and arable land area. The underlying hypothesis here is that differences in economic structures and economic performance due to the size factor are likely to be due to differences in the 'resource base' of countries as represented by the size of their capital, human and natural resources.

It is also clear that size is a relative concept; some countries can be considered to be small only because some others are large. As such, in principle, the relative size of a country on any of the above three criteria must be considered to depend on the ranking of a particular country in relation to other countries. It is, therefore, suggested that the relative size of countries on the three criteria should be measured in terms of the highest values of these criteria for all the developing countries taken together. On this basis, it is possible to construct a country size index for all developing countries with the 'largest' country on each criterion taken as 100. The separate indices can be combined into an overall composite index of size by assigning either equal weights or differential weights. Unfortunately, at the present state of our knowledge, it is not possible to estimate the relative contribution of these three factors to the production potential of a country. As a first approximation, therefore, it may be appropriate to construct a combined index of size by assigning equal weights to the three factors, although it must be readily conceded that there is no firm empirical basis for doing so. Appendix Table A.1 shows the size index for 111 countries calculated according to the following formula:

$$I_i = \frac{100}{3} \left[\frac{P_i}{P_{max}} + \frac{A_i}{A_{max}} + \frac{Y_i}{Y_{max}} \right]$$

Where

I_i is the country size index for individual country i, with i running from 1 to 111;

P, A and Y are population, arable area and GNP of each country respectively;

P_{max}, A_{max} and Y_{max} represent the highest values of population, arable area and GNP respectively.

It will be seen that the country size index for a large number of countries is indeed very small, and the mean and the median values of the index for the whole sample are only 3.1 and 0.8 (on a scale from 0 to 100). There is also a discontinuity at the end of the series of country size indices and there are four countries (viz. Argentina, Mexico, Brazil and India) whose index values are exceptionally high. In view of the skewed distribution and the predominance of small values, a convenient way of dividing countries into categories of small and not so small may be to use the median value of the index as a cut-off point. According to the data presented in Appendix Table A.1, Paraguay constitutes the dividing line for distinguishing between small and other countries. The highest values of population, arable area and GNP for countries which have a size index below that of Paraguay are 4.7 million, 22,850 sq.km. and US$ 2.9 billion respectively.

However, there is a problem in combining these three indices into a single index of size. There is an implicit assumption that the consequences of the smallness of one variable (e.g. population) will be compensated by the larger value of another variable (e.g. area or income). This is, of course, not true. In order to get over this problem, it is suggested that population, arable area and GNP should be considered as three independent measures of size, and that the highest values of these in the sample of countries with an aggregate size index below that of Paraguay should be taken as the boundaries for classification of small economies.[6] In other words, all countries which have populations of 4.7 million or less, arable areas of 22,850 sq. km. or less, and GNPs of US$2.9 billion or less may

43

be classified as 'small'. In order to avoid giving a misleading impression of precision, these figures may be rounded to 5 million, 25,000 sq. km. and US$3 billion respectively. An illustrative list of countries which satisfy all these three criteria is given in Table 1.

TABLE 1

AN ILLUSTRATIVE LIST OF SMALL DEVELOPING ECONOMIES

Antigua	Guam	Papua New Guinea
Bahamas, The	Guinea-Bissau	Paraguay
Barbados	Guyana	Reunion
Belize	Haiti	Rwanda
Bermuda	Honduras	St. Kitts-Nevis
Bhutan	Jamaica	St. Lucia
Botswana	Jordan	St. Vincent
Burundi	Lesotho	Sao Tome and Principe
Cape Verde	Liberia	Seychelles
Comoros	Macao	Solomon Islands
Congo	Maldives	Somalia
Costa Rica	Malta	Surinam
Cyprus	Mauritania	Swaziland
Djibouti	Mauritius	Togo
Dominica	Namibia	Tonga
El Salvador	Neth.Antilles	Trinidad & Tobago
Equ.Guinea	New Caledonia	Vanuatu
Fiji	Nicaragua	Western Samoa
Gambia, The	Pacific Islands	Yemen (Dem.)
Grenada	Panama	

Source: Appendix Table A.1

Of the 59 countries listed above,[7] as many as 21 countries have a size index of below 0.1, which is one-eighth of the value of the index for Paraguay. The highest values of population, arable area and GNP for this group of 21 countries are: 370,000, 2,300 sq. km. and US$460 million respectively. These very small countries are likely to constitute a class by themselves and for an analysis of their special problems, it is necessary to classify small countries further, into two categories of, say, 'micro states' and 'small states'. A rough sub-classification of countries into these two groups can be derived by adopting cut-off values of population, arable area and GNP of, say, 400,000, 2,500 sq.km., and $500 million respectively.

It is true that the criteria suggested above are not invariant with respect to time. However, this is not a serious objection if one can assume that the ranking of countries according to these three criteria will not change dramatically within the foreseeable future. The composition of different categories will change only after a long period of time, as indeed is likely to be the case in respect of present categories of developed and developing countries. For the present, the procedure suggested here should provide a workable basis for further research and analysis on problems of small economies.

44

NOTES

1. For a detailed discussion, see Svennilson (1960).

2. See Robinson (1960, p. xv).

3. See Selwyn (1975, p.11).

4. See paper by Thomas on 'Industrialisation Experience of Small Economies' in this volume.

5. In particular, see paper by Lloyd and Sundrum on 'Characteristics of Small Countries' in this volume.

6. The use of multiple criteria for classifying countries is similar to the approach adopted by the United Nations for identifying the least developed countries. According to the United Nations criteria, a least developed country is one which had a per capita GDP of US$100 or less in 1968; a share of manufacturing in GNP of ten per cent or less in 1968; and a literacy rate of 20 per cent or less for persons above 15 years (1968).

7. Some small countries which may satisfy these criteria are not included in Appendix Table A.1 because of lack of reliable data.

REFERENCES

Chenery, H.B., and Syrquin, M, 1975, "Patterns of Development, 1950-70", London: Oxford University Press.

Demas, William G., 1965, "The Economics of Development in Small Countries with Special Reference to the Caribbean", Montreal: Mcgill University Press.

Food and Agriculture Organization (FAO), 1979, "Production Yearbook", Vol.33, New York.

Kuznets, S., 1960, 'Economic Growth of Small Nations'. In E.A.G. Robinson, ed., "Economic Consequences of the Size of Nations", London: Macmillan.

Robinson, E.A.G., ed., 1960, op. cit.

Selwyn, Percy, ed., 1975, "Development Policy in Small Countries," London: Croom Helm.

Svennilson, I., 1960, "The Concept of the Nation and its Relevance to Economic Analysis". In E.A.G. Robinson, ed., op.cit.

The World Bank, 1979, "World Bank Atlas", Washington, D.C.

TABLE A.1

INDICATORS OF SIZE IN SELECTED COUNTRIES

Country	Country Size Index	Population (in thousand)	Arable Area (in sq. km)	GNP (US$ million)
St. Kitts Nevis	0.011	50	140	30
Maldives	0.012	140	30	20
Dominica	0.014	77	170	30
St. Vincent	0.015	103	170	30
Seychelles	0.016	62	50	60
Antigua	0.018	73	80	60
Grenada	0.019	105	160	50
Sao Tome & Principe	0.020	82	360	40
Tonga	0.023	92	530	40
St. Lucia	0.024	118	170	70
New Hebrides	0.034	101	950	50
Cape Verde	0.035	313	400	50
Belize	0.037	130	510	100
Solomon Islands	0.038	205	540	80
Western Samoa	0.042	154	1,190	50
Djibouti	0.042	300	10	130
Pacific Islands	0.047	129	590	140
Comoros	0.051	370	900	70
Equ. Guinea	0.088	338	2,300	120
Macau	0.091	291	20	370
Bermuda	0.097	54	50	460
Gambia, The	0.106	554	2,650	120
Barbados	0.109	248	330	440
Swaziland	0.115	511	1,670	270
Bahamas, The	0.120	213	160	520
Guinea-Bissau	0.122	747	2,850	130
Guam	0.127	94	120	590
Bhutan	0.137	1,231	2,540	110
New Caledonia	0.142	145	100	650
Malta	0.146	333	140	620
Neth. Antilles	0.153	244	80	680
Surinam	0.174	381	460	710
Lesotho	0.201	1,250	3,550	320
Mauritania	0.202	1,503	1,990	410
Mauritius	0.205	906	1,070	670
Guyana	0.205	817	3,790	430
Fiji	0.236	589	2,330	780
Yemen (Dem.)	0.265	1,717	2,650	600
Liberia	0.312	1,684	3,710	740
Reunion	0.322	499	570	1,450
Congo	0.351	1,423	6,670	710
Cyprus	0.359	644	4,320	1,180
Namibia	0.373	926	6,550	960
Botswana	0.385	728	13,600	390
Somalia	0.490	3,660	10,660	430
Papua New Guinea	0.518	2,857	3,560	1,460
Rwanda	0.563	4,379	9,550	710
Burundi	0.581	4,156	12,720	550
Jamaica	0.617	2,101	2,650	2,230
Panama	0.636	1,771	5,650	2,120
Honduras	0.642	3,322	9,150	1,410
Haiti	0.643	4,749	8,700	1,090
Trinidad & Tobago	0.686	1,118	1,570	2,930
Togo	0.706	2,350	22,850	650
Costa Rica	0.789	2,061	4,900	2,870
Paraguay	0.796	2,810	11,200	2,100
Jordan	0.820	2,888	13,650	1,960
Nicaragua	0.848	2,411	15,050	2,090
El Salvador	0.879	4,256	7,310	2,510
Benin	0.889	3,229	29,500	680
Malawi	0.919	5,597	22,780	860
Angola	1.081	6,575	18,300	1,840
Yemen (Arab)	1.088	4,982	15,700	2,540
Sierra Leone	1.106	3,210	40,980	640
Senegal	1.152	5,240	24,040	1,980
Guinea	1.287	4,989	41,700	1,000
Central Afr. Rep.	1.351	1,867	59,100	440

INDICATORS OF SIZE IN SELECTED COUNTRIES

Country	Country Size Index	Population (in thousand)	Arable Area (in sq. km)	GNP (US$ million)
Dominican Rep.	1.357	4,980	12,300	4,190
Uruguay	1.376	2,876	19,100	4,170
Madagascar	1.383	8,085	29,290	1,870
Mozambique	1.386	9,691	30,800	1,320
Bolivia	1.423	5,154	33,050	2,460
Nepal	1.453	13,332	23,140	1,450
Singapore	1.454	2,319	80	6,540
Zimbabwe	1.465	6,683	24,800	3,070
Upper Volta	1.547	5,465	56,130	760
Sri Lanka	1.629	14,097	21,310	2,290
Chad	1.714	4,221	70,000	560
Lebanon	1.727	2,939	3,480	7,390
Zambia	1.734	5,128	50,080	2,350
Guatemala	1.782	6,436	18,000	5,350
Ghana	1.895	10,634	27,050	3,940
Kenya	2.092	14,614	22,700	4,300
Tunisia	2.184	5,899	44,100	4,940
Uganda	2.364	12,049	55,380	3,140
Mali	2.398	6,129	98,000	720
Cameroon	2.535	7,882	73,800	3,280
Tanzania	2.567	16,363	51,000	3,440
Hong Kong	2.660	4,536	90	11,890
Afghanistan	2.979	14,304	80,500	3,150
Ivory Coast	3.358	7,463	91,600	5,710
Niger	3.401	4,862	150,000	950
Sudan	3.517	16,919	74,950	5,650
Zaire	3.648	25,694	61,800	5,290
Peru	3.939	16,363	34,330	11,800
Chile	4.380	10,553	58,280	13,160
Burma	4.511	31,512	99,990	4,330
Malaysia	4.522	12,961	64,800	12,600
Morocco	4.775	18,310	78,400	11,140
Ethiopia	4.965	30,245	137,300	3,280
Egypt	5.185	37,796	28,310	12,950
Colombia	6.197	24,605	55,050	18,760
Bangladesh	7.407	81,219	91,250	6,520
Philippines	8.092	44,473	81,000	20,410
Korea Rep.	9.486	35,953	22,310	35,150
Thailand	9.555	43,326	176,500	18,660
Pakistan	11.012	74,905	203,000	15,070
Argentina	18.169	26,036	350,000	48,710
Mexico	22.905	63,319	232,200	73,720
Brazil	47.472	116,100	407,200	163,880
India	87.043	631,726	1,694,000	100,180

Note: All figures are for 1977. Please see text for the formula used for calculation of the country size index.

Sources: The World Bank, 1979, "World Bank Atlas"; and FAO, 1979, "Production Yearbook", Vol.33.

3. Problems of Long-term Growth in Small Economies: a Theoretical Analysis

Amit Bhaduri, Anjan Mukherji and Ramprasad Sengupta

Evidently, the 'smallness' of a country is a multidimensional concept. Usually one particular aspect of smallness is chosen depending on the context. Thus a country may be called 'small' because of its geographical size; or it may be 'small' because its population is small. In a somewhat different context, a country may be considered 'small' because of its narrow natural resource base or because it has a relatively small domestic market. The former notion of a 'small' country is thus based on the natural characteristics of the country; the latter on its economic characteristics.

ECONOMIC 'SMALLNESS' AS A MULTIDIMENSIONAL CONCEPT

A little reflection will show that there may be a conflict between 'smallness' defined on the basis of <u>natural</u> characteristics like area or population and that defined on the basis of <u>economic</u> characteristics such as natural resource base or domestic market.[1] For it is possible to imagine and find examples of countries whose natural 'smallness' stands in a somewhat inverse relation to their relevant economic characteristics (e.g. some of the oil-producing countries of West Asia may be 'small' in terms of area or population, but relatively 'large' in terms of natural resource base or the size of the domestic market). Under these circumstances it will not be possible to find any statistically satisfactory composite index of 'smallness', involving both the natural and the economic characteristics.

At another level, any attempt to define the index of 'smallness' of a country encounters difficulties of another nature. For example, even a simple index like population is satisfactory only in a more or less static sense; obviously, with a growing population, a country which is small to-day in terms of population need not remain small at a somewhat distant future date. Similarly, a small domestic market need not imply smallness of the market for all time to come. All this seems to point to the fact that neither the cut-off point nor the ordering of countries in terms of some specific indices of 'smallness' is likely to remain invariant over time.

To sum up: (a) a statistically satisfactory composite index of 'smallness' is unlikely to be found because the various relevant characteristics are not, in general, positively correlated in any significant sense; and (b) the ordering of countries in terms of some of their relevant indices of 'smallness' (e.g. population, market-size, per capita income, etc) is unlikely to remain invariant over time.[2] Similarly, many arbitrarily chosen cut-off points for 'smallness' (e.g. population of less than five million) are also time-dependent.

The above mentioned difficulties, and a host of similar ones, make it evidently worthwhile for us to explore other avenues for characterising the economic 'smallness' of a country. In approaching the problem from an economic point of view, it appears that there are two rather distinct elements or components which need to be combined in the characterisation of smallness. On the one hand, a 'small' economy is typically an economy which is relatively open to international trade (although the obverse is not necessarily true) and this <u>international aspect</u> of smallness should be built into the characterisation. On the other hand, the techno-economic aspect of smallness can almost always be related to some scale factor, i.e. in the presence of economies of scale and increasing returns, smallness of scale must result in certain distinct disadvantages. One could imagine this scale-effect to be a typical characteristic of the national production aspect of a small economy. The avenue which we wish to explore in the economic characterisation of 'smallness' consists of these two distinct aspects of a typical small country, namely its international aspect of relative openness to foreign trade and its national production aspect dominated by the effect of scale of operation.

It is clear that, for the purpose of economic analysis, one could set out various alternative postulates to capture the international and the national production aspects of a small economy mentioned above. For example, within the static framework of conventional international trade theory, one would have tried to deal with the international aspect in terms of 'relative factor endowments'. But to our way of thinking, this would have immediately come into conflict with the other aspect, namely production dominated by scale-effect. For increasing returns is a classic example of a dynamic economic phenomenon involving time in an essential manner,[3] which hardly fits into the static framework of conventional trade theory. Such difficulties compel us to view 'comparative advantage' from international trade and the phenomenon of 'increasing returns to scale' in an integrated manner in an attempt economically to characterise smallness.

Comparative advantage in international trade over time, or in a dynamic sense, is essentially related to the concept of the rate of growth of productivity of labour. Other things being equal (in particular, the rise in wage rates across countries), the country or group of countries with a faster rise in labour productivity over time will be gaining in competitive position in the international market.[4] In a similar manner, the scale-effect over time or dynamic increasing returns to scale is a phenomenon best captured by relating increasing labour productivity to the scale of operation (or output) over time. Thus, in the dynamic context, the effects both of scale and of comparative advantage point to the crucial importance of a single factor, namely the rate of growth of labour productivity over time, and it is from this point of view that an economically integrated approach can be attempted to characterise the problem of smallness of a country. It should be stressed that such a characterisation is set essentially in a dynamic context and focuses on the problem of sustainable growth in labour productivity in a small country. We present below a stylised model, based on not too unreasonable assumptions, to focus sharply on this problem of sustainable growth in labour productivity faced by a small country.

A FORMAL IDENTIFICATION OF CRITICAL MINIMUM SIZE

In order to capture the limits to sustainable growth in labour productivity in a small economy, we must explicitly introduce the postulate of increasing returns to scale. This is captured in our formal analysis by assuming that both the productivity of labour and that of other material inputs (termed 'capital') are positively related to the size of investment. But since investment typically influences the productive capacity of the economy at the margin, i.e. mostly for new plant and equipment,[5] we can more legitimately assume that the incremental output-capital ratio (β) and the incremental output-labour ratio (θ) are increasing functions of the scale of investment (I), i.e.

$$\beta = \beta(I) \; ; \; \beta'(I) \equiv \frac{d\beta}{dI} > 0$$

$$\text{and} \quad \theta = \theta(I) \; ; \; \theta'(I) \equiv \frac{d\theta}{dI} > 0 \quad \Bigg\} \quad \ldots\ldots\ldots\ldots\ldots(A.1)$$

In order to focus exclusively on the effect of the scale and size of a country on the sustainable growth in labour productivity, we also abstract from the Keynesian problem of effective demand and the Marxian problem of realisation of profits through adequate market size. In terms of modern national income accounting, this implies that all savings are automatically invested and there is no independent investment function. Needless to emphasise, as a description of reality, this pre-Keynesian assumption leading to an abstraction from the effective demand problem is not justifiable. Nevertheless, this assumption is made not with a view to attaining greater descriptive reality, but to isolate the problem of sustainable productivity growth from the 'supply side' (i.e. ignoring the problem of effective demand).[6] To keep the formal argument simple, we also assume that the ratio of investment (identically equal to savings by assumption) to national income is a constant (α) through time, i.e.

$$S = I = \alpha Y, \; 1 > \alpha > 0 \quad \ldots\ldots\ldots\ldots\ldots\ldots\ldots\ldots\ldots(A.2)$$

The above two assumptions (A.1) and (A.2) enable us to define the dynamic growth-path along the lines of the so-called Harrod-Domar formulation. However, it will be noted that our concern with labour productivity compels us to introduce employment explicitly into the formulation (unlike in the Harrod-Domar equation, where it is subsumed). Thus we have, from definitions

$$\frac{dY}{dt} = \beta(I) . I, \text{ where } Y = \text{total output} \quad \ldots\ldots\ldots (1)$$

and $\frac{dE}{dt} = \frac{1}{\theta(I)} . \frac{dY}{dt}$, where E = total employment $\ldots (2)$

or, using (2) in (1),

$$\frac{dE}{dt} = \frac{\beta(I)}{\theta(I)} . I \quad \ldots\ldots\ldots\ldots\ldots\ldots\ldots\ldots\ldots\ldots\ldots\ldots (3)$$

Also from the definition of average labour productivity (p), we have

$$p = \frac{Y}{E}$$

so that (from logarithmic differentiation) we obtain the rate of growth of labour productivity as

$$\frac{\dot{p}}{p} = \frac{\dot{Y}}{Y} - \frac{\dot{E}}{E} = \beta(I) \frac{I}{Y} - \frac{\beta(I)}{\theta(I)} . \frac{I}{E} \quad (\text{from (1) and 3)})$$

and, using assumption (A.2),

$$\frac{\dot{p}}{p} = \beta(I) \left[\alpha - \frac{I}{\theta(I).E} \right] \equiv G (I,E) \ldots\ldots\ldots\ldots (4)$$

Thus, in (4), the rate of growth of labour productivity is seen to be explicitly determined by the level of investment and the level of employment in the economy.

It is clear that the rate of growth of labour productivity will be positive only when

$$\frac{\dot{p}}{p} \equiv G(I,E) > 0, \text{ implying from (4)}$$

that $\alpha > \frac{I}{\theta(I).E}$,

$$\text{i.e. } \theta(I) > \frac{I}{\alpha E} = \frac{Y}{E} = p \quad (\because I = \alpha Y) \ldots\ldots\ldots\ldots (5)$$

52

or, alternatively,

$$E > \frac{I}{\alpha\theta(I)} \equiv \phi(I), \text{ as the condition for } \frac{\dot{p}}{p} > 0 \quad \ldots (6)$$

To analyse how the rate of growth of labour productivity $(\frac{\dot{p}}{p})$ is determined in this analytical framework, first note from (4) that

$$\frac{\partial G}{\partial E} \equiv G_E = \beta(I) \cdot \frac{I}{\theta(I)E^2} > 0 \quad \ldots\ldots\ldots\ldots\ldots\ldots\ldots (7)$$

Thus from (7), other things being equal, a larger volume of employment has invariably a positive impact on the rate of growth in labour productivity, somewhat in conformity with the empirically observed so-called 'Kaldor-Verdoorn' law.[7]

On the other hand, the impact of the scale of investment on productivity growth (other things being equal) can be seen to be less certain from (4). For, by partially differentiating (4) with respect to I and after suitable manipulation, we obtain

$$\frac{\partial G}{\partial I} \equiv G_I = \beta'(I)\left[\alpha - \frac{I}{\theta(I)E}\right] - \frac{\beta(I)}{\theta(I)E}(1 - e_\theta) \quad \ldots\ldots (8)$$

where $e_\theta = \frac{d\theta/\theta}{dI/I} \equiv \frac{I\theta'(I)}{\theta(I)}$,

i.e. the elasticity of labour productivity at the margin (θ) with respect to the scale of investment.

From (8), it can now be easily seen that the rate of growth of labour productivity will increase with the level of investment (other things held constant) only if

$$G_I \equiv \frac{\partial G}{\partial I} > 0, \text{ implying}$$

$$\beta'(I)\left[\alpha - \frac{I}{\theta(I)E}\right] > \frac{\beta(I)}{\theta(I) \cdot E}(1 - e_\theta)$$

which, after suitable manipulation, yields

$$E > \frac{I}{\alpha \cdot \theta(I)}\left[\frac{1 - e_\theta + e_\beta}{e_\beta}\right] \quad \ldots\ldots\ldots\ldots\ldots\ldots\ldots (9)$$

where $e_\beta = \frac{d\beta/\beta}{dI/I} = \frac{I\beta'(I)}{\beta(I)}$, i.e. the elasticity of the incremental output-capital ratio with respect to the scale of investment.

We may now use (6) in (9) to rewrite (9) as

$$E > \phi(I) \left[\frac{1 - e_\theta + e_\beta}{e_\beta} \right] \equiv \Psi(I) \quad \dots\dots\dots\dots\dots\dots\dots (10)$$

It will be noted that the right hand side of (10) is only a function of I, exactly like (6).

To make the analysis more easily tractable, we may simply assume constant elasticities,

$e_\theta = \lambda > 0$, a constant

and $e_\beta = \mu > 0$, another constant,

so that assumption (A.1) takes the more specific form

$$\beta(I) = \beta_0 I^\mu$$
$$\text{and } \theta(I) = \theta_0 I^\lambda \qquad \dots\dots\dots\dots\dots\dots\dots\dots\dots (A.1a)$$

(The 'integrability' of the functions implies that only the <u>current</u> level of investment affects the relevant parameters and that the historical path of investment is irrelevant, except in so far as it is captured in the integration constant.)

It can immediately be seen from (A.1a) and (6) that the right hand side of (6), denoted by $\phi(I)$, is an increasing function of I at a decreasing rate so long as $\lambda < 1$; and in view of the inequality condition (6), this function $\phi(I)$ separates all the possible combinations of employment E and investment I into two regions - one region where the rate of growth in labour productivity can be sustained at a positive rate and another region where it cannot be sustained at a positive rate. The function $\phi(I)$, the dividing line between these two regions, also represents the locus of all possible combinations of I and E at which labour productivity is constant,

i.e. $\dot{p}/p = 0$.

Thus, for $\lambda < 1$, we have diagram 1 based upon condition (6) specified further by assumption (A.1a).

On the assumption that $0 < \lambda < 1$ and $\mu > 0$, it can easily be seen from (10) that, for $e_\theta = \lambda$ and $e_\beta = \mu$, we must have

$$\psi(I) > \phi(I) \quad \dots\dots\dots\dots\dots\dots\dots\dots\dots\dots\dots\dots (10a)$$

54

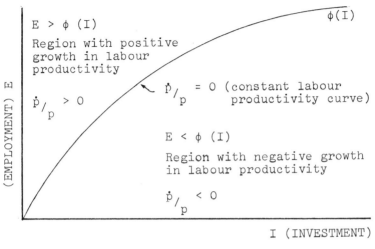

Diagram 1

case (i) $\lambda < 1$

Note on diagram 1: it can easily be checked that

$$\phi(I) = \frac{1}{\alpha\theta_0} I^{1 - \lambda} \text{ and } \phi'(0) = + \infty \text{ and } \phi'(+ \infty) = 0.$$

It will also be noted from (4) that along the locus of any <u>given</u> constant rate of growth of labour productivity,

$\dot{p}/p = G(E,I) = \bar{G}$, we must have

$$\left. \frac{dE}{dI} \right|_{G = \bar{G}} = - \frac{G_I}{G_E}$$

But, since $G_E > 0$ by (7), the sign of this contour of constant labour productivity growth curve is dependent only on the sign of G_I, which in turn, as we have already seen, depends on condition (10). Thus,

$$\frac{dE}{dI} \gtreqless 0 \text{ according to } \begin{matrix} E < \psi(I) \\ E = \psi(I) \\ E > \psi(I) \end{matrix} \Bigg\} \quad \dots\dots\dots\dots\dots(10b)$$

The implications of conditions (10a) and (10b) are more clearly exhibited by diagram 2.

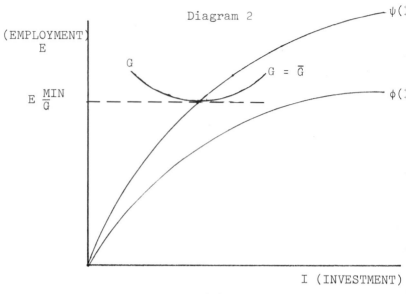

Diagram 2

(EMPLOYMENT)
E

$E \frac{MIN}{G}$

$\psi($

$G = \overline{G}$

$\phi($

G

I (INVESTMENT)

case (i) $\lambda < 1$

In diagram 2, any constant positive labour productivity growth contour GG lies entirely above the curve ϕ(I) (see diagram 1). And by condition (10b), the contour is negatively sloped so long as $E > \psi$ (I) and positively sloped when $E < \psi$(I). It reaches its critical minimum value $E_{\overline{G}}^{min}$ at $E = \psi$ (I), i.e. where the ψ(I) curve also intersects the GG contour.[8]

There are two interesting aspects regarding the size of a country revealed by diagram 2. First, it will be noted that there is a minimum employment level $E \frac{min}{\overline{G}}$ associated with every postulated constant rate of growth of labour productivity. Thus, to return to our earlier discussion, dynamic comparative advantage in international trade may require a small (and hence) relatively open economy to maintain at least a minimum growth rate in labour productivity which becomes simply unfeasible because of its limited active population size. In other words, $E \frac{min}{G}$ associated with $\overline{G}$ in diagram 2 cannot be attained, and population size begins to operate as an effective bottleneck in the context of dynamic comparative advantage in international trade for the small economy.

The second interesting aspect of diagram 2 is to exhibit that for any sufficiently 'small' combination of employment (E) and investment (I), i.e. for an economy 'small' both in terms of population size and income level (since $I = \alpha Y$), the ray through the origin and that particular combination may lie below both ψ(I) and ϕ(I), simply because the slopes of both curves are indefinitely large in the neighbourhood of the origin[9]. This implies that a sufficiently 'small' country, with a correspondingly small configuration of employment (E) and investment (I), may not be able to maintain any positive rate of growth in labour productivity (see diagram 1). At the same time, such a ray through the origin (in diagram 2) would intersect some $G(E,I) = \bar{G}$ locus in the part which is downward sloping only if the (E,I) combination was in some sense large in both the components. This seems to point to still another disadvantage of smallness in the present context: unless a country has some minimum economic size in terms of both employment (or population) and investment (or income level), in maintaining some given growth rate of labour productivity, employment and investment will not be substitutable 'factors'. Consequently, one 'factor' cannot be used as a substitute to break the bottleneck of the other, unless the country already has some minimum economic size in the above sense.

The above analysis demonstrates that, even under the assumption of only moderately increasing returns to scale over time (i.e. for $\lambda < 1$), the economic size of a country in the above sense can produce both an <u>absolute</u> (when no positive growth in labour productivity is possible) and a <u>comparative</u> disadvantage, which makes its international trading position unsustainable over time. In view of this, it is hardly surprising that the assumption of strong increasing returns to scale (i.e. for $\lambda > 1$) will tend to show similar disadvantages regarding size.

In the case of strong increasing returns to scale and $\lambda \geqq 1$, we may separate the analysis into two sub-cases. In the simpler case of $\lambda = 1$, we immediately obtain from (10)

$$\phi(I) = \psi(I), \text{ if } e_\theta \equiv \lambda = 1$$

and, from(6)and(A.1a), the two corresponding curves for $\phi(I)$ and $\psi(I)$ coincide with a constant given by $\frac{1}{\alpha \theta_0}$, i.e.

$$\phi(I) = \psi(I) = \frac{1}{\alpha\theta_0}, \text{ when } \lambda = 1 \dots\dots\dots\dots\dots(10c)$$

Further, given any value of the rate of growth of labour productivity $\bar{G} > 0$, we can obtain, in view of (A.1a),

$$G(E,I) = \beta_0 I^\mu (\alpha - \frac{1}{\theta_0 E}) = \bar{G} > 0$$

simplifying to

$$E = \theta_0 \frac{\beta_0 I^\mu}{(\alpha\beta_0 I^\mu - \bar{G})} \dots\dots\dots\dots\dots\dots\dots\dots(10d)$$

Using (10c) and (10d), we have diagram 3 in this case of $\lambda = 1$, corresponding to our previous diagram 2 in the case of $\lambda < 1$. As can be seen in diagram 3, any contour of constant positive growth in labour productivity GG has a horizontal asymptote $E = \frac{1}{\alpha\theta_0}$, which is independent of $\bar{G}$, and a vertical asymptote $(\frac{\bar{G}}{\alpha\beta_0})^{1/\mu}$, which obviously is not independent of $\bar{G}$.

Thus, in diagram 3, given $G = \bar{G}$, the level of I must be greater than $(\frac{\bar{G}}{\alpha\beta_0})^{1/\mu}$ to sustain that given constant growth in labour productivity. Consequently there is a critical minimum

Diagram 3

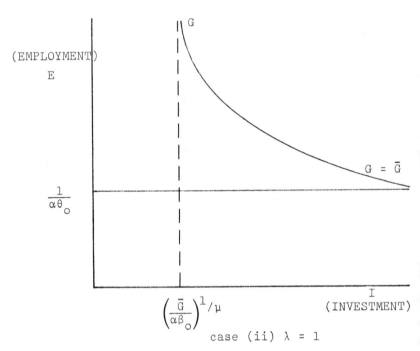

case (ii) $\lambda = 1$

level of investment which must exceed $(\frac{\bar{G}}{\alpha\beta_0})^{1/\mu}$ if a preassigned growth rate $\bar{G}$ in labour productivity is to be attained.

In an analogous manner, we shall briefly indicate that the same qualitative analysis with only slight modification holds in the remaining case of really strong increasing returns to scale characterised by $\lambda > 1$. For this case, with a pre-assigned positive labour productivity growth, $\bar{G} > 0$, we have

$$G(E,I) = \bar{G} = \beta_0 I^\mu (\alpha - \frac{I^{1-\lambda}}{\theta_0 E}) \text{ which, in}$$

correspondence with (10d) above (for $\lambda = 1$), simplifies to

$$E = \frac{\beta_0 I^{1-\lambda+\mu}}{\theta_0(\alpha\beta_0 I^\mu - \bar{G})} \dots\dots\dots\dots\dots\dots\dots\dots\dots\dots(10e)$$

58

Further, in view of assumption (A.1a), relation (6) entails

$$\phi(I) = \frac{I^{1-\lambda}}{\alpha \theta_o} \quad \text{which is positive. But since, from (10),}$$

$$\phi(I) \left(\frac{1-\lambda+\mu}{\mu}\right) = \psi(I), \text{ positivity of } \psi(I) \text{ implies}$$

$$\frac{1-\lambda+\mu}{\mu} > 0,^{10} \quad \text{and also, for positive } \psi(I), \psi(I)$$

is always less than $\phi(I)$ so long as $\lambda > 1$

Noting also that $\phi'(I) < 0$ for $\lambda > 1$ and $\phi'(I) \rightarrow \infty$ as $I \rightarrow 0$, we can now arrive at diagram 4 in this case of strong increasing returns of $\lambda > 1$.

Note from our earlier discussion (see (10b)) that the contour of any constant positive labour productivity growth is negative above the curve $\phi(I)$ in diagram 4, which from (10e) again has a vertical asymptote at $(\frac{\bar{G}}{\alpha \beta_o})^{1/\mu}$ as in diagram 3, while $E = 0$ is also an

Diagram 4

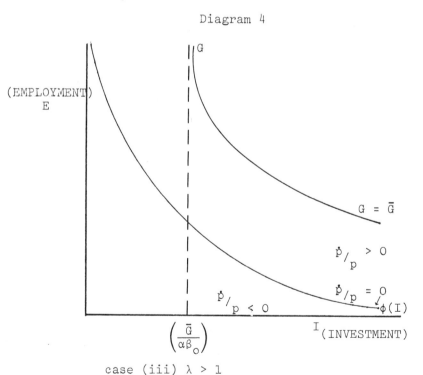

case (iii) $\lambda > 1$

asymptote for both $G(E,I) = \overline{G}$ and $\varphi(I)$. This again shows the critical minimum size of investment which has to exceed $(\frac{\overline{G}}{\alpha\,\beta_0})^{1/\mu}$ to sustain a pre-assigned positive growth rate in labour productivity $\overline{G}$, in the case of strong increasing returns characterised by $\lambda > 1$.

Thus, the formal analysis suggests the critical role of economic size - either in the form of a minimum employment level (see diagram 2) or in the form of a minimum investment level (see diagrams 3 and 4), depending on the degree to which increasing returns prevail (i.e. $\lambda \lesseqgtr 1$) - in maintaining any pre-assigned growth in labour productivity. This, in turn, shows that without some critical minimum economic size in terms of the relevant variable - employment or investment - a small country will not be able to sustain its dynamic comparative advantage in international trade over time.[11] And since 'smallness' implies 'openness' in trade under normal circumstances, the over-riding importance of the concept of a minimum economic size for a country inescapably follows from our analysis.

POSSIBLE ESCAPE ROUTES FROM THE CRITICAL MINIMUM SIZE

Going by the conventional occupational classification of an economy into primary (agriculture), secondary (industry) and tertiary (services) sectors, our preceding analysis would fit in more exactly with the industrial or secondary sector, rather than with the economy as a whole. This, in other words, means that our previous analysis points to the limits to industrialisation in a small economy placed in a relatively open international trading context. This is so, because dynamic increasing returns have typically been an empirical property of the manufacturing sector. There has been virtually no clear empirical evidence to suggest the prevalence of any distinct returns to scale in either agriculture or services.

Under these circumstances one could argue that comparative advantage in agriculture is largely guided by the 'land-man ratio'. But it must be recognised that the land in such a land-man ratio is not in natural but in efficiency units, so that the land-augmenting (in efficiency units) technological progress becomes crucial. Almost invariably, the source of such technical progress is connected with industry. Thus, in an ultimate sense, it is perhaps not too far from the truth to claim that the sustained rise in labour productivity in agriculture over time is also linked to the industrial progress in general and the rise in industrial labour productivity in particular.[12] It is in this sense that our analysis of the previous section may have some indirect relevance for the agricultural sector as well.

Leaving aside further complications of the agricultural sector, the tertiary or services sector presents an altogether different set of complications in relation to our previous analysis. To start with, except by the 'income method', there is no well-defined procedure in terms of the 'product method' to evaluate the level of productivity or its change in the services sector.[13] Consequently, any analysis centering around the productivity level and its change is bound to face statistical measurement problems of a rather special nature, and this difficulty is also faced by our analysis of the previous section. Secondly (and additionally, in the face of the statistical problems mentioned above), it is theoretically as well as empirically quite problematic to assert that the services sector is subject to dynamic increasing returns in the sense described above. In any case, there is hardly any convincing evidence to suggest that dynamic increasing returns to scale is a typical phenomenon for the services sector as a whole.

Therefore, from our point of view, the services sector in a small economy is placed in a somewhat special situation. It has neither the disadvantage of the industrial sector dominated by the scale effect, nor even the limitation of given land-man ratios which typically characterise the labour productivity of agriculture.[14] In the present context of the limitations of the economic size of a small country, it is therefore only natural to explore the potentialities of the services sector in providing an escape route for sustained economic growth in a small economy.

One of the distinguishing features of the services sector is possibly its more or less completely demand-determined character, i.e., by and large, the size of the services sector is not limited by resource availability but by the demand made for services.[15] Consequently, the role that the services sector can play in the longer-run growth process of a small economy is largely contingent upon the demand that is generated for services internally as well as externally.

We shall present a relatively simple analysis to show the link between the problems of industrial growth studied in the last section and the process of domestic demand generation for services.[16] The domestic demand for services is generated from two sources - a derived demand component which may be assumed to depend on the level of material output in the economy and a final demand component depending on income elasticities governed by Engels' Law. It stands to reason that, in a small economy constrained by its economic size in maintaining a given level of productivity growth, the components of both derived and final demand will also be correspondingly constrained to an upper limit. What this upper limit to the growth of services will be depends, in particular, on the specific manner in which the components of derived and final demand are related to changes in the level of material production. It is not necessary for our purpose here to compute how precisely the domestic demand for services increases with material production. In so far as derived demand for services is concerned, it can be assumed to grow more or less at the same rate as material production. The final demand for services depends on the rate of growth in population as well as the growth in per capita income by the usual income elasticity formula. Since, in the long run, growth in per capita income will be roughly in line with growth in labour productivity, which in turn will be restricted by the economic size of a small country (see above), there is almost certainly a well-defined upper limit to the domestic rate of growth of demand for services. To put this argument a bit more formally:

let $d^S = f(y)$ be the per capita demand for services as a function of per capita income y. Then the total final demand for services is

$D^S = N.f(y)$, where N = population, which on logarithmic differentiation gives

$$\frac{\dot{D}^S}{D^S} = \frac{\dot{N}}{N} + \left(\frac{yf'(y)}{f(y)}\right)\frac{\dot{y}}{y}$$

The term $\dfrac{yf'(y)}{f(y)} = \eta$, can immediately be seen to be the relevant income elasticity of demand for services, while the maximum rate of growth in per capita income cannot in the long run exceed the rate of growth in labour productivity G, i.e. $\dot{y}/y \le G$. These considerations together yield the upper limit to the growth domestic final demand for services as

$$d^S \le d^S_{max} = n + \eta.G, \text{ where } n = \frac{\dot{N}}{N} \quad \cdots\cdots\cdots\cdots (11)$$

Our analysis so far has shown how, in the presence of increasing returns, the growth in labour productivity in a small economy is likely to be very limited over time which, in turn, not only adversely affects its international competitive position, and thus the international marketability of its products, but also limits growth in the size of the domestic market for sectors like services, which may not otherwise be subject to increasing returns to scale. Under these circumstances, the conclusion seems almost inescapable that, without growing foreign demand for services, a small economy will be hard pressed to sustain high growth over a long stretch of time. Thus, the drift of our argument leads us to a somewhat unusual position: in the presence of increasing returns to scale in the manufacturing sector, industrialisation or trade in manufactures is unlikely to serve as the main vehicle of growth in a small economy. Instead, it is export trade in services rather than manufactures which may provide the crucial impulse for sustained growth in a small economy, which is otherwise not very favourably placed in terms of natural resources or the land-man ratio. However unorthodox this proposition may sound, casual empiricism regarding the economically more successful small economies (e.g. Hong Kong, Singapore, Panama, etc.) seems to suggest that such a thesis is not altogether without basis.

Once the main focus is shifted to the foreign demand for services, however, two important features become immediately obvious. First, a geographically or politically well-located small country (e.g. Singapore and Hong Kong respectively) will be much better poised for growth[17] if it has a relatively large or prosperous hinterland, which generates demand for its services. Indeed, perhaps in no other sphere than in the present context does the theory of economic co-prosperity apply with greater force. But, unfortunately, this is typically a given datum to a small economy over which it has little control - it can at best benefit from a process of co-prosperity with its trading partners, but it will usually be unable to create conditions for it unilaterally.

And secondly, at another level, the picture of a small economy with highly open trade policies in general and trying to benefit from services exports in particular immediately raises the question of the terms of trade: can such an economy maintain sufficiently advantageous terms of trade over time for it to benefit from its openness in trade? To see the argument in its essence, it will again be helpful to take recourse to a little formalism.

The current account balance of payments of a country is given in current prices as

Balance of Payments on Current Account (B') = Exports (X') - Imports (M'), all at current prices.

Hence at a constant 'GDP deflator' P, we have constant price balance of payments.

$$\frac{B'}{P} = B = \frac{P_X}{P} X - \frac{P_M}{P} M \quad \dots\dots\dots\dots\dots\dots\dots (12)$$

Since our small economy is relatively open by assumption, many of its inputs into production or final consumption goods originate abroad while exports also have a relatively high weightage in output. Under these circumstances, it is not unreasonable to assume that

$$\frac{P_X}{P} \simeq 1$$

so that (12) reduces to

$$B = X - \left(\frac{P_M}{P_X}\right) \cdot \frac{P_X}{P} M \simeq X - \frac{1}{T} M \quad \dots\dots\dots\dots\dots (13)$$

where $\frac{P_X}{P_M} = T$, the terms of trade.

From the accounting relation of total national income at constant prices,

Y = Domestic Demand (D) + Trade Balance (B).

Since domestic output (Q) + Imports (M) = Domestic demand (D) + Exports (X), it follows that D = Q + M - X, so that from (12)

$$Y = Q + M - X + X - \frac{M}{T} \quad \dots\dots\dots\dots\dots\dots\dots\dots\dots (14)$$

63

Assuming imports in the small economy to be a proportion of domestic output, i.e. M = m.Q, (14) can be written as [18]

$$Y = Q \left[1 + m \left(1 - \frac{1}{T} \right) \right] \quad \dots\dots\dots\dots\dots\dots\dots\dots\dots\dots\dots (15)$$

where $T = \dfrac{\text{price index of exports}}{\text{price index of imports}} = \dfrac{1}{Z}$

Relation (15) can be used to yield the corresponding growth rates of national income (Y) and output (Q) as

$$\frac{\dot{Y}}{Y} = \frac{\dot{Q}}{Q} - \left[\frac{mZ}{1 + m(1 - Z)} \right] \frac{\dot{Z}}{Z} \quad \dots\dots\dots\dots\dots\dots\dots\dots\dots (16)$$

As (16) shows, the more the terms of trade move against the small country, i.e. the higher the value of $\frac{\dot{Z}}{Z}$, the greater is the divergence in the growth rate of national income and national output. Thus, for any given output growth rate, a stronger adverse movement in the terms of trade implies a correspondingly lower growth in national income and a lower growth in the size of the domestic market.[19]

Since the critical factor is the movement in the inverse terms of trade,

$$\text{i.e.} \quad \frac{\dot{Z}}{Z} \equiv \frac{\dot{P}_M}{P_M} - \frac{\dot{P}_X}{P_X} \approx \frac{\dot{P}_M}{P_M} - \frac{\dot{P}}{P},$$

the factors governing the price levels of imports and exports over time are of crucial importance. Again, it can be seen here that the country with a higher labour productivity growth will generally be able to have the terms of trade moving in its favour over time.[20] Therefore, the small economy will again be at a double disadvantage; its international competitive position steadily declines in sectors marked by increasing returns and, at the same time, its domestic market dwindles through a declining terms of trade effect. The only likely strategy that may counter this is to concentrate on areas where 'economic size' is not a critical factor and in this sense again the role of the services sector may turn out to be crucial under many circumstances.

SUMMARY OF MAJOR PROPOSITIONS

Our three major propositions can briefly be summarised as follows:

(i) Dynamic increasing returns governing increases in labour productivity and dynamic comparative advantage governed by increases in labour productivity define the context of our analysis.

64

(ii)   In this context, to maintain its international competitive position, a small country has to maintain a minimum growth in labour productivity which may not be possible due to the limitations of its 'economic size'. We demonstrate that, with moderate increasing returns, its population size or employment may act as the fundamental bottleneck (see diagram 2) while, with strong increasing returns, its income size or level of investment can operate as the basic constraint (see diagrams 3 and 4). This provides the analytical rationale for characterising 'smallness' in economic terms using only population size or income level (total and not per capita) under certain conditions.

(iii)   Lower growth in labour productivity in a small economy places it at a double disadvantage; neither is its international competitive possition sustainable nor does its domestic market grow rapidly enough due to a continuous adverse terms of trade effect. Naturally, under these circumstances, only sectors, like services, that are not generally subject to increasing returns can provide a long-term escape route in a typical small economy. And, since its domestic market linked with domestic production grows relatively sluggishly, foreign demand for services under many circumstances may well turn out to be the critical variable to consider in formulating a longer-run development strategy in a small economy.

NOTES

1. One should make the further distinction between indices of smallness which are certain and those which are less certain. Thus, population size or geographical size are more or less certainly known. But, in many cases of particularly small developing countries, the natural resource base has not been fully explored and is not known with any degree of certainty.

2. The time-dependence of a criterion of smallness can result either from the fact that the relevant index (e.g. population) itself is a function of time or because the index is subject to the uncertainty of knowledge (e.g. natural resource base). Thus, in the latter case, geological exploration can suddenly change the picture (see note 1 also).

3. This even Marshall himself recognised, as is evident in his famous mathematical appendix H of the 'Principles'. He realised that increasing returns is an irreversible process through time, while decreasing returns can be imagined as a reversible phenomenon. See also Young (1927) for a classical analysis of this point.

4. See Joan Robinson (1956) for one of the earliest analyses of dynamic comparative advantages along these lines.

5. In terms of traditional classification, net rather than gross investment is related to capacity expansion. But, with continuous technical progress, the distinction between net and gross investment is obscure, as it becomes almost impossible to identify pure replacement investments. Therefore (as in 'vintage models'), it seems more appropriate to work with the notion of gross investment.

6. This also means we are not explicitly bringing in the problem of market size in a small economy. The underlying economic assumption is that a sufficiently strong and sustained competitive position in international trade will keep at bay the problem of effective demand. It will also be noted that in (A.2) below, the international trade aspect of savings + imports = investments + exports is not introduced on the assumption that foreign trade is in balance as a characteristic of sustainable growth.

7. More exactly, the 'Kaldor-Verdoorn law' links growth of labour productivity to the level of output in industry. Assuming employment to be roughly proportional to output, we can see its proximity to the 'Kaldor-Verdoorn law'.

8. The reader can derive the value of this critical minimum level of employment quite easily as

$$
E\frac{min}{G} = \left[\frac{1}{\alpha\theta_0} \left(\frac{1 - \lambda + \mu}{\mu} \right) \right] \left(\frac{\bar{G}}{A} \right) \frac{1 - \lambda}{\mu}
$$

$$
\text{where } A = \frac{\beta_0 (1 - \lambda)\alpha}{1 - \lambda + \mu} > 0
$$

9. For, with $\lambda < 1$, $\phi'(0) = +\infty$ and $\psi'(0) = +\infty$ (also $\phi'(+\infty) = 0$), as can easily be checked. Notice that the slope of any ray through the origin is α/p; thus rotating a ray in a counter clockwise direction implies a higher value for p, the productivity of labour, and consequently a larger base for the percentage growth in productivity.

10. In the other case ($\frac{1 - \lambda + \mu}{\mu}$) < 0 and $\psi(I) \leq 0 < \phi(I)$. So, for this case, one may neglect $\psi(I)$ from consideration.

11. Subject to the condition that the rise in the wage rate is roughly the same across countries over time. For, by sufficiently depressing the rise in the real wage rate, one can always get a competitive edge in spite of a slower rise in labour productivity. The experience of post-war Japan till the late sixties is a well-known case in point.

12. For the validity of such a general statement, one has to abstract from possible short-term rises in agricultural productivity which come from the re-organisation of the

production structure resulting from, say, land reform. However important these factors may be, their effects are not indefinitely sustainable over time, in the sense of maintaining a constant rate of growth of labour productivity. Further, one must take into account the rise in labour productivity in agriculture which may be associated with a continuous withdrawal of labour from agriculture to industry for quite a stretch of time in face of a substantial backlog of open and disguised unemployment.

13. It will be recalled that in the material national income accounting procedure of centrally planned economies the services sector is, by and large, excluded. This avoids mixing up value-added computed from the production side with that computed only from the income or expenditure side.

14. Subject to the definition of land-man ratio in efficiency rather than natural units discussed above.

15. Particular kinds of service, mostly belonging to economic overheads or infrastructure, like passenger transport, may often have a heavy capital cost. In our discussion, we are not concentrating on such sectors, but on services like banking and insurance, tourism, various distributive trading activities etc.

16. For reasons already mentioned, the role of agriculture in the process will not be explicitly analysed.

17. In a certain sense this is comparable to advantages arising from a favourable natural resource base.

18. This way of looking at the terms of trade in relation to national accounts was adopted by W. Godley and F. Cripps in their Cambridge Policy Model for the UK economy.

19 The reader can see (by suitably revising formula 11) that an adverse terms of trade movement will restrict the growth rate of final demand for services still further.

20. The country with a higher growth in productivity has the crucial advantage of being able to afford an equal rise in the money wage rate and still maintain a comparatively lower rate of inflation compared with its rivals, which, in effect, means advantage in trade arising from continuous devaluation of the currency by a corresponding percentage. Therefore, $\frac{\dot{z}}{z} \simeq (G_L - G_S) > 0$, where G_L and G_S are labour productivity growth in a large (rival) and small country respectively, so long as the money wage rises at more or less the same rate in both.

REFERENCES

Robinson, Joan, 1956, 'The Pure Theory of International Trade'.
   In "Review of Economic Studies", Vol.23.
Young, A., 1927, 'Economic Progress and Returns to Scale'.
   In "Economic Journal", Vol.37.

4. The New Role of Development Planning

Dudley Seers

The combination of rising prices for oil and manufactures, weak markets for agricultural products and increased protectionism in the industrial countries has created considerable problems for many small countries of the Third World. 'Planning' has fallen into disrepute. But in the sense of a coherent attempt at national development, it is more necessary than ever, especially in small countries, though in quite new forms.

THE WEAKNESSES IN CONVENTIONAL 'DEVELOPMENT PLANNING'

First, let us look at previous types of planning. After the war, nationalist aspirations grew in Africa, Asia and Latin America, and planning became fashionable. However, the first colonial 'development plans' were little more than the total investment programmes of government departments.

After independence, the growing political need to tackle social and economic problems required a statement of government objectives both in general terms ('reducing unemployment', etc.) and for individual sectors (e.g. 'achieving universal primary education'), illustrated by a set of projections for the following five years (plus or minus two years) for selected variables covering the economy as a whole, such as income, consumption and investment (private as well as public), accompanied by particulars of some leading projects.

But the record of such plans has not been good, especially in the past few years. Economic growth has often diverged a long way from target - indeed, in some cases it has been negative - and even where it has been fast there has been little progress towards social objectives. Many plans cease to have any administrative or even political significance after a year or two and fade out of sight. There are several reasons for this.

* I gratefully acknowledge comments by David Evans, Percy Selwyn and Michael Ward.

Technical Weaknesses

The technical quality of most development plans is poor. There is little attempt to distinguish between exogenous variables, targets, instrument variables, constraints and the residuals obtained from a national accounting framework.

Moreover, single values are usually assumed for exogenous variables, such as export prices in the last year of the plan period, whereas decision-makers would need to know the range and the implications of possible extremes, and the nature and extent of uncertainty. Indeed, the use of single values is one of the reasons why so many plans have become obsolete: any major change - e.g. a sharp climb in import prices - can make them evidently irrelevant.

Few plans in any country point out how much they are contingent, especially on external events. Indeed, they usually give the impression that the economy is far more under government control than it is in reality.

Moreover, most plans are highly aggregative, and thus evade issues of distribution - between social classes, ethnic groups, urban and rural areas, coastal regions and the interior, etc.[1] Yet these issues are usually crucial to development. The same is true of the distinction between the foreign and domestic sectors. Rarely is an attempt made to specify (in plans or elsewhere) targets for foreign capital investment, the criteria for its entry, etc., even in countries where self-reliance is put forward as a major development objective.

Plans derived from the Harrod-Domar model treat investment as the determinant of economic growth and rely heavily on incremental capital-output ratios (ICORs). Yet there is little meaning in ICORs if they cover groups of industries with very different levels of technology, less still if they cover the whole economy. They are moreover subject to great variation, especially over periods as short as five years. They can range from over 15 to less than 2. Indeed, although they are usually derived from past experience, a major object of policy should be precisely to reduce them by choosing appropriate technologies, and investing in activities with low ICORs. Moreover the use of ICORs is open to a more basic question: how can one justify assuming that investment is the sole determinant of growth? This diverts attention away from many other important causes, such as maintenance of existing capital, improvements in the health of the workforce, technical training, etc.

The statistical basis for plans is often very weak anyway. It is impossible to estimate production at all precisely, or how fast it grows, in sectors such as agriculture and services, if there is no regular, at least annual, collection of data, especially where much of the sector's activity is not marketed, or only marketed illegally.

There are three consequences. First, most national income estimates and therefore growth rates are the product of hypotheses rather than facts (which lays them open to political manipulation). Secondly, plans (and policies) using national income data ignore what are often the main economic changes - the destruction of the household and village economies, which are not at all adequately measured, and their replacement by a monetised, national economy.[3] Thirdly, the growth of 'black markets', 'informal' activities, etc., is also largely overlooked, imparting a serious bias to policy.

Lack of Effective Commitment

A more basic problem which helps explain the technical weaknesses, including the presumptions of plans and the neglect of statistics, is lack of commitment to development. Leaving aside those cases, not numerous, where the political leader has merely plundered the country for the sake of himself and a few relatives and associates, many other governments do not give much priority to social progress. Rhetorical references may be made to increasing equality and eliminating poverty. Governments may even call themselves 'revolutionary'. But policies actually operating permit or even encourage the concentration of the benefits of growth in those sectors, areas or social classes (sometimes ethnic groups) which are already relatively affluent. Other sections of the community have little voice in shaping the process of planning.

In such situations there seems no role for a self-respecting planning office: yet surely it should persevere in its work until in due course the political wheel turns and a government comes to power eager to draw on its services.

Lack of Rationality in Decision-making

Especially where there is no commitment to development, the leadership typically takes decisions on exchange rates, wage rates, etc., ad hoc, without concern for their effect on the pattern of development, an effect which may well be considerable. Indeed, very often decisions may be taken without even consulting the director of planning.[4]

This is not to say that political leaders will accept the advice of the development planner (or even ought to): they always take into account other considerations, some of which may be quite legitimate in any political philosophy, but not necessarily easily quantifiable (the benefits of self-reliance, for example). They have the right, however, and even the duty to listen to advice on the measurable costs and benefits of a particular short-term policy decision in the light of long-term development needs. What is required could be called 'informed intuition'.

There is often no channel through which they get such advice. Many planning offices work in a sort of administrative vacuum, neither being consulted by the political leadership at all frequently nor enjoying access to it. Some do little more than absorb the output of the economics faculties, and add a pseudo-professional patina to government policies which are decided elsewhere.

Rationality requires consistency. The prime purpose of planning is, according to the textbooks, to make government policies in different sectors more consistent with each other and with the main policy goals. It is only one of the means to this end. The principal instrument for introducing coherence across the whole range of government policies, and thus making planning effective, is regular inter-departmental meetings at ministerial and 'lower' levels, participants at which accept the obligation to reach agreements and to implement them.

Anyone familiar with the way governments actually work knows that the reality is often quite different. Ministries usually treat certain conventional policy areas as their sole responsibility. Moreover, a Minister with a personal power base that is indispensable to the government is under little compulsion to defer to a meeting of colleagues. Most planning offices lack the authority to obtain the co-operation of other ministries. In particular, unless they have strong political support they will be unable to match the strength of the Treasury which tends to concentrate on short-term needs. Planning is hardly likely to make policy coherent if there is no effective framework for inter-ministerial co-operation.[5]

False Conceptions of Planning

Linked to the other weaknesses, especially lack of commitment, are various unhelpful characteristics of the way in which planning has been perceived. First, the short time-horizon of the typical plan means that the development issues can hardly be considered. After all, decisions on the crucial determinants of development, such as the content of education or the system of land tenure, or even major capital works such as irrigation schemes, are not likely to show their effects in less than a decade. The transformation of society is a very lengthy process. A plan for a few years only makes sense within a much longer perspective.

Secondly, partly because of the shortness of the planners' horizons, critical issues of development, such as the content of education and the system of land tenure mentioned in the last paragraph, are often ignored - indeed the economic dimension tends to be greatly exaggerated. After all, economic growth is merely one among the means to 'development', and is by no means sufficient in itself.[6] This would imply nowadays not just growth but a society free of poverty, united, peaceful, egalitarian, democratic, self-reliant, sufficiently strong to withstand external threats, and with the internal dynamic to continue improving itself in these respects. And to achieve these ends not merely economic policies are needed, but associated social and administrative policies.

Thirdly, the functions of a planning office are also widely misconceived. Its main responsibility is seen (even by itself) as being to give birth every five years or so to a <u>plan</u> for publication. Consequently the office engages in a burst of frenetic activity every few years, putting on one side its other responsibilities such as project evaluation, preparation of annual investment plans, etc. Paradoxically the work of planning offices is often badly planned.

The object of these publications is apparently to demonstrate to the public (and perhaps to the aid agencies) a degree of government commitment to development (which may in fact hardly exist). If a planning office were actually dealing with the real issues of development, such as the distribution of income in its social, geographic or ethnic dimensions, its output would principally take the form, not of publications, but of direct advice to the decision-makers.[7]

Some policy issues might well be illustrated by quantitative projections, and some of the projections might well be put before the public. Publishing medium-term plans is one way of doing this. However, neither the preparation nor the publication of medium-term plans is essential to planning, properly conceived.

THE NEED FOR NEW DEVELOPMENT STRATEGIES

The case for a thorough reconsideration of 'planning', due to such defects, has now been reinforced by recent events.[8] While the 'oil shocks' and related increases in the prices of manufactures, much greater than those for many primary products, have effectively undermined many existing development plans, they have also opened new horizons for planning offices.

The Effect of the 'Oil Shocks'

In the first place, most oil-importing countries find that foreign exchange is a constraint more dominant than ever (especially the poorer ones that cannot borrow on a significant scale from private banks[9]), and that in particular oil imports need to be minimised. Short-term policy-making has therefore become primarily dependent on the allocation of foreign exchange, and costly errors can be made if the planning office is not consulted on the implications, both short- and longer-run, of foreign exchange budgets.

The task of optimising the scale and pattern of imports, especially of oil, can be facilitated by elaborating input-output tables so as to show the oil and total foreign exchange content of different types of final expenditure in some detail. (Such tables are by now common; where they do not exist, the oil crisis underlines the need to create them.) In addition such research can be helpful in attempts to minimise the immediate effect of the sharp rise in oil prices. It would assist, for example, decisions on whether petrol should be rationed, whether kerosene should continue to be subsidised (as it often is, because of its importance for rural households) and whether crops should be converted into ethanol.[10] Such research can now be facilitated by using mini-computers to re-run models.

The need to simulate the effects of different assumptions about oil prices has also now become inescapable. Whether the terms of trade become 25 per cent worse or 25 per cent better by 1985 will make a great deal of difference to what governments can do. Indeed contingency plans are needed for a situation in which oil suddenly became unobtainable due to a major disruption (for whatever reasons) in supplies from the Middle East.

The implications of the 'oil shocks' for planning offices are, however, much more far-reaching than the need for a refinement of existing techniques. Fundamental questions are posed about their functions.

The Outlook for the 1980s

The foreign exchange crises are not transient. While there will doubtless be occasional declines in the price of oil in the years ahead, the outlook is for underlying strength despite conservation, the discoveries in Mexico and the gradual emergence of alternative sources of energy (e.g. solar power and ethanol). World consumption is rising,[11] depletion policies in OPEC members are becoming more conservative, and the political situation in the Gulf is chronically unstable. Yet prices of other primary commodities will remain weak until there is a revival of activity in the industrial countries - but that will hardly relieve the foreign exchange shortage of most commodity exporters because it will set the stage for further price rises in oil.

Moreover an additional problem lies ahead. When a transition to new sources of energy becomes economically practical, as can be confidently predicted, it will be far from easy for countries already in a chronic foreign exchange crisis to afford the necessary equipment.

The Nature of New Development Strategies

This prospect suggests, indeed compels, a thorough re-examination of the development strategies that were adopted while energy was cheap, and thus of the role of planning - just as the politico-economic changes of the 1950s did earlier. Governments of various political ideologies in the past quarter-century treated industrialisation as virtually synonymous with development and fell into the convenient practice of relying primarily on imported technologies. These are usually energy-intensive as well as capital-intensive. Many sectors came also to rely on oil-based inputs (especially textiles, chemicals and agriculture). Governments allowed foreign life-styles to be copied, so - in view of the heavy concentration of income - consumption also became highly energy-intensive.

This type of economic growth always raised serious questions because of its effects on employment and income distribution. Moreover in most cases it has led to a chronic dependence on food imports. The issue now, however, is no longer whether it is desirable but whether it is possible. When the price of imported oil quadrupled in 1973-74, this meant in most countries reductions in reserves and indebtedness rising at a very fast (in some cases unsustainable) rate for those governments able to borrow. Some promoted exports, if they could, and reduced superfluous imports. Many were forced to cut capital investment and social expenditure.

There was a partial recovery in foreign exchange positions after 1975, but when oil prices started to soar again after the Iranian Revolution early in 1979, a number of governments were in a much worse state than when they were struck by the first oil price rise. Many of the buffers (reserves, borrowing capacity, export expansion, easy import-cuts) had been used up already, and industries which were oil-intensive became hard to sustain. Among the consequences many governments put much more emphasis on agriculture and reduced consumer activities such as motoring.

These effects have, however, not been parts of consistent strategies, but by-products of numerous ad hoc emergency decisions of various departments, often taken on very short-term grounds. The objective need for a more purposive approach to basic structural changes is now in many countries overwhelming. This starts with studying, partly by cross-examination, the plans and policies of individual departments (a process which would also make their personnel more aware of national objectives).

As pointed out above, such changes will take far longer than the few years covered by medium-term plans. An appropriate horizon might be about the end of the century: a longer time-span would involve too big a range of projections of 'exogenous' variables. After 13 years, for example, the size of the population of working age begins to be affected by births that have not yet taken place.

Long-term strategic possibilities can be illustrated by scenarios (e.g. Interfutures, 1979). These would not only incorporate some of the elements of conventional plans, but would also show additional dimensions. An important one now would be distributional, particularly in view of the relationship between income and the oil-intensity of different patterns of consumption and production. In many countries, issues of urban-rural balance are more pressing than ever.

In addition, non-quantitative elements, such as the extent and nature of decentralisation of decision-making, would also be covered. Indeed, realistic scenarios would take account of illegal activities too (doubtless without numerical precision) where these are a major influence on the pattern of the economy. (No development strategy that ignored magendo, for example, would be of much use for Uganda.) Projections in less numerical detail would not merely avoid a misleading appearance of the degree of government influence over the economy: they would also permit a proper emphasis on the rural sector, especially in view of its resilience in the face of the 'oil shock'. (It might be a major aim of development strategy to find ways of reinforcing such resilience.)

Perhaps the most important dimension for some countries of certain alternative strategies is that they require not merely social changes within a country but reassessment of external relations: for example, more autonomous strategies may provoke the hostility of foreign powers.

Administrative Implications

Consideration of alternative development paths underlines the importance of continuous contact between political leaders and development planners, on almost a day-to-day basis. Governments committed to development will be demanding studies of the longer-term aspects of various issues, especially those that cut across departmental frontiers, treating the planning office in fact as an official 'think tank'. Development planners need more than ever direct access to the government to help ensure that the alternatives they explore are not entirely impractical.[12] It is true that such a working relationship will still not be initiated by many political leaders, and may even be resisted by them. But it will be made increasingly necessary by the logic of the economic crisis.

Planning offices could perform functions like those of a military general staff, which include preparing not only contingency plans to cover sudden emergencies (based on 'war games'), but also long-term strategies and medium-term plans of organisation, re-equipment and training to implement them. The strategies are sketched in the light of possible changes in military technology, according to the expectations and policies of governments with respect to (e.g.) relations with neighbours and great powers. This requires (and normally involves) regular discussion with the political leadership about the strategic alternatives.

Military planning not merely offers analogies to development planning. The two forms of planning should be linked in obvious ways (how much can be afforded for defence?): indeed, development strategy needs to be coherent, incorporating military, economic and social dimensions. For example, an 'open door' strategy is more easily compatible with a pro-US than a pro-Soviet military alignment.

These considerations imply that naive 'rate of return' cost-benefit analysis is less use than ever. Factors such as the extent to which a project reduces dependence (and which of its technological options would reduce it most) need to be taken into account, usually by allowing for them qualitatively after the quantitative exercises have been performed.[13]

Work of this type on development options would require new types of staff - not merely economists but also sociologists and ecologists, because the long-run problems are now obviously not exclusively economic. It would also need new statistical priorities. Since maximising the national income would be less significant, that variable would cease to be central to the programme of a statistical office. Work on particular sectors would be of greater importance, especially on the production and consumption of energy (see above). There would also be other tasks which would be specific to the country concerned - e.g. estimating how much land lay uncultivated (which might be available for growing substitutes for imported foodstuffs).

THE STRATEGIC OPTIONS IN SMALL COUNTRIES

The choice facing governments of many small countries is bleak. The development options for dealing with their current economic crisis are constrained by realities. Political, economic and cultural constraints are implicit in the work of many analysts, especially dependency theorists. Geographical determinants of development strategy have, however, been very little discussed by social scientists of any school.[14] These determinants do not change at all, or do not change significantly, within, say, 20 years. They limit for any particular country the range of feasible scenarios - whether it is ruled by a conservative military dictatorship or a revolutionary junta. One such determinant is location (especially close proximity to countries with overwhelming military power). Another, which is relevant for our present purposes, is size.

The Implications of Size for Planning

Size can, of course, as other papers for this conference will undoubtedly explain, be defined in various ways[15] - geographical, demographic and economic. The government of a country with a small area has fewer options because it is unlikely to have a very diversified resource base, in particular much arable land - in contrast to Canada, say, or Australia or Brazil. Nowadays the extent of territorial waters is also important in view of the importance of fishing and sub-sea mineral potential in a country's 'economic zone'.

Area, however, does not mean much except in relation to the population inhabiting it. If the area is small in relation to the population (even though that is also small), the country is likely to be dependent on imports for supplies of strategic commodities, which might include iron ore (or steel), copper, wood, cereals and livestock products - above all, oil.

Unless the governments of such countries were able to find a dynamic strategy (as in Singapore), population pressure has historically been reduced by emigration. This has often been encouraged by government policy: Malta and Mauritius are cases in point. But it creams off some of the most enterprising and highly skilled people (an effect only partially compensated by remittances they subsequently send home). Anyway, the opportunities for large-scale migration have mostly disappeared, through tightening of controls in the recipient countries, except for temporary labour permits in countries of the Middle East that have small populations in relation to their oil reserves (and even these governments are increasingly apprehensive about their heavy dependence on foreign labour).

But, if size of population matters, then population policy forms an important part of strategic planning. This does not necessarily mean, as it has often meant in the past, a policy of population limitation. If the resource base is adequate, the economy has been needing immigrants and the government's development strategy involves external risks,[16] there would be arguments for a pro-natal policy.[17] On the other hand, if chronic emigration has been signalling a shortage of resources, and particularly if this is ceasing to be feasible, while military threats are remote, the indicated policy would be anti-natal. This evaluation would determine attitudes to family allowances, and of course contraception and abortion, as well as policies in many other fields which affect population growth in one way or another - e.g. housing and female education.

The structure of the manufacturing sector is influenced by the third possible criterion of size, the magnitude of the market, for which the estimated national income can be a proxy. This is ultimately a matter mainly of population: the national income equals population multiplied by per capita income, but the former factor has a much greater variation internationally than the latter.

Industrialisation can hardly be based mainly on a home market that is relatively small. If it amounts to less than some US$ 10 billion (corresponding to a population of 5 to 50 million, say, according to per capita income), it would hardly support industries producing intermediate products such as steel, aluminium, heavy chemicals, etc., especially since many of the necessary materials would have to be imported, and thus paid for in foreign exchange. So the only feasible development strategy in small countries, with limited natural resources, lies in creating export-oriented industries or services (in view of the drawbacks of emigration - and its limits).

It is very hard for such a government to create these at all rapidly without foreign capital and technology, the main channels for which are the transnational corporations (TNCs). Only in a large country (e.g. India) do local companies export goods which have a local market sufficient to enable economies of scale to be enjoyed, and overhead costs to be written off. Moreover, TNCs also provide access to the necessary markets abroad. Planning in a small country, in almost any sense of the word, is therefore obviously somewhat restricted, because many of the important decisions about output and investment are taken overseas. Moreover, tax revenues depend partly on how much the TNCs concerned choose to resort to 'transfer pricing'.

Small Countries and Large Companies

But this does not mean the government need be entirely dependent on the TNCs. The crucial need in a small country, especially one arriving at greater independence, is to develop the technological and administrative capacity for an industrial policy that is both deliberate and selective. Typically it is neither. Industries that can provide little foreign exchange or employment for the country (if import requirements and profit remittances are deducted from export proceeds) are often allowed to enter, sometimes actually subsidised by tax concessions, cheap land, even power.[18] Indeed, industrialisation policy may be purely reactive - saying 'yes' or 'no' (almost always 'yes') to whatever corporation in whatever industry based in whatever country happens to send executives.[19] The result is a ragbag of industries, with virtually zero integration (not even producing much for one another).

Technological and administrative capacity are needed not only to select suitable industries but to monitor their performance subsequently. Many industrial development corporations request information about a firm's plans for employment, production, exports, etc., before deciding whether or not to grant tax concessions, for example, but then subsequently make no effort whatever to see whether the promises are in fact being fulfilled.

One aim of a selective long-term strategy may be to reduce foreign influence over the industrial sector, either directly via joint ventures, or indirectly through requiring the participation of citizens in ownership and/or management, or lending money to local entrepreneurs to buy their way into a sector. (They would be more sensitive to national needs than TNC subsidiaries which have to conform to the worldwide policies of their corporation.)

A purposive industrial policy can of course only be derived from an overall development strategy. As indicated above, planning offices could play a major role in shaping this, but whether this is actually feasible depends on the perceptions and political skills of the leadership. There is little point in requiring potential foreign investors to justify their projects if the government is committed, overtly or de facto, to an 'open door' strategy, or if it is not able or willing to negotiate effectively.

Countries that have industrialised during the cheap oil period have proved highly vulnerable to recent increases in the price of oil and other industrial inputs (and associated recessions in the industrial countries). It is true that the immediate impact is less severe than on other types of economy, because they have a greater capacity to borrow foreign exchange from private banks (Hong Kong and Singapore, for example) and their manufactured exports have continued to grow, especially to the Middle East. But their borrowing capacity can hardly increase indefinitely, and they face rising protective barriers in the industrial countries.[20]

For them, therefore, as for most small countries, it is not easy to devise a plausible long-term strategy. To 'delink' to any considerable extent from the world economy would involve heavy social costs. Limiting, for example, imports of industrial inputs threatens the livelihood of the workers; so not merely do the firms concerned resist such policies, the trade unions do so, too. It may even be difficult to raise corporate taxes (or start collecting them once a 'tax holiday' expires) without provoking a decline in production, possibly complete withdrawal. Jamaican experience with TNCs in the period 1975-80 illustrates some of those constraints. Various other forms of retaliation are possible, even military.[21] (Governments, especially of small countries, which have not yet linked themselves to the world economy, might consider such possible eventual consequences.)

A Self-reliant Strategy?

The range of development options to be considered by planning offices is not great in small countries which have already become habituated to cars, television programmes, etc. and types of food that cannot be produced locally. (In many tropical countries, for example, dietary customs incorporate bread manufactured from wheat.) Typically a small country shows a severe incompatibility between its patterns of consumption and production.[22] It is of course the function of trade to reconcile these, but, especially in the 1980s, the prospective costs (in various senses) of dependence on trade point to searching for ways of increasing self-reliance. Since on the supply side the possibilities are very limited now, planners might turn their attention more to the structure of demand. For example, it is absurd for governments of oil-importing countries to permit advertisements for energy-intensive forms of consumption, such as motoring. Yet restraints on such consumption, and especially attempts to reduce it by altering the distribution of income significantly, may be incompatible with a government's political base or administrative capacity.

A drastic plan of autonomy would, moreover, involve external, ultimately military, risks, and countries with small populations have by definition only a limited military capacity. It is true that the potential size of military manpower is less important today, in view of the sophistication of technology, which requires not so much large armies as high-level skills and expensive equipment, but the very foreign exchange problem that induces more self-reliant strategies also rules out such technology, unless it can be obtained without unacceptable political strings. If a government's military equipment comes from a 'great power', it is dependent on spare parts and technical assistance from that source and thus cannot avoid external influences on its policies; but if it turns elsewhere for arms this may be treated as provocative (e.g. Guatemalan experience in the mid-1950s). A small country with a military establishment too limited to withstand attack by a big power can, however, hope to deter such intervention by making it expensive - for example, by developing a militia that could be converted into guerillas, equipped from local small-arms production.

Other Possible Strategies

There are two possibilities to be considered, which may extend the range of scenarios in some countries. One is the development of service industries, if the location is suitable. Examples are banking (Bahrain) or tourism (Bermuda). Perhaps the contrasts with industrialisation are not really so great: again it may be necessary to rely to a greater or lesser extent on the capital and expertise of transnational corporations (in banking, transportation and hotels).

The alternative possibility, for some small countries, is to link up with others, thus adding resources, increasing the military potential, widening the market and strengthening the technological base. Not merely would planning then be able to show a greater variety of strategic options; but also the possibility would be opened up of co-operation, at least, between planning offices, and formulation of co-ordinated policies (e.g. agreements not to compete with tax concessions).

To go into pros and cons would not be appropriate here. It is just necessary to make two points in the light of international experience about the basic viability of a scheme of integration. This depends in the first place on machinery for redistributing some of the benefits gained by the larger, more industrialised members: such machinery has rarely been of much significance.[23] Secondly, its survival may depend on cultural compatibility: moreover, in the absence of this, the price paid by a small country for economic integration is ultimately a weakening of its cultural identity.

For some planning offices a major task is to work on the

implications of possible integration schemes in terms of industrial structures, educational programmes, etc.

Size and the Role of a Planning Office

Weaving the various policies into a consistent whole, compatible with constraints (internal and external) and with exogenous variables, and deciding what issues should be put to the particular political leadership, is a central task of a planning office, but especially important in small countries, where the penalty for strategic mistakes can be high.

The government's budget and the number of professional personnel available are related to a country's size, and in a small country a highly elaborate system of alternative detailed strategies, with various time-horizons, can hardly be envisaged.[24] The government will also lack a wide range of expertise to formulate and implement policy, especially vis-a-vis foreign firms.

Yet, in a small administration the planning office is less likely to remain forgotten, in political limbo. Moreover, face-to-face contact between the political leaders and the people is much more feasible than in a large country. This can provide the political solidarity required for a development strategy - especially for the forced self-reliance that may lie ahead for some countries. Such contact is, however, far from a sufficient condition for this. What is also needed is political leadership capable of finding a way forward for a small country, taking advantage of political opportunities, linking policies to political reality, mobilising support for them, and exploiting what room to manoeuvre there is. Then it may become possible to broaden the range of development options. Leadership is a more important factor than in a large country.[25] The work of a planning office (provided it does not concentrate on preparing 'plans') can, however, provide useful support.

NOTES

1. A conspicuous exception is Malaysia, where successive development plans (since the second) have shown targets for poverty groups, and for each of the main races.

2. This can be true even for a decade. For the period 1960-70 the aggregate ICOR ranged from 16 for Uruguay to 1.8 for Saudi Arabia (UN, 1972, p. 29).

3. There are anyway serious conceptual problems in defining the national income in economies where many activities are internal to the household or the village economy which elsewhere would be marketed (e.g. river fishing, rice milling, handloom weaving, furniture making, nursing, etc.).

4. Thus, when governments decree big increases in the wages and salaries of civil servants, those taking the decision ought to

receive a brief pointing out the likely consequences, unless there were a compensating devaluation. The brief could cover such issues as what would happen to port congestion (and thus the rate of investment), to the demand for cars (and thus the need for investment in roads, etc.) and to wages and salaries in other sectors (and thus to the feasibility of self-sufficiency in foodstuffs and of import substitution in manufactures).

5. Usually the only real instrument for achieving a degree of coherence is the annual budget; yet, since departmental estimates are in the first place agreed bilaterally between the Treasury and other departments, they too reflect the balance of political power and the personal effectiveness of ministers.

6. The national income aggregates conventionally used are not necessarily appropriate anyway. Increases in some types of output are always needed, but the price-weights used to produce estimates of growth reflect distributions of income and consumer tastes which may be the chief obstacle to development.

7. The tendency of technical assistance experts in economic and social fields, especially those on 'missions', to see their role as preparing reports for publication indicates their remoteness from the real process of policy-making. (Would legal or military experts work in this way?) The primary role of technical assistance, especially in macro-economic policy, is clearly often to assist a government's public relations.

8. I am referring here to oil-importing economies. In countries that export oil the need for a coherent development strategy is by no means less urgent, indeed in some ways more so, but it raises different issues.

9. See Killick (1981).

10. All these issues raise other questions according to local circumstances. For example, could the administration cope with petrol rationing, in view of the opportunities for corruption? Would making kerosene more expensive accelerate deforestation to a dangerous extent? What would be the opportunity costs in terms of food foregone if crops are grown for fuel?

11. Especially in OPEC: the volume of exportable surpluses will soon, for this reason, fall significantly in those members with large populations and where sectors other than oil are economically important (Indonesia, Venezuela and, especially, Nigeria).

12. Naturally, a close advisory relationship to politicians implies that such studies will not automatically be published, though release of summaries or extracts would certainly in some cases help make outside opinion more knowledgeable and enable it to be consulted.

13. Attempts to quantify all relevant factors, as in some forms of 'social cost-benefit analysis', lead to highly artificial assumptions (e.g. the attempts of the Roskill Commission, investigating a site for a possible third London airport, to value historic churches). They stem fundamentally from a dubious attempt to simplify choices that are inherently very complex.

14. I have discussed these in Seers (forthcoming). As I point out there, the tendency of development theorists to ignore size may be due to ideological doctrine - some of them would not find it easy to accept that, in certain circumstances, geographical factors rule out far-reaching social change.

15. So also can the word 'small'. This does not, however, affect my argument much, since I am mainly talking about how much associations between size and other characteristics affect the scope of planning.

16. In a period of struggle for resources, a 'great power' may even attack a small country that lacks any resource interest, simply to obtain the use of airfields, ports, etc., so that it can deploy its forces against some completely different objective. (The German army invaded Belgium twice, for example, to obtain access to northern France.)

17. Even to consider the need for military mobilisation and pro-natal policies will shock many of those (in the industrial countries) working on development problems. Are there not global dangers in excessive military expenditures and fast population expansion? These are, however, not relevant questions for policy-makers (or planners) in small countries, which have to concern themselves with their own national interests - until the seemingly remote time when there is some world political authority that can provide for their security and economic needs. It is clear that the United Nations cannot do this.

18. Now that the price of oil has gone up, many of these industries may involve net foreign exchange costs.

19. To predict the pattern of industrialisation in a small country in the 1980s it may well be more useful to study the registers of the leading hotels in the 1970s than the government's industrial policy statements. Contrast Japanese policy during the early stages of their highly professional industrial strategy: foreign businessmen who had the presumption to take the initiative were firmly snubbed.

20. Notably the Multi-Fibre Arrangement, which may be extended to small countries adhering to the Lome Convention. There are also bilateral pressures to limit exports of textiles and clothing 'voluntarily' (e.g. by Britain on Mauritius).

21. Though such retaliation often seems to be provoked as much by rhetoric (especially in the field of international affairs) as by actual policy changes.

22. See Wyeth (unpublished).

23. There has been an attempt in the Andean Pact to arrange for the poorer countries to obtain some new industries. See Tironi (1980). The fiscal machinery of the European Community, on the other hand, has if anything redistributed revenue from the poorer countries to the richer. See Seers and Vaitsos (1980).

24. However, the need for such sophistication may also be less, because there will be fewer options that can realistically be considered (see above). Moreover, a country which is small (at least in terms of area) has less need for regional planning.

25. Mr. Mintoff once told me that the government of a small country had to decide what trump cards it held and then play them for all they were worth, advice apparently based on his own experience in Malta.

REFERENCES

Interfutures, 1979, "Facing the Future", Paris: OECD.

Killick, Tony, 1981, 'Eurocurrency Market Recycling of OPEC Surpluses to Developing Countries; Fact or Myth?' In Christopher Stevens, ed., "The EEC and the Third World: a Survey", London: Hodder and Stoughton.

Seers, Dudley, forthcoming, 'Development Options: The Strengths and Weaknesses of Dependency Theories in Explaining a Government's Room to Manoeuvre'. In Dudley Seers, ed., "Dependency Theory: a Critical Re-assessment" London: Frances Pinter.

_____, 1980, 'Conclusions: the EEC and Unequal Development'. In Dudley Seers and Constantine Vaitsos, ed., "Integration and Unequal Development: the Experience of the EEC", London: Macmillan.

Tironi, Ernesto, 1980, 'A Case Study of Latin America'. In Dudley Seers and Constantine Vaitsos, op.cit. United Nations, 1972, "Trade Prospects and Capital Needs of Developing Countries During the Second United Nations Development Decade", TD/118/Supp.3/Rev/1, New York.

Wyeth, John, unpublished, "Development Strategies and Specialisation in Small Countries: a Case Study of Belize", doctoral thesis, University of Sussex.

5. Growth Experience of Small Economies

Boris Blazic-Metzner and Helen Hughes

Despite changing perceptions of what constitutes a 'small' country, the hypothesis that such countries, however defined, are handicapped in development, persists.[1] It is argued that internal and external economies of scale are necessary for the growth of firms and economies. The development, adaptation and utilisation of advanced technology and hence the growth of labour productivity are thought to be associated with economies of scale. The economic model underlying such arguments is in essence that of a closed economy, and a small autarkic country would, indeed, have growth difficulties. However, when the model is opened up, it seems that, provided small economies become specialised with a relatively high participation in international trade, migration and capital flows, there is no minimum scale for a territory on the basis of economic reasons. A territory's political aspirations may impose minimum size constraints in terms of manpower and national income available to fulfil national objectives, but these should be analysed separately from economic constraints, although in practice countries may wish to combine economic with political objectives in charting their growth.

Perhaps the strongest lesson of the development experience of the last 30 years is that no matter how well or ill countries are endowed naturally (in terms of minerals, climate, location etc.), their economic performance depends primarily on their commitment to growth and the appropriateness of the policy framework they evolve to implement their growth strategy.[2] The determination of national economic strategies and the policies to implement them is a political process which depends on a national social and political consensus about the objectives of development and how they may be reached. It is true that such a consensus often seems difficult to

* The authors are grateful to Reza Farivari and Huseyin Goksal for assistance in preparing this paper and to Arabindu Kundu for advice on the analysis. The views and interpretations, however, are theirs and should not be attributed to the World Bank, to its affiliated organisations, or to any individual acting on their behalf.

Social cohesion ≠ democracy in Singapore

attain even in a small country, but if all other things are equal, a
relatively small population is more likely to be able to reach social
and political agreement than a large population. Small countries tend
to be more homogeneous and more equity-oriented than large
countries. Their governments are therefore likely to be more
democratic and more stable than those of large countries. All this
makes economic objectives easier to achieve.[3] Thus, because there
are diseconomies as well as economies of scale, small countries also
have advantages associated with their very smallness.

During the last 30 years, all countries have had wide and
growing access to world markets. This has, of course, been much
more important for small than for large countries, for it has largely
offset the economic consequences of their smallness. Participation
in international trade, labour and capital flows has had costs, but
experience, particularly in the 1970s, suggests that these have been
much less than the benefits of 'openness' by a considerable margin.
Participating in international economic relations has not led either
to economic or to political dependence. On the contrary, political as
well as economic advantages appear to accrue from exposure to the
harsh winds of international competition. Countries that do so have
more, not less, development choices. The study of rent-seeking
behaviour indicates that as an economy builds up economic activities, commensurate vested interests, whether in the private sector
among entrepreneurs and workers, or in the bureaucracy, develop.[4]
If production is predominantly, or even partially, for the domestic
market, many of these vested interests will be protectionist,
resisting competition, change and adjustment. It has been well
established that producers tend to be better organised than
consumers, and the producers' case tends to be reinforced by
defence arguments for economic self-sufficiency. Nationalist
arguments tend to be particularly high in newly independent
countries. The larger the country, the greater the scope for
protectionist pressures that often lead to high costs. In a small
country, in contrast, vested interests tend to be trade-oriented
from an early stage of development. Self-sufficiency is clearly only
attainable at very low standards of living. Instead, competition
becomes a way of life. The efficiency impacts of ensuing trade
growth reinforce the vested interest pressures for the process of
continuous adjustments that makes it possible, resulting in a flexible
and dynamic economy that tends to more than offset the costs
arising from fluctuations in the international economy.

On balance, the advantages of smallness could in theory
outweigh the disadvantages. Some small countries could be expected
to grow rapidly. The first section of this paper, indeed, indicates
that not all small countries grow rapidly, and that small countries
as a group do not always grow more rapidly than large countries,
but some small countries have been among the most rapidly growing
developing countries. The second section discusses the costs and
benefits of 'smallness' in relation to small countries' experience
during the last 15 years. The evidence suggests that small
countries can grow very rapidly, if they tailor their economic

TABLE 1

GDP GROWTH BY POPULATION SIZE OF DEVELOPING COUNTRY, 1965-78[a]

Population	Total number of Countries	Countries for which data available		1965-73		1973-78	
		Total	Petroleum Importers	Total	Petroleum Importers	Total	Petroleum Importers
				(Average annual growth rates in percent)			
Less than 1 million	60	21	17	6.9	6.5	6.2	4.2
1 - 5 million	34	30	27	6.5	6.0	3.5	3.8
Total, 5 million or less	94	51	44	6.6	6.0	4.7	3.9
More than 5 million	59	58	44	6.8	6.3	5.9	5.0

[a] GDP in 1978 prices.

Note: petroleum importers are defined as countries that are net importers of petroleum and those whose petroleum exports are less than 10 per cent of total merchandise and service exports.

Source: World Bank data.

policies to their size as well as to other characteristics; however, if they do not, they are likely to stagnate and also to have serious social and political problems. The third section reviews the international context. There are now so many small independent countries that each cannot be regarded as marginal to the world economy. Their future development is dependent on the continuing expansion of liberal international economic relations. The paper concludes with a discussion of the policies that small as well as large countries must pursue if prospects for the small countries' growth are to continue to be favourable.

GROWTH EXPERIENCE

The dearth of data on small, and particularly very small, countries and territories limits quantitative analysis.

Table 1 suggests that while countries with populations of more than five million grow faster than those with populations of five million or less, among the latter the very small countries (with populations of less than one million) grow faster than the small ones (with populations of one to five million) and often faster than large countries (with populations of more than five million).[5]

Some caveats are needed before these results can be interpreted. GDP growth data were only available for 21 of the 60 very small countries and territories, and 30 of the 34 small countries, whereas coverage was almost complete for large countries, with only Iran missing out of the 59 countries in this category. Many of the countries for which data are not available have experienced political difficulties and consequently low growth. Others, however, are very small countries which have only recently become independent; here growth experience has been more mixed, so that it is not certain whether the missing data exert an upward or downward bias. It would seem to be safer to say that there appear to be no major differences in the growth experience of countries by size, and this is confirmed by regression analysis. Size does not explain growth (Table 4).[6] Some small economies have been among the most rapidly growing developing countries during 1970-78: Macao (18.8%), Botswana (15.5%), People's Democratic Republic of Yemen (14.8%), Lesotho (11.9%), Malta (11.6%), Jordan (10.5%), American Samoa (9.3%), Hong Kong (9.0%), Mauritius (8.3%) and Singapore (8.2%) all grew at more than eight per cent per year. Only Taiwan (11.2%), Republic of Korea (10.1%) and Brazil (9.0%) among the large developing countries, Iraq (11.1%) and Saudi Arabia (8.4%) among the capital surplus petroleum exporting countries, and Japan (9%) among the industrial countries, have grown as rapidly (World Bank, 1980). Many small countries, however, experienced low growth in the 1960s, and for some, growth fell further in the 1970s as increases in petroleum costs, the industrial countries' recession and the resulting fall in demand brought the inappropriateness of economic policies to a head.

When growth is viewed in per capita terms, the importance of population trends becomes evident, as can be seen in Table 2.

TABLE 2

POPULATION AND PER CAPITA GDP GROWTH BY POPULATION SIZE, 1965-78

(AVERAGE ANNUAL GROWTH RATES IN PERCENT)

	1965-73		1973-78	
	Population	Per Capita GDP[a]	Population	Per Capita GDP[a]
Less than 1 million	1.7	5.1	1.8	4.3
1-5 million	2.4	4.0	2.5	1.0
More than 5 million	2.4	4.3	2.3	3.5

[a] Per capita GDP in 1978 prices.

Source: World Bank data.

Relatively higher per capita income growth rates for the very small countries are consistent with the view that a demographic transition from low life expectancy/high fertility to higher life expectancy/lower fertility tends to take place fastest in countries that are growing relatively rapidly and have relatively equitable social policies. It seems that welfare policies are implemented relatively early in the development of some of the very small economies, accentuating the speed of the demographic transition.

Regional growth differences among countries with a population of less than five million are interesting in terms of both per capita income and income growth. From Table 3 it can be seen that in Southern Europe and East Asia throughout the 1960s and 1970s, and in the Middle East and North Africa during 1965-73, the small countries grew more rapidly than the large countries. In the Caribbean in both periods, and in Africa, south of the Sahara, during 1965-73, they grew more slowly than the large countries. The growth of the small countries dropped sharply in Oceania from 1965-73 to 1973-78, and it was low in the Caribbean for both periods. The reasons for these relationships vary from region to region, often with the changing experience of one or two of the larger countries in the 'small' group.

TABLE 3
PER CAPITA GDP GROWTH BY POPULATION SIZE AND REGION, 1965-78

	Number of countries		1978 Average Per Capita GDP[a]		Average annual growth rates in percent			
					1965-73		1973-78	
	Population		Population		Population		Population	
	more than 5 million	5 million or less	more than 5 million (US$)	5 million or less (US$)	more than 5 million	5 million or less	more than 5 million	5 million or less
Capital Surplus Petroleum Exporters	2	3	4,270	10,040	9.1	5.6	9.2	4.5
Southern Europe	5	2	2,410	2,140	6.5	7.8	4.1	5.6
Central and South America	11	9	1,490	1,040	6.8	4.2	4.9	4.6
Caribbean	1	6	920	880	8.5	4.5	5.4	1.3
East Asia	6	2	640	3,242	8.2	9.7	8.2	8.3
Oceania	-	3[b]	-	2,182[c]	-	6.9	-	1.0
Middle East and North Africa	6	5	710	2,220	5.8	10.8	7.9	4.5
South Asia	6	-	170	-	4.0	-	5.0	-
Sub Saharan Africa	21	21	540	330	5.8	4.7	3.9	3.9

a Per capita GDP in 1978 prices.

b Note that Nauru, Niue, New Caledonia, Tokelau and Tuvalu are included in the calculation of per capita income but not in growth rates.

c Excluding Nauru, per capita income is $1,680 for this group.

Source: World Bank data.

SMALLNESS AND GROWTH

As the growth experience of small developing countries suggests that the most important sources of growth are associated with human resource development and national cohesion, and with the formulation and administration of economic policies to carry out well defined development strategies, an analytical framework that examines their sources of growth should be specified in these terms. Such hypotheses are, however, very difficult to formulate in testable terms. The attempt that has been made here is discussed in the following pages and summarised in Table 4. Large countries were analysed for comparison.

Size

Size can be measured in terms both of population and area: in economic terms it is the resource endowment and the size of the domestic market that matters. Whatever the definition, however, the argument of the trade-offs between the (largely social and political) economies of small scale versus the (economic) diseconomies of small scale suggests that there would be no significant correlation (positive or negative) of scale with growth for small and large countries. This proved to be the case. The sign varied with the definition of size and the size of country, and the results were not significant.

Natural Resource Endowment

Rich mineral resources have not been an unmixed blessing for the small (as well as the large) developing countries. The existence of mineral rents (to the extent that they have been appropriated by the host country) has distorted prices and hence economic signals in an economy, making it difficult for enterprises and workers in sectors not enjoying high rents, such as agriculture, industry and tourism, to compete. The result has usually been a one product export economy which was very vulnerable to external fluctuations. Alternative policies of restraining the inflow of mineral rents into the economy, if necessary by investing them abroad, were often not implemented. Some small countries, allowing unrealistic expectations generated by the existence of mineral wealth to overide policy formulation, even made the situation worse by borrowing in boom times. Then, in cyclical downturns when there was a real need for borrowing, they were 'borrowed up'. With the exception of the capital surplus petroleum exporters that have received very large rents indeed, resource-rich countries have not been among the consistently rapidly growing ones.

The group of petroleum exporting developing countries that have been able to appropriate the bulk of mineral rents accruing to their mineral endowment, but have not been able to absorb the resulting income domestically, represent special development problems. The group include two large countries (Saudi Arabia and Iraq), two small countries (Kuwait and Libya) and several very small

TABLE 4

DETERMINANTS OF DEVELOPING COUNTRY GROWTH

Exogenous Variable	Endogenous Variable	Gross Domestic Product	
		Countries of 5 million or less	Countries of more than 5 million
Population in 1970 (-)		+0.0006 (0.1987)	-0.0001 (-0.4044)
Area (square kilometres) (-)		-0.0012 (-1.5100)	+0.0001 (0.8627)
Adult Literacy Rate (+)		-0.0073 (-0.58021)	+0.0057 (0.6117)
Growth of Agriculture (+)		+0.0344 (0.4711)	+0.3551** (3.2476)
Growth of Manufacturing (+)		+0.1050 (1.5642)	+0.2853** (3.3711)
Growth of Gross Domestic Savings (+)		+0.0609** (4.0400)	+0.0743** (3.4853)
Flow of ODA (+)		-0.00923 (-0.4659)	-0.0010 (-0.0723)
Net Flow of Net Direct Foreign Investment (+)		+0.0148 (0.9783)	-0.0042 (-0.2701)
Net Flow of Net Medium-and Long-Term Capital (+)		-0.0246 (-1.4161)	+0.0139 (1.2287)
Increase in the Consumer Price Index (-)		-0.0852* (-2.6307)	-0.0085 (-0.6353)
Growth of Merchandise and Service Exports (+)		+0.4047** (7.8103)	+0.0577 (1.4041)
Growth of Population (-)		-0.4084 (-1.2747)	+0.0534 (0.2940)
Constant (+)		+3.9319** (3.6657)	+0.0378 (0.0482)
Adjusted R^2		0.7617	0.7338
Standard Error of Estimate		1.531	1.283
F Statistics		11.12	11.80
No. of Observations		39	48

(+) or (-) are the signs expected in the regression.
** = Significant at 1% level of probability.
 * = Significant at 5% level of probability.

Note: GDP was used instead of GNP to avoid problems caused by financial flows in small countries' incomes. All variables with the exception of population and area are growth rates for 1965-78. The figures in parentheses are t values.

countries (Bahrain, Brunei, Oman, Qatar, United Arab Emirates). The principal constraint on these countries' growth lies in their lack of human resources: all of these countries are short of skills despite substantial flows of immigrants. It is not therefore surprising to find that the smaller countries grew less rapidly than the larger ones. The small capital surplus petroleum exporting countries' development problems could become pressing in the longer run as petroleum reserves run out, but at $10,000 per capita average annual income, such problems do not seem acute at present. They do, however, underline the rationale for the petroleum exporting countries' petroleum conservation policies.

It seems impossible to predict how a mineral-rich country will perform in practice, and even more to the point, no satisfactory measure of mineral 'intensity' has been devised. This variable was therefore not tested.

Location

Because of the importance of trade, location might be thought to be very important to small developing countries. That is, small countries such as those of the Caribbean and Central America that are close to large markets would appear to have a considerable advantage in transport costs, while those scattered out of the way of principal shipping and airline routes would be at a disadvantage. But while distance from markets may be a disadvantage for some small countries, it did not prevent Hong Kong, Singapore and Mauritius from developing worldwide markets. It seems unlikely that location can be used to predict growth. Moreover, given the large range of markets, from very low income to industrial countries, that the small developing countries have found in practice, a meaningful location measure could not be found.[7]

Human Resource Development

The development of every country, small or large, presents a unique problem that has to be solved in the light of particular natural endowments, locations, levels of development in relation to other countries, and so on. Devising a development strategy is generally much easier in a small than in a large country, even if the small country is poorly endowed. The range of options is usually narrower, and the solutions required are much simpler. The opening of mines (Jamaica, Liberia, New Caledonia), half a dozen export-oriented saw-mills (Belize, Surinam), tourist resorts (Antigua, St. Lucia, St. Maarten), banking (the Bahamas, Cayman Islands) can provide the impetus needed for growth, break balance of payments constraints, and directly and indirectly solve employment problems if it is accompanied by a suitable macro-economic policy framework. Vested economic interests are relatively few and can be reconciled much more easily than in a large country. Fluctuations in earnings from trade (for example fluctuating primary product prices or flows of tourists) can be smoothed out relatively easily by investing abroad revenues obtained in good years from resource rents and similar taxes. Monetary, trade and labour management are relatively simple. Planning and implementing investment in the social and physical infrastructure is much less complex in small than in large countries.

The relative ease of such a development solution is, however, deceptive. Simple as such problems may appear to, say, the Governments of China or of Brazil, to the political leaders and managers of small countries, such problems usually loom very large, because of the lack of skilled people. Tasks governments have to carry out, like economic activities, have economies of scale. A country needs only one prime minister or president no matter what its size; the number of ministers and government departments needed to take care of economic development is not proportional to a country's size (and is often inflated in small countries). The costs of running a country are lower where small territories are close to other countries (Monaco, Macao) than in isolated island economies and they diminish as population increases and with income growth. As more people become educated and experienced, the available human resources increase. Nevertheless very small communities eventually have to make choices between the cost of running their own government infrastructure (and sometimes living in relative isolation), or becoming part of a larger community, using a larger country's currency, postal system, trade regulations and so on to enable sufficient resources to be devoted to economic growth. An appropriately conceived regional grouping could provide such 'overhead' services.[8] In extreme cases a whole community, or a substantial portion of it, may wish to relocate. It has been suggested, for example, that the inhabitants of some of the very small and isolated Pacific communities might be well advised to accumulate the aid expenditures now being expended on them as cash grants to help them move to larger neighbouring countries. Other people will want to continue to live in small island communities (such as Norfolk Island and Pitcairn Islands) in spite of their isolation. In all such cases communities will rely on their cultural traditions to mark their national identity.

The lack of adequate human resources is particularly acute in countries at low levels of development. It is reflected in political as well as economic organisation and hence in the capacity for formulating economic strategy and policy. Countries with inappropriate economic policies and administrative capacities tend to grow very slowly even if they are well endowed and well located. This is true of many countries in sub-Saharan Africa. Relatively low infrastructure investment, modest increases in agricultural productivity and a few resource-based competitive enterprises could make for markedly accelerated growth. Aid flows have been concentrated on these countries so that funds for public investment are generally available, but their productivity is low. Transnational corporations are sometimes interested in the economic opportunities available in natural resource development, but the lack of negotiating experience on the country's side makes for exploitative situations. Human resource development is thus often the principal bottleneck in economic development.

The experience of other small countries that are better endowed with skills suggests that growth is possible with relatively small populations. Most of the small countries that have grown particularly well have had populations with considerable skills at both the 'blue collar' and intellectual end of the spectrum, and upgrading skills has been a key economic objective. The desire for economic growth has been well articulated, and the achievement of high living standards has been linked to the effort required. The countries concerned were relatively cohesive, and became more so in the development process. Government has played an important role in developing human resources, in providing the necessary physical infrastructure, and in designing and administering appropriate 'rules of the game' for efficient production. This has been true, for example, in 'laissez faire' Hong Kong. While there has been emphasis on efficiency in production, care has been taken to distribute the fruits of growth reasonably equitably, both directly through earnings, and indirectly through taxation and the provision of welfare services. Singapore and Malta are two examples of this type of development.

Where human resources have not been developed on appropriate lines, and where economic and social policies were not appropriate, development has been stalled. Slow growth and stagnation have led to other troubles, ranging from civil unrest to wars with other countries. With inappropriate policies income distribution became less equitable, there was little social surplus and welfare was neglected. Political pressures sometimes put off unrest by raising incomes ahead of productivity, by borrowing abroad and/or by inflationary policies, but such measures have made the ultimate achievement of sustained growth even more difficult.

Finding a proxy for the complex represented by 'human resource development' is, of course, impossible. Secondary education levels, often used, do not cover 'blue collar' skills and work ethic requirements, and are sometimes much more an outcome of, than an input into, development. Adult literacy was thought to be too general a concept to prove useful, and this was indeed the case. The results were not significant, and were counter-intuitive, the relationship being negative for small countries. A high degree of literacy probably only leads to growth if macro-economic policies are appropriate. Otherwise it is more likely to lead to migration.

Migration and Workers' Remittances

The quickest way to raise living standards for poor people from developing countries would be to end international migration barriers: migrants usually reach the living standards of the host countries within a generation. A great deal has been written about the costs of emigration to the migrant, but people continue to migrate when they can. Long waiting-lists and illegal migration indicate a large pent-up demand. There is also little evidence of a net loss to the home countries in the long run, unless the country concerned follows foolish policies. Countries such as Malta have prospered with high levels of permanent and temporary emigration;

Caribbean countries have done less well. Three of the high-growth small countries - Botswana, Yemen Arab Republic, and Lesotho - owe their growth to a considerable degree to emigrants' remittances. This is not to say that migration is without cost to the home or host country, particularly in social terms. If nationality per se is valued highly, permanent migration (which is usually preferred by the people concerned), would be a heavier loss to a small than a large country. The benefits nevertheless appear to exceed the costs for both individuals and countries.[9]   Data on remittances were too inadequate to test the relationship between migration and growth, but it would have been expected to be positive.

Sectoral Structure

Most small countries were traditionally agricultural producers, and for many agriculture is still the predominant economic activity. In these countries diversifying agricultural output and raising agricultural productivity have been the prime development tasks. In some countries, however, notably in the Caribbean, the growth of minerals, tourism and manufacturing (and rents from these sectors) has led to a neglect of agriculture, with ensuing high costs of food imports and with unemployment and balance of payments problems (Chernick, 1978).

Industry has often been seen as the leading development sector. It has been argued that countries would have to go through an import substitution phase before (if ever) being able to compete internationally in the export of manufactured goods. Such hypotheses have not been borne out by actual development experience. A number of countries have used exports as a basis for industrialisation (Hong Kong, Singapore, Mauritius and Malta). In others, though industrial activity is limited, it is largely for export (Haiti, Puerto Rico). It is true that industrialisation in a small country has to be specialised, efficient and internationally competitive. This may require the participation of transnational corporations, though not necessarily in the form of equity investment. In countries with a well developed human resource base, foreign investment can usually be 'unbundled' if it makes economic and financial sense to do so.[10]

Some of the most successful 'manufacturing' industries in small countries have a strong services orientation. Printing is an example. Indeed, service industries have been shown to be particularly well suited to small economies because they tend to have low internal transport costs. In the 1970s banking was a prime example. Tourism is another major service activity that has had high private and social returns in some small countries. Those with a strong human resource base (Switzerland, Singapore or Hong Kong) have, moreover, found its associated social costs negligible. For others, however, the social costs have been considerable.

The relationship of agriculture and manufacturing to GNP growth was tested. Signs were positive as expected, but only for large countries were they significant. Service industries may have outweighed both in the small countries.

The Policy Framework

Testing the impact of policy on growth is of course very difficult. Innumerable proxies can be used. Four main areas were defined as indicative of approximate policy choice. Capital mobilisation was the first area examined. It was divided into the following two sub-groups:

(i) The growth of domestic savings was thought to be the most important of the capital indicators, with an expected positive relationship. The correlation had the expected sign and was significant for both groups of countries.
(ii) Aid, direct foreign investment and other private medium-and long-term capital flows are the other components of capital mobilisation. The relationship between aid and growth was negative for the period covered, though not significant for either small or large countries. Presumably this is because the bulk of aid goes to the poorest countries, some of which have been growing slowly. The flow of private direct foreign investment had a positive association with the growth of small countries, but not with that of large countries; but neither result was significant. It is possible that the greater openness of the small economies, leading to more competitive conditions for foreign investors, also contributed to this result. Moreover, the role of foreign investment in large countries is much smaller than in small countries. The flow of other private capital also did not have a significant association with growth, and the correlation was negative for small countries, though positive for large. With the exception of countries such as Hong Kong, Singapore and Malta, the flows to small countries were too small to have an impact. Most small countries are not yet sufficiently creditworthy to borrow from international capital markets on a large scale.

It was extremely difficult to find a proxy measurement for the effectiveness of monetary, fiscal, trade, income and other policies. However, given the existence of international inflationary trends in the 1970s, the relative increase in consumer prices in each country seemed to be a reasonable proxy for the overall effectiveness of domestic management. The relationship was of course expected to be inverse: the better the domestic management, the lower the cost of living increase and the higher the rate of growth. The relationship tested had the correct sign and was significant for small countries, though not for large. It seems likely that small countries cannot tolerate high inflation rates, but that some large countries can grow quite rapidly in spite of high rates of inflation. The experience of, say, Brazil and Chile seems to confirm this hypothesis.

Given the importance of specialisation and hence of trade for small economies, policies leading to openness seemed important. The growth of merchandise and service exports was therefore examined. The relationship was, as expected, positive for both small and large countries, but it was only significant for small countries, 'for which it proved to be the most significant result. This hypothesis, too, seems sensible. The larger the country the relatively less important would 'openness' be. However, a rapid growth of exports has in practice also proved essential to the growth of such large countries as Brazil, Chile, Korea and Yugoslavia.

The growth of population was taken to be a proxy for welfare policies. It was thought that the higher the population growth, the less effective were welfare policies. The sign was expected to be negative, and this was the case for small countries, though the results were not significant. Large countries can evidently tolerate a greater degree of population growth (and the poor social policies this implies). Again, not much can be attributed to the positive sign because it was not significant.

As was expected, in so far as it can be concluded that favourable economic trends follow from appropriate policies, policies that lead to high savings, stable prices and a rapid growth of exports lead to high growth rates in small countries. It was also to be expected that price stability and export growth are more important for small than for large countries. The evidence also suggests that large countries have more room for manoeuvre in policy formulation, but they probably need it because the formulation of appropriate policies may be more difficult.

Statistical Validity of the Results

Given the inability to specify the variables thought to be the critical ones, the overall adjusted R^2 seems quite high, though this no doubt results from the upward GDP trend (see the constant). The F statistic is also reasonable for the number of observations, and the Durbin-Watson statistic was very significant in all the equations, with values of 2.019 for countries of five million or less and 2.046 for countries of over five million. It was thought that log relationships might have provided a better fit, but the regression could not be run in log form because of negative growth rates for several variables and countries.

THE INTERNATIONAL ENVIRONMENT

Small countries can only grow and develop in a liberal international economic environment. While each country is individually only a marginal participant in world markets, together and in particular markets, their impact can be quite marked. Hong Kong itself (exporting more manufactures than India, for example) has had a large enough impact on clothing markets in industrial countries to be subjected to quantitative import controls. Trade in goods and services, migration and international capital flows are both complementary and competitive. Some countries prefer to focus on trade (Japan), while others use all in various combinations, and for small countries, and particularly those poorly endowed with natural resources, migration and participation in capital markets are very important.

Trade in Goods and Services

The last 30 years have seen a turning away from the protectionism of the 1930s (and its concomitant worldwide low growth) by the industrial countries. Trade is now more free among them, and access to their markets is greater than it has been at any time since the years leading up to World War I.

A 'new protectionism' did emerge with the slowing down of the industrial countries' growth in the late 1960s but it was and still is mainly directed at other industrial countries, notably Japan. Protection against imports from developing countries has been mainly directed at the textile, clothing and footwear exports of the East Asian countries, which have, nevertheless, continued to increase their share of industrial country and other markets (Hughes and Waelbroeck, 1981). While it is very important to be alert to further attempts to erode the 'openness' of the trading environment, it is equally important not to exaggerate it, or to use it as an excuse not to overcome developing country supply constraints. Countries such as Malta and Mauritius, that have overcome these constraints, had export growth of 20-30 per cent a year in the 1970s. The negotiation of the Codes of Conduct in the Tokyo Round of GATT multilateral trade negotiations gives developing countries a strong negotiating position (if they join the system). Regional and other developing country organisations can play an important role in negotiations if they focus on technical details rather than on generalities. Negotiations in the area of trade in services will be important in the 1980s if liberal rather than restrictive conventions are to be adopted. Many small countries have demonstrated that, for them, trade liberalisation makes a great deal of sense, even if other countries continue to be protectionist. Singapore is an example of a country which reversed a protectionist trend, at some cost, but with almost immediate results. For small countries with high protection, such liberalisation is difficult, but without it they are not likely to be able to grow rapidly. The growth of inter-developing country trade is going to put pressure on the protectionism of large developing countries. Without more liberal access to their markets their trade growth will be confined to that determined by the three per cent or so of GNP growth of the industrial countries rather than their own five to eight per cent growth.

Migration

Temporary emigration has been an important source of economic growth for countries with very undeveloped human resources, and it is likely to continue to be needed at least through the 1980s. For very small counries, permanent migration is likely to be important. Given the very large flows of migrants to Europe, to North America, and to the Middle East during the past 20 years, the small countries' needs are again marginal. If migration were to become more restricted, however, they would be hurt more than proportionately because they have more limited domestic economic opportunities than large countries.

The Flow of Capital

The development of international capital markets following the freeing of capital flows among countries has been the most unexpected and successful development in the international economy. It has served countries with surplus savings and those with investment requirements, and several small developing countries have benefited directly as host countries to the intermediation activities that have had to take place to accomplish this. The same needs are likely to arise in the future, and mineral-rich countries, or others earning high rents, can use the international capital markets to balance out the fluctuations in their economies.

International capital markets are still expanding, with several small developing countries now playing a direct role in the development of international intermediation. Hong Kong, Singapore and Bahrain are examples, and others such as Kuwait are likely to follow.

Small and Large Countries

A relatively high exposure to international markets is risky. Markets are far from perfect. Fluctuations must be expected. The situation changes very rapidly. This is difficult for countries with poorly developed human resources to handle. But the many small countries that now exist have to take part in the international economy or stagnate. The co-operation of large countries is needed to maintain the present liberal international environment and to improve it further to give the small countries scope for growth. This is not a cost, for they too will benefit.

NOTES

1. In the late 1950s countries of ten to fifteen million people were thought to be 'small'. See Robinson (1960); Chenery and Syrquin (1975) also took a population of fifteen million as the cut-off point for 'small' economies. With economic growth and the independence of many small territories, the five million cut-off point, used in this volume, to distinguish between 'small' countries and other countries has become widely accepted.

2. C.f. Chenery and Syrquin, op.cit., who took such factors as natural endowment as the principal parameters of growth analysis.

3. This was noted by Simon Kuznets (1960, pp.28-31).

4. See Anne Krueger (1974) for a description of vested interests' influence on economic policy. Such issues have been discussed by Olsen (1978) and in the literature on the market for protection; see Anderson and Baldwin (forthcoming) for a summary.

5. See World Bank (1980) for country detail.

6. C.f. Chenery and Syrquin (1975, p. 88).

7. See Bennathan in this volume.

8. Most attempts at regional integration to date have been more ambitious than successful. See Vaitsos (1978) and Hughes (1980).

9. The literature on this subject is large and emotive. For a summary of the economic impact of migration, see Swamy (1981).

10. See Lall and Ghosh in this volume.

REFERENCES

Anderson, Kym and Baldwin, Robert E., forthcoming, "The Political Market for Protection in Industrial Countries", World Bank Staff Working Paper.

Chenery, Hollis B. and Syrquin, M., 1975, "Patterns of Development, 1950-1970", London: Oxford University Press.

Chernick, Sidney, E., 1978, "The Commonwealth Caribbean: The Integration Experience", Baltimore: Johns Hopkins University Press.

Hughes, Helen, 1980, 'Inter-Developing Country Trade and Employment', Session IV, Mexico City: IEA Sixth World Congress on "Human Resources Employment and Development".

_____ and Waelbroeck, Jean, 1981, 'Can Developing Country Exports Keep Growing in the 1980s?' In "The World Economy", Vol.4, No.2.

Krueger, Anne, 1974, 'The Political Economy of the Rent-Seeking Society'. In "American Economic Review", Vol.64, No.3.

Kuznets, Simon, 1960, 'The Economic Growth of Small Nations'. In E.A.G. Robinson, "Economic Consequences of the Size of Nations", London: Macmillan.

Olsen, Mancur, 1978, "The Political Economy of Comparative Growth Rates", mimeo.

Robinson, E.A.G., 1960, "Economic Consequences of the Size of Nations", London: Macmillan.

Swamy, Gurushri, 1981, "Remittances of Migrant Workers: Issues and Prospects", World Bank Staff Working Paper.

The World Bank, 1980, "World Bank Atlas", Washinghton D.C.

Vaitsos, Constantine V., 1978, 'Crisis in Regional Economic Co-operation (Integration) Among Developing Countries: A Survey'. In "World Development", Vol.6, No.6.

6. The Industrialisation Experience of Small Economies

Ian Thomas*

It is generally agreed that industrialisation, in the sense of creating an efficient and expanding manufacturing capacity, makes a vital contribution to accelerating economic growth and development. Manufactured goods tend to have higher income elasticities of demand over a wider range of income than other products, and are produced by techniques which generally involve more linkages and greater possibilities of diversification and specialisation than those of other sectors. Statistics show not only that production in the manufacturing sector has grown faster than in other sectors, both in developed and developing countries[1], but that on average the growth has been fastest and the relative importance of the sector has been greatest at intermediate levels of income (approximately $500 to $1,000, in 1975 dollars) when countries have been on the threshold of 'take-off' into self-sustaining growth and development[2].

In attempting to build their manufacturing sectors almost all developing countries have encountered production problems, caused by such factors as inadequate labour skills, inappropriate technologies and insufficient capital, and marketing problems, caused mainly by a deficiency of effective domestic demand. But countries with small populations as well as low incomes have had in addition to confront the problems of insufficient labour, insufficient potential markets domestically and, in certain cases, insufficient land.

Because manufacturing depends more on factor specificities relating to labour and capital than to land, it tends to be more mobile than most other economic activities (e.g. farming or mining). Equally, because it is usually more capital-intensive than most other activities (e.g. farming, banking, tourism), economies of scale and factor indivisibilities tend to be more important. It follows that countries with small domestic markets caused by small populations as well as low incomes are generally at a disadvantage, compared with larger countries, in undertaking manufacturing activities. Yet a few of these small countries have developed flourishing manufacturing sectors which have made very substantial contributions to GDP and have continued to grow swiftly, mainly on the basis of a successful export performance.

*The author is grateful to Bimal Jalan and Sanjaya Lall for comments on an earlier draft.

There has, as yet, been no systematic analysis of the experience of manufacturing development in these countries. There have, of course, been many studies of the industrialisation process, both in general and in specific countries, including small countries; there have also been a number of statistical studies of the changing economic structure of countries which normally accompanies a rise in income, with population size as one of the characteristics which might explain differences between country groups[3]. There is widespread agreement that, as incomes rise, resource allocation processes produce generally predictable changes in the composition of domestic and external demand and in the structure of production. These changes result from an interaction between the effects of rising incomes on demand - principally the proportionately greater increase in the propensity to consume manufactures than primary products, and on supply - principally the different factor proportions in changes in production technologies caused by the growth of physical and human capital in relation to population.

There is less consensus on the degree to which the structure of production (and thus the relative importance of the manufacturing sector) differs from one country to another because of its size (population), irrespective of its income level. Chenery (1960) had calculated that, at a constant per capita income of $300 (1953 dollars) and with a 'normal' composition of output, a country with a population of ten millions would produce, per capita, 38 per cent more manufactures than would one with only two millions, while a population of 50 millions would raise the differential to 90 per cent. However, Chenery and Syrquin (1975) calculated that, at a constant income of $500 (1964 dollars), the industry-oriented small country (defined as having a population in 1960 of 15 millions or less) derived 31 per cent of its GNP from manufacturing, only two points less than the large country but seven points more than the primary-oriented small country. They also concluded that differences between the productive structures of large and small countries were not significant at the lowest income levels (below $100) and that they tended to converge at the highest income levels (above $1,500). Kuznets (1971), on the other hand, had calculated the share of manufacturing in GDP to be lower in small countries (population in 1958 of less than ten millions but more than one million) than in large ones at all 'bench-mark' levels of income between $70 and $1,000 (1958 dollars). Similarly, UNIDO (1979) concluded that the proportion of 'commodity GDP' (i.e. excluding services) derived from manufacturing (value-added basis) was lower in small countries (population in 1970 of less than 20 millions) than in large ones at all indicated levels of income between $100 and $3,000 (1970 dollars). The difference was most marked at low levels and became progressively less important as incomes rose.

Regarding the relative importance of income and population as explanatory variables of the changing structure of a country's economy, Chenery (1960) concluded that about 70 per cent of the variations between countries in the relative share of manufacturing in GDP was caused by difference in income, and that the difference in market size was only one of a number of factors accounting for the remainder. The regression results obtained by Chenery and Taylor (1968) also showed income to be a very much more significant variable than population in determining the relative importance of the manufacturing sector.

The general conclusion of these statistical investigations, therefore, is that the size effect on economic structure is far smaller than the income effect, and the differences between rich and poor small countries are much the same as between rich and poor large countries. At its face value, such a conclusion would seem to suggest that the processes of industrialisation in small countries need not be any different from those in large countries, and that higher income countries are likely to be better placed than lower income countries. Such a generalisation leaves unanswered the question of what the poorer developing countries should be doing to raise their incomes and levels of industrialisation. As Chenery (1960, p.650) admits, "the association between industrialisation and rising income tells us very little about the factors causing the rise in income itself".

The purpose of the present paper is a modest one. It presents available data on some of the major variables concerning the manufacturing sector, including its share of GDP, rate of growth and composition, the extent to which it provides employment, and the importance to the sector of exports. The data reveal striking differences among small developing countries and between them and larger developing countries, among which there are also significant differences. The paper also attempts to examine the validity of some of the commonplace suppositions regarding the reasons for success or failure in the development of manufacturing in small countries. A concluding section briefly summarises some of the main findings and makes a few short comments on the possible future prospects for manufacturing in small countries.

Finally, it should be mentioned that in the paper, unless otherwise stated, the term 'small countries' has been restricted to developing countries (whether or not politically independent) whose populations in 1978 were below five millions; the term 'large countries' refers to developing countries (outside the centrally planned economies) whose populations in that year were above 30 millions[4]. 'Manufacturing' is defined as all activities included in Section 3 of the International Standard Industrial Classification of All Economic Activities (ISIC). These definitions have been adopted purely for reasons of convenience.

MANUFACTURING IN DEVELOPING COUNTRIES

Share of Manufacturing Sector in GDP

Table 1 presents the available data of the share of the manufacturing sector in GDP for a number of small countries.* It shows a tendency for this to be largest where incomes are highest,

---

* All tables are at the end of the Chapter.

as in Israel, Singapore and Hong Kong, and smallest where they are among the lowest, as in The Gambia, Guinea-Bissau and Solomon Islands. The major exceptions are found among countries where natural resources dominate the economy: in those where the resource is of high value but is marketed without processing (e.g. crude oil exported from Gabon), incomes are comparatively high but the contribution of manufacturing to GDP is relatively low; in those where the value-added by processing the resource is relatively small (e.g. in the case of sugar, fruit and wood in Swaziland), incomes are comparatively low but the proportion of GDP from manufacturing is relatively high. The relationship between the share of manufacturing in GDP and the level of population is by no means as marked, although it should be noted that almost all the small countries where the manufacturing share is 15 per cent or more of GDP have populations of between one and five millions while almost all those in which it is seven per cent or less have populations of under one million.

Data from the World Bank (1980) show that in large countries, too, there is a tendency for the manufacturing sector's share in GDP to be positively related to the level of per capita income. The tendency is not as marked as in the small countries, however, and there are notable exceptions. Countries in which incomes are abnormally low compared with manufacturing share include India and Pakistan, while those in which it is abnormally high include Nigeria and Indonesia, where oil distorts the position. In general there seems to be no significant relationship between the share of manufacturing in GDP and the level of population among this group of countries. Nevertheless, the manufacturing sector accounted for ten per cent or more of GDP in nearly three-quarters of the large countries but in only one-half of the small ones, and for 20 per cent or more of GDP in over one-third of the large countries but in only one-sixth of the small ones. Also apparent is the tendency for the sector to constitute a relatively lower share of GDP in small countries than in large ones at similar levels of income.

Growth of Manufacturing Sector

Available data on the increase in output of the manufacturing sector in small countries during two representative periods, given in Table 2, show that growth has varied very considerably, both between countries and between the two periods concerned. Data from the World Bank (1980) indicate similar variations in the case of large countries. But while growth seems to have been rather faster on average during 1970-78 in large countries (8.1 per cent) than in small ones (5.9 per cent)[5], it appears to have shown no statistically significant relation to the relative share of manufacturing in GDP, level of income, or size of population. Relatively fast growth was recorded both in small countries with high incomes where manufacturing was already of significance to the economy at the start of the 1960s (e.g. Singapore and Costa Rica), and in those with low incomes where it was of comparatively little importance even at the end of the 1970s (e.g. Lesotho and Liberia).

It was also registered both in countries with populations approaching the five million limit (e.g. Haiti and Hong Kong) and in those with less than a million (e.g. Belize and Guyana). On the other hand, relatively slow growth was registered both in middle-income small countries in which manufacturing is of considerable significance to the economy (e.g. Congo) and in poor ones in which it is not (e.g. The Gambia); both in the more populous small countries (e.g. Rwanda) and in the less populous ones (e.g. Trinidad and Tobago, where growth was negative). In most countries for which data are available, manufacturing output grew more slowly during the 1970s than the 1960s, particularly in Panama, Mauritania and Cyprus; in Trinidad and Tobago and Jamaica it declined. In a few countries, however, including Botswana, Guyana and Haiti, a marked acceleration was apparent between the two decades.

The reasons for these disparities are doubtless diverse, but in general it would seem that the potential growth of the manufacturing sector depends on the technical possibilities of profitably producing and marketing an increasing volume of goods whose demand is characterised by high income elasticities and/or, where they can be sold at prices which undercut competitors, by price elasticities which are greater than unity and thus result in expanding market shares. These production possibilities depend on a country's basic characteristics, such as its location, resource availabilities, labour supplies etc., and on the extent to which it can maximise their value by creating, purchasing or otherwise obtaining use of the technological knowledge, expertise and other labour skills, capital plant and equipment, and infrastructural facilities necessary for manufacturing. The degree to which growth actually occurs depends on the adequacy with which these production factors are harnessed and utilised and thus, at one remove, on the intensity of market demand for the different manufactured goods which they can be used to produce.

Governments of small countries which have had the greatest success in fostering the growth of manufacturing appear to be those whose fiscal and financial policies towards industry have been clear, stable and consistently applied, and which have not led to resource misallocation through distortions of the price mechanism. Because of the inadequacies of the domestic market potential, small countries whose governments promoted import-substitution of manufactures through a high level of protection and subsidies to capital usually experienced severe foreign exchange constraints and relatively low growth (e.g. Uruguay during the 1960s). By contrast, those which operated more balanced policies, which emphasised exports at least as much as import-substitution, usually experienced comparatively high growth (e.g. Hong Kong and Singapore).

Another factor of general relevance to a country's manufacturing potential seems to be location. It appears that most small countries in which manufacturing has made a relatively large contribution to GDP or has grown comparatively quickly are either favourably located in relation to large dynamic markets (e.g. Malta's proximity to EEC) or are well situated in relation to an expanding supply of potentially skilled labour (e.g. Hong Kong) or to world trade routes (e.g. Singapore). Conversely, in those which are unfavourably located in relation to large dynamic markets by reason either of remoteness (e.g. the small island countries of the Pacific) or of terrain (e.g. some of the small land-locked countries of Asia, Africa and Latin America), manufacturing is little developed.

The proximate effects of some of the other major factors influencing manufacturing, such as the availability of natural resources, skilled labour, capital, etc., are on the composition of the sector, and are considered below.

Employment in Manufacturing Sector

Available data on employment in manufacturing in small countries are given in Table 3. This shows that during the 1970s employment trends were generally upward but that in some small countries there were substantial fluctuations (e.g. in Jamaica, Panama and Singapore during 1975), which were probably caused at least in part by variations in external demand for products manufactured primarily for export. The table also shows the great disparities which exist in the relative importance of manufacturing as a source of employment. The share of the sector in the total ranged from nearly one-half in Hong Kong, through more than one-quarter in Uruguay, Singapore and Malta, to one-twentieth in the Bahamas. Data from the International Labour Office suggest that in most large countries the fluctuations in employment in manufacturing were less severe, reflecting these countries' lower external economic 'dependence'. However, the relative importance of the sector as a source of employment also varied considerably, its proportion of the total ranging from over two-fifths in Turkey and Brazil, to under one-twentieth in Bangladesh and Ethiopia.

An adequate supply of labour is clearly basic to the development of manufacturing. The evidence suggests that where a country's population is below a certain level (possibly of around 50,000) its labour force will be so small as to make it very difficult - in some cases almost impossible - to create the requisite skills and to provide the necessary infrastructures to develop any significant and profitable manufacturing capacity[6]. Equally important is the growth of population through 'natural increase' (higher birth rates/lower death rates) or net immigration, or both. During the 1960s, the expansion of the labour force among small countries was fastest (more than three per cent annually) in Israel and Hong Kong (largely through net immigration) and in Costa Rica and Panama (largely through high net birth rates); these countries were among those in which manufacturing production rose most swiftly. Conversely, the labour force rose very slowly in Haiti, where manufacturing production declined. A third factor of importance is the degree of concentration of population. All other factors remaining equal, manufacturing is more likely to develop in geographically small countries with high densities of population (e.g. Hong Kong, Singapore and Malta) or in geographically larger countries with highly skewed distributions of population (e.g. Uruguay), than in small countries in which the density of population is low and relatively uniform (e.g. Gabon and Botswana).

Composition of Manufacturing Sector

The main product groups which comprise the bulk of the value-added in the manufacturing sector are shown in Table 4 for a selection of small and large countries and for some medium-sized ones in which manufacturing output grew especially quickly during the 1970s. The available information shows that the composition of the sector varies considerably, both within these categories of country and between them, but that two major features are apparent.

First, the degree of concentration of manufacturing by product group tends to be much higher in the small countries than in the others. It tends to be particularly high in those countries in which there is an easily processed dominant local resource, as in Mauritius or Fiji, where over three-fifths of the manufacturing value-added (and more than three-quarters of the gross output) is accounted for by the food, drink and tobacco group, which in those two countries is dominated by sugar milling, or in Trinidad and Tobago, where over four-fifths is provided by the chemicals group, which in that country is dominated by petroleum refining. The narrowness of manufacturing in some of the poorer small countries compared with the others is exemplified by the diffferences in the share of total output taken by the leading four product groups: this exceeded 90 per cent in Rwanda and Central African Republic but was less than 50 per cent in Israel.

Secondly, the proportion of the manufacturing sector's output accounted for by what are generally considered to be first-stage industries, producing mainly consumer goods, tends to be much higher in most of the small countries than in the others. This tendency is especially marked in the case of the food industry, which in 1975 was the largest single component of the sector in 17 of the 22 small countries for which details are available. First-stage industries are usually based on local resources and tend to be small-scale, technologically simple and capital-unintensive, with few vertical or horizontal linkages, or external economies; they often result in comparatively little value being added to the production factors. Conversely the share in the total of second-stage industries producing mainly investment goods, such as base metals, machinery and transport equipment, and intermediates such as chemicals (excluding petroleum products), tends to be much lower in most of the small countries than in the others. These industries are usually based as much on imported raw materials as on local ones, are often large-scale, technologically complex and capital-intensive, and have more linkages and external economies; they usually involve substantial value being added to the production factors.

The products of the first group of industries are generally recognised as being of diminishing relative importance within the manufacturing sector as industrialisation proceeds and incomes rise. Chenery (1960) showed that a rise in incomes from $100 to $600 (1953 dollars) would be accompanied by a fall from 68 per cent to 43 per cent in consumer goods' share of the sector total and a rise from 12 per cent to 35 per cent in that of investment goods. He estimated (1960) their growth elasticities[7] as being 1.29 for the consumer goods group and 1.64 for the investment goods group. More recently, UNIDO (1979) has shown that, both in large countries (populations of 20 millions or more in 1970) and in small ones, growth elasticities during the period 1969-73 were significantly higher for industries producing investment goods, such as machinery and equipment, iron and steel, paper, and chemicals, than for those producing consumer goods, such as food, beverages and tobacco, textiles, and leather and leather products (including footwear). It showed co-efficients to have been rather lower on average in small than in large countries, which was probably a reflection of the generally less advanced development of most small countries and the extent to which their manufacturing sectors were dominated by one or two relatively low-growth industries such as food. The study also showed the variations in growth elasticities between different industries to have been substantially greater in small countries: in general, co-efficients were higher in those countries categorised as having 'ample' resources and a 'primary orientation' than in those with only 'modest' resources or with 'ample resources' but an 'industrial orientation'. The differences were particularly marked for resource-based industries, such as leather (including footwear), wood products, glass and non-ferrous metals.

Several studies have also made estimates of size elasticities[8]. Chenery (1960) showed these to be much higher for capital goods and intermediates than for consumer goods. He concluded that industries with significant economies of scale produced about 40 per cent of the output of the manufacturing sector at an income of $300 but 57 per cent at one of $600 (1953 dollars). UNIDO (1979) showed co-efficients during 1969-73 to have been generally higher for small countries than large ones. It concluded that for small countries with 'ample' resources, market size was most important for base metals, electrical machinery, transport equipment, glass and paper, while for those with only 'modest' resources, it was most important for textiles, non-electrical machinery, leather products and rubber products. For large countries, it was significant only for non-electrical machinery, professional and scientific goods, transport equipment, iron and steel, and rubber products.

Overall, therefore, growth elasticities were generally higher for the same range of products for which size elasticities were most significant, viz. the chemical and engineering products of heavy industry, for which substantial factor indivisibilities and economies of scale mean both high minimum and optimum levels of output. The differences in the composition of the manufacturing sector between 'typical' small and large countries would thus appear to have put the first group of countries under a 'structural' disadvantage, in as much as global demand for these capital goods industries tended to rise significantly faster than for most of the more simple consumer goods industries, such as the food industry[9]. Only in a few small countries (notably Singapore, Israel and, to a lesser extent, Hong Kong) was the share of the machinery, transport equipment and other metal products industries comparatively important, while that of the base metal industry was not significant in any of them except Israel. The chemicals group, on the other hand, was an important element in several small countries (notably Trinidad and Tobago, Singapore and Uruguay); petroleum refining dominated the group in almost all of them, and between 1960 and 1974 petroleum products were the fastest growing products manufactured by developing countries, with a growth rate almost three times that of food products. It appears that no small country produced a majority of the twenty manufactured products whose output by developing countries has been shown by UNIDO (1979) to have risen fastest during 1960-74, and some did not produce any of them. Although the production of most of these products is resource-based, for almost all of them it is characterised by substantial economies of scale, while for a significant proportion it is also subject to high minimum levels, complex technologies and high levels of skill.

But if 'structural' factors do not seem generally to have been favourable for fostering the growth of manufacturing in small countries, they could still grow quickly as a result of 'competitive' factors. To the extent that an enterprise could profitably produce and market an expanding volume of manufactures which in terms of price, quality (including technical specification), delivery date, etc. are superior to those of its competitors, or which were marketed in a more effective manner or had better conditions of market access than its competitors, then it could enlarge its market share and raise its output. This has been especially important in the case of exports, and much of the expansion of manufacturing in the faster growing small countries has resulted from the more competitive position of their goods in major markets. The importance of exports to these countries is discussed in the next section.

Exports of Manufactures

Importance to production

The tendency is well known for the ratio of a country's foreign trade to its GDP to be higher the smaller is its economy. The extent to which a producer is dependent on exports for selling his manufactures obviously varies, but would appear to be greater, the smaller is the domestic market and the more capital- or skill-intensive the product. The proportion of a country's output of manufactures which is exported therefore depends in part on the product composition of the manufacturing sector. Unfortunately, lack of published data in many small countries on the gross value of production of the manufacturing sector (as distinct from value-added within the sector) precludes the calculation of comprehensive statistics of the proportion of manufacturing output which enters international trade. However, enough information is available (see Table 5) to conclude that the proportion is generally higher in small countries which have no natural resources except human skills (e.g. Hong Kong and Singapore), or which have one predominant natural resource which is relatively easy to process or which has to be processed before export in order to reduce weight or bulk (e.g. refining of petroleum in Trinidad and Tobago or milling of sugar cane in Barbados, Fiji and Mauritius), than it is in those countries with several natural resources, whether the countries are middle-income (e.g. Panama and Nicaragua) or low-income (e.g. Rwanda and Central African Republic). By comparison, the proportion of the manufacturing sector's output exported from large countries is much lower (e.g. nine per cent in India and Nigeria in 1975).

Size and growth

Inter-country comparisons show the relative size (value) of manufactures exported from small countries to bear a broadly similar relation to the relative size of GDP or relative importance of manufacturing. This is apparent from Table 5 in which small countries are ranked in order of value of manufactured exports in 1975: those in the Caribbean, Pacific and Africa are generally lower placed than those in Asia and Latin America, although countries which refine for export imported crude petroleum (e.g. the Netherlands Antilles and the Bahamas) constitute a major exception.

The relative size of exports of manufactures at any particular time depends upon production possibilities and demand levels, and thus on a combination of structural factors, notably the product and market composition of the exports, and competitive factors, embodied in a country's ability to enlarge its market share. Unfortunately no comprehensive time-series data are readily available on which to show trends in exports of manufactures from small countries. Some data are available, but they usually define manufactures[10] in such a way that they are not comparable with production. This anomaly is especially important in the case of small countries, where much of the output of the manufacturing sector often consists of simple processed foodstuffs which are excluded from the conventional definition of manufactured exports. For countries in which manufactures account for almost all exports (e.g. Hong Kong, Malta, Fiji, Barbados), trends in total exports are a satisfactory substitute for those of manufactures, but for countries in which the latter account for, say, only a half or less of the total (e.g. Israel), they are not.

As far as product composition is concerned, Table 6 shows the major product groups which in most small countries account for the bulk of exports of manufactures. It reveals a generally high degree of concentration which is usually highest among the smallest countries. Manufactured exports from some of these very small countries consist entirely or almost entirely of one product, e.g. semi-processed vegetable oils from St. Vincent and The Gambia or petroleum products from Antigua. But the degree of concentration is only a little less in some of the larger small countries which specialise in resource-based manufacturing for export. Examples include cane sugar from Fiji, Guadeloupe, Belize, Reunion, Mauritius and Guyana; petroleum products from the Netherlands Antilles, the Bahamas, and Trinidad and Tobago; ferro-nickel from New Caledonia; and alumina from Jamaica and Surinam. In these cases, overall performance of exports from the manufacturing sector necessarily depends overwhelmingly on domestic availabilities of, and external prices for, the particular product concerned. Where these two characteristics have varied substantially (e.g. for cane sugar), receipts from exports of manufactures have inevitably fluctuated markedly. For example, comparing 1965-70 and 1970-73, average growth in (total) exports from Fiji was 7.3 per cent and 28.4 per cent respectively, whereas that from Mauritius was -0.3 per cent and 30.3 per cent respectively. On the other hand, concentration on exporting a product in buoyant demand and readily available and stable supply can lead to consistently high growth, as in the Netherlands Antilles, whose exports rose in value by over 25 per cent annually on average during the first half of the 1970s.

All other factors remaining equal, exports from a country should tend to rise faster, the more it was able profitably to concentrate on producing those manufactures for which import demand was rising fastest. A study by UNCTAD (1977) showed that during 1970-76, aggregate imports from all sources by the major developed market-economy countries (which are the largest outlets for most exporters of manufactures from small countries) rose most quickly for petroleum products, followed by clothing, leather and footwear, road motor vehicles, rubber products and chemicals. Imports into these countries from developing countries grew fastest for road motor vehicles (but from a very low base), followed by other engineering and metal products, clothing, pulp, paper and board, leather and footwear, petroleum products, and rubber products. But it should be noted that since 1977, clothing, leather and footwear would have occupied a lower position as non-tariff barriers to these products (and others, notably textiles) constrained access and therefore export growth.

The UNCTAD study found that for some small countries (including Hong Kong and Israel) the rate of growth of exports during 1970-76 was the same as, or very similar to, that which could have been expected as a result of their product structure at the start of the period. With a curtailment in market access for Hong Kong's chief products (clothing and textiles) as a result of the Multifibre Arrangement, this meant that the country's exports grew much more slowly during the 1970s (4.8 per cent on average from 1970 to 1978) than during the 1960s (12.7 per cent on average from 1960 to 1970). But for other countries (including Singapore) the growth in exports was significantly different from that indicated by their initial product structure, and no general correlation was found between the two. Between 1970 and 1975, exports from Singapore rose four times faster than their initial product structure would have indicated. This suggests either that the country considerably improved its competitive position vis-a-vis its rivals, or that it swiftly adjusted its product composition to changing circumstances, or a combination of both. In fact the last mentioned possibility is the most likely, but in the second half of the decade the product composition of Singapore's exports - in which petroleum products and electrical machinery loomed large - almost certainly helped maintain the buoyancy of the total. The overall result was that (total) exports from Singapore grew faster during the 1970s (9.8 per cent on average from 1970 to 1978) than during the 1960s (4.2 per cent on average from 1960 to 1970).

As far as external market composition is concerned, the high degree of concentration of many small countries is a well known characteristic. It is particularly marked where exports of manufactures consist predominantly of simple processed products, e.g. cane sugar, which are shipped under special arrangements, e.g. from the ACP countries to the EEC. In general it appears that the more diversified the manufactures exported by a country, and the greater their degree of processing or transformation (in terms of added-value), the less concentrated will be their markets, although this tendency is almost inevitably modified by a country's location and history.

Finally, with regard to competitive factors, it is clear that growth in exports of manufactures depends also on enlarging market shares. In the case of goods which are price elastic, such as textiles and clothing, this involves a manufacturer's ability to export profitably at prices which are lower than his competitors or on terms which are in other ways superior. It depends on various considerations concerning costs and on the provision by governments of appropriate infrastructures and policy frameworks. In the last of these, the maintenance of a competitive exchange rate and the negotiation of preferred access to external markets is particularly important. As far as goods with a price inelastic demand are concerned, such as machinery and equipment, technical factors, delivery dates, and after-sales service, etc. become important.

AN ECONOMETRIC INVESTIGATION

On the basis of the kinds of consideration set out above, concerning the relationship between returns to scale in manufacturing industry and the size of market, it might be expected that the shares of the manufacturing sector in GDP and total employment, as well as its rate of growth, would be constrained in small countries. Yet it has been shown that the sector accounts for a significant proportion of GDP and employment in a considerable number of these countries. Plausible explanations for this are that the size constraint has been overcome by such factors as an advantageous location, an ability to attract substantial amounts of foreign investment, the possession of significant quantities of a natural resource suitable for processing domestically, or the existence of a skilled labour force. One or a combination of these factors might be expected to enable a small country to overcome its size constraint by making it possible to sell a substantial proportion of its production abroad. In order to test these hypotheses, regression analyses were undertaken for those small countries for which the relevant data were available.

Regression equations based on a linear function were estimated using ordinary least squares for a number of dependent variables, including the share of the manufacturing sector in GDP and in total employment, the rate of growth of the sector, and the share of manufactured exports in GDP. In view of the lack of data, many of the indicators used to measure the different explanatory variables had to be indirect. The proxies used included the following: repatriated earnings from direct foreign investment in all sectors of the economy as a substitute for all foreign investment in manufacturing; secondary school enrolment ratios and newspaper circulation (per 1,000 of population) as measures of the level of industrial skills; distance from the nearest OECD country as a measure of location; share of the mining sector in GDP as a measure of the natural resource base; and the difference between the shares of manufactured exports in total merchandise exports in 1970 and in 1975 as a measure of the growth of manufactured exports.

Relatively few of the above hypotheses were supported by the regression results. The share of manufacturing in GDP did not show a significant relationship with the variables chosen to represent size, location, skills and direct foreign investment, although there was a positive and significant relation to urbanisation, which is hardly surprising. The sector's share in total employment displayed a positive and significant relationship with the proxies for skill and natural resource base, but not with the other variables. The growth of manufacturing had, as expected, a positive and significant relationship with the growth of domestic investment and the inflow of long-term capital; its relationship to the proxy for direct foreign investment was significant but, surprisingly, negative; it did not show any significant relationship with market size or skills. The share of manufactured exports in GDP showed a positive and significant relationship with urbanisation, but not with size, location, skills or direct foreign investment.

Because of the limitations of the data and the sensitivity of the results to the type of equation specified, the form of the variables and the sample size, these results should be interpreted with caution. It is important to emphasise that they do not indicate that independent variables such as size, location, foreign investment or labour skills have no influence on determining the level or growth of manufacturing output, employment or exports in particular countries, but only that they are not a sufficient condition for industrialisation. Other types of equation can be specified and different variables incorporated. The more interesting of the results of using alternative specifications for some of the above variables and for others can be seen in the paper by Banerjee elsewhere in this volume[11].

CONCLUSIONS

The experience of the last quarter-century shows that it is possible for a country with a small population and an initially low average level of income so to transform its economy that it grows quickly and the manufacturing sector makes a substantial contribution to that growth. But this phenomenon is sufficiently rare and is usually the product of such special circumstances that doubts must be entertained as to whether its ingredients can be generalised or easily replicated. In the three most obvious examples - Singapore,

115

Israel and Hong Kong - special demographic and location-cum-strategic considerations were at work, and it is not until consideration is extended to some more 'normal' but less spectacular cases, such as Malta or Costa Rica, that a certain measure of guarded optimism may be expressed regarding the potential for growth of manufacturing in certain other small countries.

This potential will continue to depend on the usual 'supply factors', such as the development of a skilled and productive labour force and the ability to generate domestic savings and attract foreign capital on mutually beneficial terms. It will also remain dependent on the evolution of demand, both by market and by product.

As far as markets are concerned, there is a great potential for promoting exports of manufactures among small countries and from them to other developing countries. Nevertheless, the industrialised countries will probably remain a vital outlet for most of them. Much of the future market potential of this group will depend on reversing the current trend towards the adoption of increasingly protectionist policies. These are not only leading to a reduction in the growth of incomes and the impairment of welfare generally, but for many small countries they may mean the difference between poverty or even starvation on the one hand and a reasonable standard of living on the other.

As far as products are concerned, growth in global demand for manufactures during the quarter-century before 1974 tended to be fastest for investment goods which were capital-intensive and not profitable to produce except in large amounts and for long runs. The situation may be changing, however, and it is possible that the most dynamic manufactures during the remainder of the century may have rather different characteristics. One example could be the goods connected with the communications and information industry, which are usually skill-intensive but not necessarily capital-intensive. Another is the possibility of further disaggregating production processes internationally, so that more small countries can attract transnational enterprises undertaking assembly-type operations, either directly or through sub-contracting to local enterprises. To the extent that this is the case, small countries may not be under the same structural disadvantage during the next generation as during the last one. In addition, they can help themselves by orienting their education systems towards training more skilled workers, particularly technologists who could adapt current production processes in such a way that they become technically feasible and financially viable at much lower levels of output. Governments can also assist by adopting more appropriate policies which foster the development of an efficient and competitive manufacturing sector.

Nevertheless, it does appear doubtful whether the most disadvantaged of the small countries, which have tiny populations, are remote from large or dynamic markets and possess few if any natural resources, can overcome either the demand constraint of small national and regional markets or the supply constraint of inadequate labour. These countries seem unlikely to develop a manufacturing sector which can be operated profitably and comprise a significant proportion of GDP. As far as future growth prospects are concerned, their salvation may lie in the services sector, not only in tourism but also in the operation of knowledge industries, e.g. financial services (as in the Cayman Islands), although the amount of employment generated by the latter would not be large in absolute terms.

NOTES

1. During the period 1960-75, output in the manufacturing sector of developing countries rose on average by 7.4 per cent annually, compared with 2.8 per cent for agriculture and 6.1-6.6 per cent for other sectors (UNIDO, 1979, p.43).

2. During the period 1960-75, the average annual growth of the manufacturing sector was 5.2 per cent in countries whose GNP per capita in 1975 was under $265 but 8.6 per cent in those where it ranged between $521 and $1,075; the share of the manufacturing sector in GDP in 1975 was 13.8 per cent for the first group of countries and 22.8 per cent for the second. See UNIDO (1979, pp.39, 43-44).

3. For a general analysis, see, for example, Balassa (1980) and Sutcliffe (1971). For statistical studies, see, for example, Chenery (1960); Chenery and Taylor (1968); Chenery and Syrquin (1975); Kuznets (1971); and UNIDO (1979).

4. On this definition, the large developing countries (outside the centrally planned economies) comprise Bangladesh, Brazil, Burma, Egypt, Ethiopia, India, Indonesia, Korea (Rep. of), Mexico, Nigeria, Pakistan, Philippines, Thailand and Turkey.

5. The two averages shown are unweighted arithmetic means of growth during 1970-78 in the countries listed in Table 2 and note 4 above.

6. The concept of a critical minimum size of population for developing a manufacturing sector of significance is investigated in other papers in the present volume. See, for example, Bhaduri, et al., and Lall and Ghosh.

7. Growth elasticity is the per capita incremental value-added in manufacturing divided by the per capita increment in income. It thus measures the effects of an increase in income not only on demand but also on supply, e.g. a change in factor proportions brought about by an increase in the amount of capital per worker or an improvement in the type and degree of skills available.

8. Size elasticity is the per capita incremental value-added in manufacturing divided by the increment in population. It

represents the effects of larger domestic markets (caused by increased populations), both on costs of production through economies of scale and on increases in demand deriving from other sectors (Chenery, 1960, p.631).

9. See UNIDO (1979, p.68).

10. In international trade analyses, manufactures are usually defined as those products within the SITC categories 5-8, often with the exclusion of divisions 67 (iron and steel) and 68 (other base metals); in production statistics, manufactures are usually defined as products from activities within the ISIC category 3. This second definition embraces a much wider range of goods than does the first one.

11. See also the second section of the paper by Blazic-Metzner and Hughes in this volume, particularly Table 4.

REFERENCES

Balassa, B., 1980, "The Process of Industrial Development and Alternative Development Strategies", Washington, D.C: The World Bank.
Chenery, H.B., 1960, 'Patterns of Industrial Growth'. In "American Economic Review", Vol.50.
_____, and Syrquin, M., 1975, "Patterns of Development, 1950-70", London: Oxford University Press.
_____, and Taylor, L., 1968, 'Development Patterns: Among Countries and Over Time'. In "Review of Economics and Statistics", Vol.L. No.4.
International Labour Office, 1980, "Yearbook of Labour Statistics", Geneva.
Kuznets, S., 1971, "Economic Growth of Nations", Mass: Harvard University Press.
Sutcliffe, R.M., 1971, "Industry and Underdevelopment", London: Addison-Wesley.
The World Bank, 1980, "World Development Report", Washington, D.C.
_____, 1980, "World Tables", Washington, D.C.
United Nations, 1978, "Yearbook of Industrial Statistics", New York.
_____, 1978, "Yearbook of International Trade Statistics", New York.
_____, 1978, "Yearbook of National Accounts Statistics", New York.
United Nations Conference on Trade and Development, 1977, "Trade in Manufactures of Developing Countries and Territories, 1977 Review", New York, U.N.
United Nations Industrial Development Organization, 1979, "World Industry Since 1960: Progress and Prospects", New York, U.N.

TABLE 1

SELECTED SMALL DEVELOPING COUNTRIES: SHARE OF MANUFACTURING SECTOR
IN GDP, AND LEVEL OF INCOME AND POPULATION

	Manufacturing Sector (% of GDP) 1960	1978	GNP ($ per capita) 1978	Population (millions) 1978		Manufacturing Sector (% of GDP) 1960	1978	GNP ($ per capita) 1978	Population (millions) 1978
Malta	15	30e	2,170	0.3	Burundi	n.a.	9	140	4.5
Israel	23	26e	3,500	3.7	Benin	3	9	230	3.3
Singapore	12	26e	3,290	2.3	Cent. Afr. Rep.	4	9	250	1.9
Swaziland	8b	26c	590	0.5	Togo	8	9	320	2.4
Uruguay	21c	26e	1,610	2.9	Comoros	2	9e	180	0.4
Hong Kong	25	25e	3,040	4.6	Papua N. Guinea	3	8	560	2.9
Mauritius	12	21a	830	0.9	Chad	5	8e	140	4.3
Costa Rica	14	20e	1,540	2.1	Somalia	3	7	130	3.7
Nicaragua	16	20e	840	2.5	Djibouti	4	7e	450	0.3
Jamaica	15	17	1,110	2.1	Botswana	8f	7a	620	0.8
Paraguay	17	17	850	2.9	St. Lucia	n.a.	7e	n.a.	0.1
Lebanon	13	n.a.	n.a.	3.0	Liberia	n.a.	6	460	1.7
Honduras Rep.	13	17	480	3.4	Sierra Leone	n.a.	6	210	3.3
Jordan	n.a.	16	1,050	3.0	Equ. Guinea	3	6e	n.a.	0.4
Congo	10	16	540	1.5	Surinam	n.a.	5d	2,110	0.4
El Salvador	15	15a	660	4.3	Gabon	n.a.	5a	3,580	0.5
Cyprus	12	15a	2,120	0.7	Seychelles	n.a.	5e	1,130	0.1
Rwanda	1	15a	180	4.5	Grenada	n.a.	4d	530	0.1
Panama	13	14a	1,290	1.8	Dominica	n.a.	4e	n.a.	0.8
Trinidad & Tob.	24	14a	2,910	1.1	Western Samoa	n.a.	3g	n.a.	0.2
Haiti	10	13a	260	4.8	Sao Tome	1	3e	490	0.1
Guyana	9	12a	560	0.8	Lesotho	n.a.	2e	280	1.3
Fiji	n.a.	12c	1,420	0.6	Cape Verde	1	2e	160	0.3
Mauritania	3	11e	270	1.5	The Gambia	2	1c	230	0.6
Belize	n.a.	10a	n.a.	0.2	Guinea Bissau	0	1e	290	0.6
Barbados	n.a.	10a	1,960	0.3	Solomon Is.	n.a.	1g	430	0.2
Niger	4	10	220	5.0					

a 1976. b 1965. c 1973. d 1975. e 1977. f 1964. g 1972.

Sources: IBRD, "World Development Report", 1980; UN, "Yearbook of National Accounts Statistics", 1978.

TABLE 2

SELECTED SMALL DEVELOPING COUNTRIES: GROWTH OF MANUFACTURING SECTOR
AND OF GDP

	Manufacturing sector (% p.a.)		GDP (% p.a.)	
	1960-70	1970-78	1960-70	1970-78
Botswana	4.7	17.9	17.2	9.5
Mauritius	-1.5	11.0a	1.6	8.5g
Benin	n.a.	10.4b̄	2.6	3.8
Belize	n.a.	9.3ā	n.a.	6.0
Singapore	13.0	9.2⁻	8.8	8.5
Guyana	2.6	9.1	3.7	3.9h
Costa Rica	10.6	8.8a	6.5	6.0ā
Liberia	11.7c	8.7⁻	5.1	1.5⁻
Lesotho	n.a.	8.7a	4.6	6.5a
Togo	7.3d	7.6ā	8.5	4.2⁻
Niger	13.9⁻	7.2ā	2.9	2.4
Paraguay	4.9e	6.8⁻	4.3	7.5
Somalia	14.3⁻	6.7a	1.0	3.1
Haiti	-0.1	6.6⁻	0.1	3.9
Barbados	n.a.	6.5a	6.3	2.0
Surinam	n.a.	6.5f̄	n.a.	2.7
Nicaragua	11.1	6.3ā	7.2	5.8a
Israel	11.6d	6.1⁻	8.1	4.5⁻
El Salvador	8.8⁻	6.1	5.9	5.2
Honduras Rep.	4.0	5.8	5.1	3.3
Chad	n.a.	5.7a	0.5	1.7a
Hong Kong	18.6d	5.6ā	10.0	8.2ā
Burundi	20.5d̄	5.3⁻	4.4	2.9⁻
Cent. Afr. Rep.	5.4⁻	5.1a	1.9	3.2
Sierra Leone	n.a.	4.6⁻	4.2	1.3
Swaziland	35.3	3.8a	9.6	6.2
Uruguay	1.5	3.2⁻	1.2	1.9
Fiji	5.4d	3.0a	4.6	5.2a
Mauritania	18.0⁻	2.9ā	8.1	2.3⁻
The Gambia	6.6	2.5f̄	6.2	8.2
Rwanda	n.a.	2.4b̄	2.7	4.8
Congo	6.8	2.3⁻	2.7	3.5
Cyprus	8.7	1.8a	7.2	-1.5a
Panama	10.5	-0.5⁻	7.8	3.4⁻
Jamaica	5.6	-0.9	4.6	-0.8
Trinidad & Tobago	n.a.	-1.1a̲	3.9	3.4a̲

a	1970-77.	e	1962-70.
b̄	1972-77.	f̄	1973-77.
c	1964-70.	g	1970-75.
d̄	1965-70.	h̄	1970-76.

Sources: IBRD, "World Development Report", 1980;
IBRD, "World Tables", 1980;
UN, "Yearbook of National Accounts Statistics", 1980.

TABLE 3

SELECTED SMALL DEVELOPING COUNTRIES: EMPLOYMENT IN MANUFACTURING SECTOR
(in Thousands and as Percentage of Total Employment)

	thousands							%
	1970	1974	1975	1976	1977	1978	1979	Latest Year
Hong Kong	549.2	600.1	678.9	773.7	755.1	816.7	870.9	47.1
Uruguay a	n.a.	n.a.	n.a.	129.6	139.5	142.6	141.8	29.3
Singapore	n.a.	234.2	218.1	234.0	245.5	270.6	294.7	28.9
Malta	24.8	31.8	32.5	33.2	36.5	32.9	n.a.	28.3
Israel b	233.3	274.8	274.5	274.1	277.6	285.0	298.3	24.0
Nicaragua	22.2	25.0	26.1	30.5	32.1	29.2	26.6	20.5
Cyprus	24.8	n.a.	n.a.	27.8	30.7	34.5	35.6	20.0
Trinidad & Tobago c	65.7	65.0	67.1	n.a.	72.6	75.4	n.a.	19.6
Fiji	9.1	11.8	12.8	11.4	13.1	13.5	14.1	17.8
Mauritius d	7.8	20.8	22.5	29.3	33.2	32.5	35.0	16.7
Costa Rica	n.a.	n.a.	n.a.	88.8	102.5	103.6	113.9	16.1
Paraguay	n.a.	130.6	112.8	119.5	124.0	128.9	132.3	14.5
Barbados	n.a.	n.a.	n.a.	13.8	14.8	12.7	n.a.	13.9
Jordan	8.3	11.8	11.8	12.0	12.5	n.a.	n.a.	13.7
Gabon	9.3	n.a.	11.9	15.6	17.1	n.a.	n.a.	12.3
Swaziland	5.4	7.5	9.0	8.2	8.4	8.7	n.a.	12.2
Sierra Leone	5.7	5.9	5.8	6.3	6.0	6.0	7.7	11.3
Jamaica	n.a.	81.3	74.0	75.6	76.2	78.9	n.a.	11.1
Liberia	2.9	2.4	2.0	3.0	1.5	6.1	13.2	10.4
Panama	42.6	51.2	42.9	47.9	48.0	48.6	n.a.	9.7
Papua New Guinea	9.2	11.5	10.6	12.2	12.2	n.a.	n.a.	8.9
The Gambia	n.a.	2.6	2.3	1.7	n.a.	n.a.	n.a.	8.8
Burundi	n.a.	2.5	2.7	2.5	2.8	2.8	2.8	8.3
Botswana	n.a.	3.3	3.9	4.3	4.2	4.4	n.a.	6.3
Haiti	118.7	121.5	122.3	115.9	116.6	117.2	n.a.	6.2
The Bahamas	n.a.	n.a.	n.a.	3.4	3.9	3.8	3.9	5.4

a Montevideo only. b Including mining and quarrying and occupied territories.
c Excluding sugar distilleries and petroleum refineries. d Excluding sugar and tea factories.

Source: ILO, "Yearbook of Labour Statistics", 1980.

121

TABLE 4

SELECTED DEVELOPING COUNTRIES: COMPOSITION OF VALUE-ADDED IN MANUFACTURING
SECTOR BY MAJOR PRODUCT GROUPS, 1975
(Percentages of Total, including Other Product Groups)

	Food, beverages & tobacco	Textiles, apparel, leather & products	Chemicals, energy prod., rubber and plastic prod.	Iron and steel, non-ferrous metals	Metal prod. machinery, transport equip. etc.
Small countries a					
Trinidad & Tobago	6.6	0.8	86.8d	-	3.4
Fiji	69.4	2.6	4.3	-	10.5
Mauritius	63.1	12.0	6.3	-	9.4
Honduras Rep.	57.4	9.3	8.7	n.a.	5.8e
Panama	56.1	8.4	7.3f	0.7	6.6
Nicaragua	51.0	11.3	16.4	n.a.	6.3e
Singapore	7.0	5.5	25.6	1.8	47.8
Cent. Afr. Rep.	47.6	40.5	3.5	-	5.5
Jamaica f	47.3	8.0	13.7f	n.a.	12.3e
Hong Kong g	5.4	47.3	10.5	1.2	25.1
Somalia	43.9	11.6	10.7	-	1.2
Papua New Guinea	29.9	0.9	4.4	n.a.	40.3e r
Haiti	40.2	11.6	1.4	-	13.4
Israel h	12.5	11.2	15.3	3.6	38.0
Malta	20.4	37.9	8.7	n.a.	16.4e
El Salvador i	32.0i	37.7	15.4	1.2	4.4
Barbados i j	36.9i	13.6	8.0	-	18.6
Uruguay	32.2	22.8	24.3	0.7	9.3
Swaziland j	31.6	2.8	n.a.	-	n.a.
Cyprus	30.4	22.2	10.3	-	8.9
Jordan k	18.5	20.8	21.9	n.a.	16.1e r
Large countries b					
Philippines l	48.3	8.4	18.6	3.5	9.4
Ethiopia m	41.3	36.7	10.9	2.3	1.1
Indonesia	40.9	17.8	14.9	0.2	13.2
Egypt l n	18.0	36.9	16.1	4.3	15.1
Bangladesh	36.1	35.4	13.9	4.7	5.4
Turkey	21.6	14.3	27.3	9.0	17.4
Nigeria	26.5	19.2	22.0.	1.7	14.3
India	10.9	19.3	20.2	13.4	26.3
Brazil l	13.5	11.3	19.2	14.4o	21.9o
South Korea	21.2	22.1	21.8	4.7	16.3
Other countries c					
Syria	13.7	47.7	13.7	n.a.	10.8e
Ecuador	39.2	15.2	15.6	1.3	11.3
Kenya	37.1	9.1	19.4	1.0	18.1
Tunisia p	25.3	18.4	19.7	4.8p	9.4
Malaysia l q	23.6	5.3	23.2	3.6	21.8

a Population of under five millions. b Population of over 30 millions.
c Population of 5-30 millions, countries selected on basis of fast growth of manufacturing (annual average of 10% or more during 1970-78). d Includes non-metallic
mineral products but excludes plastic products. e Includes iron and steel and
non-ferrous metals. f Excludes petroleum products. g 1976. h Total excludes
diamond cutting. i Excludes sugar factories. j 1973. k East Bank only. l 1974.
m Total excludes paper and glass. n Total excludes glass and professional and
scientific instruments. o Metal products included in iron and steel and non-ferrous
metals. p Excludes non-ferrous metals. q West Malaysia only. r Including motor
vehicle repair services.

Source: Calculated from UN, "Yearbook of Industrial Statistics", 1978.

TABLE 5

SELECTED SMALL COUNTRIES: EXPORTS OF MANUFACTURES, 1975 d

	Value of exports of manufactures ($mn)	Exports of manufactures as proportion of total exports (%)	Exports of manufactures as proportion of production (%)
Hong Kong	5,592	92.9	84
Singapore	4,510	83.9	81
Neth. Antilles	2,337	97.5	
Trinidad &Tobago	1,170	66.6	60
Bahamas	1,099	43.8	
Israel	939	51.2	55e
Jamaica	655	80.4	
Lebanon a	410	82.4	
Mauritius	294	98.5	74
Uruguay	265	69.1	28e
Guyana	259	72.4	
New Caledonia	257	78.0	
El Salvador b	231	45.1	27
Costa Rica	230	46.7	
Panama	202	70.6	21
Nicaragua	183	48.8	22
Malta	164	98.0	63
Fiji	157	98.8	68
Surinam b	156	58.1	
Honduras Rep.	115	39.3	23
Paraguay	106	60.4	
Barbados	103	96.7	93
Togo	98	7.8	
Sierra Leone b	98	6.7	
Cyprus	83	54.8	29
Belize	63	93.9	
Reunion	58	98.8	
Guadeloupe	51	60.6	
Haiti	47	58.9	
Jordan	40	26.2	15
Bermuda	36	99.9	
Antigua	27	98.3	
Congo	25	13.7	
The Gambia	20	40.8	
Niger	16	17.3	
Somalia	15	17.0	25
Liberia	13	3.4	
Benin b	12	39.0	
Chad	12	25.9	
St. Vincent b	12	14.9	
Mauritania c	10	8.4	
Mali	9	16.9	
Gabon	9	1.1	
Cent. Afr. Rep.	8	16.1	12
Upper Volta	7	16.0	
St. Lucia b	5	32.0	
W.Samoa	5	6.6	
Papua N. Guinea	4	8.4	18
Solomon Islands	3	19.9	
Burundi	2	5.0	
Rwanda	2	4.7	6

a 1973. b 1974. c 1972. d Manufactures defined as products produced by activites within the category ISIC 3.

Source: Calculated from UN, "Yearbook of International Trade Statistics", 1978, and UN, "Yearbook of Industrial Statistics", 1978.

TABLE 6

SELECTED SMALL COUNTRIES: COMPOSITION OF EXPORTS OF MANUFACTURES BY
MAJOR PRODUCT GROUPS, 1975

	($mn)	(percentages of total, including other product groups)				
	Total a	Food etc. b	Textiles etc. c	Wood etc. d	Chemicals etc. e	Metal products etc. f
St. Vincent	12	100.0	-	-	-	-
The Gambia	20	99.7	0.1	-	-	0.1
Neth.Antilles	2,337	-	0.2	-	98.7	1.1
Antigua	27	0.1	0.1	0.1	97.2	1.0
Fiji	157	97.0	0.1	1.0	0.4	0.2
The Bahamas	1,099	1.4	0.1	-	96.3	1.4
Guadeloupe	51	94.2	0.3	-	1.7	3.0
New Caledonia	257	0.2	-	0.1	0.4	3.3
Belize	63	93.2	4.6	2.0	0.1	0.1
Reunion	58	92.0	0.4	-	5.4	1.9
Gabon	9	3.0	-	91.0	3.0	3.0
Mauritius	294	88.8	6.7	-	0.2	4.1
Guyana	259	87.7	0.3	0.1	11.3	0.3
Trinidad & Tobago	1,170	8.4	1.1	-	87.4	1.7
Somalia	15	81.2	n.a.	n.a.	n.a.	16.4
Congo	25	16.1	-	4.4	77.4	1.6
Bermuda	36	0.8	0.6	-	76.5	6.4
Sierra Leone g	98	76.1	1.5	-	17.9	4.0
Papua New Guinea	4	70.2	-	23.8	3.6	1.2
Surinam g	156	0.4	0.2	2.8	69.4	-
Barbados	103	69.0	16.9	-	4.9	7.8
Jamaica	655	30.2	1.0	-	65.8	1.4
Panama	202	29.7	2.7	-	64.6	1.6
Malta	164	8.1	64.1	-	7.8	16.8
Solomon Islands	3	61.3	n.a.	5.0	n.a.	1.0
Mauritania h	10	36.9	1.2	-	-	60.7
Paraguay	106	58.9	2.0	26.3	10.1	-
Upper Volta	7	58.1	15.6	-	11.3	8.7
Nicaragua	183	58.0	10.9	4.1	18.2	4.5
Togo	98	21.8	57.7	-	1.3	12.8
Cent. Afr. Rep.	8	16.1	2.5	57.1	23.6	0.6
Hong Kong	5,592	2.3	49.5	0.3	7.4	27.0
Niger	16	48.0	14.5	0.5	-	33.5
Singapore	4,510	7.4	5.8	3.3	44.2	32.4
Costa Rica	230	43.3	9.8	1.3	24.0	10.9
Uruguay	265	43.0	41.0	-	4.9	4.1
Western Samoa	5	18.2	42.4	18.2	-	9.1
Burundi	2	42.0	10.0	-	2.0	10.0
Mali	9	24.3	40.8	-	6.5	22.5
Rwanda	2	40.4	n.a.	n.a.	n.a.	n.a.
Lebanon i	410	11.0	16.9	1.8	11.9	37.4
St. Lucia	5	34.4	8.1	-	4.4	12.8
Chad	12	35.9	6.2	0.3	32.4	24.0
Honduras Rep.	115	29.3	5.9	34.8	21.4	3.6
Haiti	47	32.2	24.6	1.5	10.4	25.1
Benin	12	19.5	30.0	0.3	13.8	16.4
El Salvador g	231	27.5	29.3	-	16.0	11.8
Israel	939	12.5	16.2	0.4	29.3	29.5
Jordan	40	19.8	19.1	-	26.7	9.5
Cyprus	83	25.9	19.0	1.3	2.9	23.0
Liberia	13	23.5	n.a.	14.5	20.5	17.5

a All product groups, including those not specified. b Food, beverages and tobacco (ISIC 31).
c Textiles, apparel, leather and leather products (ISIC 32). d Wood and wood products
(including furniture) (ISIC 33). e Chemicals, energy products, rubber products and plastic products (ISIC 35). f Metal products, machinery (including electric), transport equipment, and
professional and scientific goods (ISIC 38). g 1974. h 1972. i 1973.

Source: Calculated from UN, "Yearbook of International Trade Statistics", 1978.

7. Agriculture in the Economic Development of Small Economies

B. Persaud*

In the context of agriculture, it is not very useful to start with a multi-criteria definition of small and large countries and then proceed to discuss the agricultural characteristics and problems of the group defined as small. States, rich and poor, face a variety of economic circumstances - of resource endowment and of levels of development - and it is doubtful whether in agriculture, or even generally, one could get very far with any such general classification.

Land is an important factor of production in agriculture. Size, in the geographical and spatial sense, is therefore of great relevance in discussing agricultural problems. Geographical size seems attractive as one criterion for determining the economic size of countries, and in fact it has been so used.[1] However, the production unit in agriculture is the farm, and the land available to individual farms depends not only on the total land area of the country concerned, but also on its population and the size distribution of the farms. Thus, on its own, the total arable area of a country has no relationship to the internal scale economies that could be achieved at the farm level. It should be recalled that in manufacturing the size issue has an important bearing on the scale economies that are possible in individual firms.

It is possible that countries with large arable areas may tend to have larger farms than those with small areas. But even if this is the case, land area is not the only determinant of the volume of output or the gross or net value of output. Land can be used more intensively, not only in terms of inputs of labour, fertiliser and water per hectare of crops, but also in terms of the extent of multi-cropping or the types of crop grown. Market gardening and extensive grazing indicate the range of land-use possible.

But the size of the agricultural sector of a country, in terms of the area of arable land, is not without economic significance. A large agricultural area offers greater opportunities for crop specialisation, and the wider the climatic and soil range, the greater the scope for a more diversified agricultural sector and

*The author is grateful to J. Karunasekera for his assistance in the collection of data for this paper.

more stable agricultural development. Agriculture is very demanding of public services, and services such as administration, research and extension do enjoy scale economies. Farms also benefit from direct external economies, e.g. in the more efficient distribution of farm inputs and in the better organisation of the marketing of their output, which are possible where the agricultural sector is large.

However, in considering the role of agriculture in the economic development of small states, the more important question is not the economics of production in large and small agricultural sectors. Agriculture has changing inter-relationships with other sectors in the course of development. The appropriate adjustment of the sector to changing economic circumstance is crucial for successful development. The interesting issues arise from differences in these inter-relationships and adjustment requirements between small and large states.

From the standpoint of agriculture, it would appear therefore that a useful starting point for size classification would be to group states according to their population size, and to proceed to analyse the role of agriculture in the economic development of small communities according to their land endowment, their level of development and their resource endowment for other sectors. Since the concern is with economic development, a priority aspect of the problem should be the special problems of agricultural development in the poorest small communities. Any composite measure of size would blur distinctions which might be important for the analysis. For instance, if land area is included, then particular situations such as small population and large land area may not receive the attention they deserve. Such a measure also raises the question: if land area is included, why should other resource endowments be excluded?

In the light of these considerations, we grouped states for the purposes of the paper according to population size, using five million as the line of demarcation. The countries included were those for which data were available. One hundred and eleven developing countries were used, of which 71 were classified as small and 40 as large. Although no special attention was given to the poorest small states, some comparative data are presented for them.

AGRICULTURE AND ECONOMIC DEVELOPMENT

It is now widely accepted that agriculture has an important role to play in economic development and that, in the absence of an agricultural strategy which ensures an efficient growth path, one which takes into account the inter-relationships between agriculture and industry at different stages of economic development, the whole economic transformation process could be delayed or frustrated. That the industrial sector normally grows faster than the agricultural sector has, in the past, led to emphasis on industrialisation to accelerate development. There is increasing recognition, however, that agricultural development can play a critical role in supporting industrial development and in ensuring that labour is not prematurely released from agriculture to aggravate urban overcrowding and unemployment. Any consideration, therefore, of the consequences of size for agricultural development must pay special attention to the implications of size for the structural transformation process, and to the role of agriculture at different stages of development.

In the early stages of development, agriculture tends to be the largest sector, occupying the vast majority of the employed population. Its domestic market is therefore small. If, for instance, 70 per cent of the population is in the agricultural sector, a not unusual proportion, then an 'average' farm family of five has a market outside the rural sector of just over two persons. Productivity increases in agriculture could encourage greater specialisation in the economy and the expansion of the non-agricultural sectors, but these productivity increases require the stimulation which comes from greater demand for agricultural products. The interaction between the agricultural and the industrial sectors at this early stage of development could be encouraged by agricultural exports. As the traditional sector, and because of its low requirements of capital and skills, agriculture could more easily provide exports at this stage than the industrial sector. Agricultural exports provide foreign exchange which enables purchases of vital capital and other inputs for the further development of the agricultural and manufacturing sectors.

Investment in industry at the early stage of development tends to emanate from the surpluses earned by the agricultural sector. And as the income of the agricultural sector increases, its purchases expand the market for manufactured goods and stimulate industrial development. Because of the large relative size of the agricultural sector, its purchases could have a significant effect on the development of the smaller industrial sector. At this stage, many of the purchases of the agricultural sector take the form of consumer goods. However, the agricultural sector becomes relatively smaller in the course of an economy's development, and its demand shifts more to capital goods and intermediate inputs such as fertilisers and chemicals, the supply of which tends to require large production units and may therefore be less easily provided domestically. The agricultural sector could also assist industrial development by developing forward linkages through the increased processing of its output.

Because of the large proportion of the labour force in farming, it is necessary for agricultural employment to continue to expand until a fairly advanced stage of economic development. If 80 per cent of the labour force is in the agricultural sector, and the labour force is increasing at two per cent per year, then the non-agricultural sectors would have to increase their employment by ten per cent if they are to absorb all the addition to the labour force. This increase would have to be faster still if the absolute size of the population engaged in agriculture begins to decline at.this early stage. Just to absorb one per cent of the agricultural labour force would require a four per cent increase in the non-agricultural employment.

This situation indicates the crucial importance for economic development of what happens in agriculture at the early stages of development. Agriculture's large contributions to employment and GNP mean that, although it tends not to be the most dynamic sector, the whole economy becomes sensitive to what takes place in it. If policies cause premature declines in these contributions, they severely constrain the development process.

Agriculture's substantial role in promoting development is through labour absorption; providing cheap food which keeps down the wage costs of the manufacturing sector; expanding its purchases from the manufacturing sector; providing surpluses in the form of savings and foreign exchange for capital and foreign inputs for industrial development; and supplying raw materials for processing. Although industry tends to be the more dynamic sector, the realisation of this dynamism depends greatly on the support of the agricultural sector. The experience of Japan, Taiwan and South Korea bears out the important role that agriculture can play in helping to accelerate economic development.

SIZE CONSIDERATIONS

Table 1 shows that on average the per capita arable area in small countries is not lower than in large countries. However, these averages involve some distortion of the general pattern of the availability of land because of the influence on them of the very large land areas of a few countries with very small populations. This is confirmed by Table 2, which provides a frequency distribution of the per capita arable area in the groupings of small and large countries. It shows a higher proportionate incidence of low per capita arable area in small states. But even this frequency distribution does not provide any strong indication that farms are smaller in smaller countries. Even if it did, it should be noted that the prospects for scale economies at the farm level depend not only on average farm size but also on the size distribution of farms and on the cropping pattern. Where there is less land it may be used more intensively. On the whole, the figures in these Tables on per capita arable area do not indicate any significantly greater scope for scale economies at the level of farm operation in the large countries than in the small ones. This is supported by data on per capita farm production and on growth rates of agricultural output.

But while the evidence does not show that farms on the average are larger in large countries, the bigger agricultural sector of large countries does provide scope for external economies. Agriculture is very demanding of public services, and the per capita cost of these services tends to be high in small states. In the case of research expenditure, returns tend to be higher the wider the area over which resulting innovations are adopted. And the effectiveness of both research and extension in small states is impeded by an inability to attract and use fully the services of agricultural specialists. These problems are ameliorated to some

128

TABLE 1

SELECTED ECONOMIC DATA ON SMALL AND LARGE COUNTRIES

Categories	Small Countries	Large Countries
Developing Countries		
Per capita arable area (ha)	0.59	0.32
Population density (per sq. km.)	11	38
Per capita agricultural exports (US$)	85.00	27.00
Share of agriculture in total exports		
simple average (%)	56.1	59.8
weighted average (%)	21.3	48.1
Share of agriculture in GDP		
simple average (%)	27.4	32.4
weighted average (%)	17.4	22.0
Share of two largest agricultural exports		
simple average (%)	33.5	29.3
Annual growth of agricultural output,		
1970-78(%)	2.6	2.3
Low Income Developing Countries		
Per capita arable area (ha)	1.0	0.3
Population density (per sq. km.)	9	65
Share of agriculture in total exports		
simple average(%)	67.3	71.2
weighted average (%)	54.6	48.1

Note: Data presented are for the latest year available - usually 1977 or 1978.

Sources: Commonwealth Secretariat (1980); The World Bank (1980) and UNCTAD (1980).

TABLE 2

FREQUENCY DISTRIBUTION OF PER CAPITA ARABLE AREA
IN SMALL AND LARGE COUNTRIES

| Class Interval | Small Countries | | | Large Countries | | |
| | Frequency | | Cumulative Frequency | Frequency | | Cumulative Frequency |
(ha)	(no.)	(%)	(no.)	(no.)	(%)	(no.)
0 - 0.49	50	70	50	26	65	26
0.5 - 0.99	15	21	65	9	22	35
1.0 - 1.49	2	3	67	4	10	39
1.5 - 1.99	2	3	69	1	3	40
2 and over	2	3	71	0	0	40

Source: FAO (1978).

TABLE 3

FREQUENCY DISTRIBUTION OF GROWTH RATES OF AGRICULTURAL
OUTPUT (1970-78)

| Class Interval | Small Country Group | | | Large Country Group | | |
| | Frequency | | Cumulative Frequency | Frequency | | Cumulative Frequency |
(%)	(no.)	(%)	(no.)	(no.)	(%)	(no.)
Less than 0	11	21	11	5	13	5
0 - 1.9	11	21	22	7	19	12
2 - 3.9	16	31	38	14	38	26
4 and above	14	27	52	11	30	37

Source: Commonwealth Secretariat, op. cit., and The World Bank,
op. cit.

extent by crop specialisation. They are sometimes also reduced in significance by regional co-operation. In the Caribbean, for instance, there is a long history of co-operation in some areas of agricultural research and training. Breeding work on sugar cane is done regionally and the small banana exporting islands - Dominica, St. Lucia, St. Vincent and Grenada - co-operate in banana research through the Windward Islands Banana Growers Association.

Besides public services, physical inputs for the agricultural sector - capital equipment, fertilisers and other chemicals - could be supplied more cheaply where requirements are large. There is scope for scale economies in the procurement and distribution of these inputs. However, in small countries, diseconomies in internal transportation and distribution may be mitigated by a compact location pattern of farm holdings.

External economies could also be significant in forward linkages. Scale economies are possible in collection, transportation, storage, processing and marketing. In the case of export marketing, minimum volumes may be critical for exportation to be possible. This may be the case because of the perishability of the products and the need, therefore, for specialised shipping arrangements. In the case of bananas, volumes must be such as to make possible frequent scheduled shipping, otherwise wastage would occur through inconsistency between the regularity of shipping and the rate of maturity of the crop. In the Eastern Caribbean, banana exportation from the small islands has been made possible by the participation of four islands in production for export. Production from one island alone would not have been sufficient for the regularity of shipping required. Inadequate volumes, made worse by hurricanes and disease, have been one of the main causes of the decline of banana exports from Fiji, Tonga and Western Samoa to New Zealand (Ward, 1979). Until the mid-1960s, these countries supplied the entire New Zealand market but, since then, New Zealand has turned to Ecuador for supplies despite the longer distance involved.

In the case of marketing, product differentiation in agriculture is not as pervasive as in manufacturing, and this eases the difficulty of penetrating marketing networks in importing countries. Agricultural markets are on the whole less imperfect, and market organisation therefore poses less severe entry problems for small countries. Small countries are likely always to be price-takers, but this has not proved a significant disadvantage, since for few agricultural products exported by developing countries has supply control by producers been effective in influencing prices. Where such control has been adopted, small producing countries have tended to benefit. Their participation in supply control is often not vital for its success, and their non-participation tends to result in gains to them through increased prices, and possibly also an increased volume of sales.

The diseconomies resulting from small export volumes could be alleviated by product concentration and more intensive production. Small countries tend to have greater concentration in agricultural exportation - see Table 1 - and this might have been encouraged by scale economies in production and marketing. For some products which are intensively produced, such as vegetables, scale problems in exportation scarcely arise because large volumes can be produced from a small area. In fact some major exporters are small countries. Specialisation could assist also in encouraging processing ventures which tend to provide scope for scale economies. Large countries have the further advantage for processing industries that they have large local markets. It is not obvious, however, that the extent to which raw materials and food products are processed is less in small countries. Scale economies are less important in food and fibre processing than in mineral processing. While scale economies may deter some forms of processing in small countries, e.g. oil-seed crushing and the making of coffee and cocoa products, they do not deter others, e.g. fruit and vegetable canning, and some small states have developed substantial canning industries for export markets. Very small states can, however, be disadvantaged in this area of activity. The canning of orange juice and pineapples in the Cook Islands, for instance, is adversely affected by the need to transport perishable fruit from outlying islands to Rarotonga (ibid.) where the processing plant is located.

Small countries tend to depend less on agricultural exports than do large countries. Table 1 shows that the share of agriculture in the exports of small countries was much less - 21 per cent compared with 48 per cent. This does not imply, however, any disadvantage in agricultural production. In fact, among the poorest countries, according to the same Table, small states have a greater dependence on agricultural exports. The small size of local markets for industrial development has encouraged some small countries to adopt export-oriented industrial development, and success in this policy has led to large exports of manufactures and relatively high levels of development. It is this success which has resulted in the lower share of agricultural exports for the whole group.

MAN/LAND RELATIONSHIP

Countries differ in their resource endowment for agricultural development, and small states are no exception. An appropriate strategy for agricultural development would depend on the circumstances of the state concerned. However, a broad characteristic which might be useful for discussing general policy options for small states is the man:arable land ratio. Where land is relatively abundant, it might be possible to have a dualistic agricultural structure with both family farms and large commercial farms. Where land is scarce, however, a 'unimodel' family farm structure tends to be the appropriate form of organisation to facilitate optimum resource use, labour intensity and cropping pattern. Impediments to the evolution of such a structure can have dangerous consequences for both agricultural and general economic development. Unlike production units in manufacturing, farm sizes cannot easily adjust to changing economic circumstances. Government intervention is usually required to assist the process, e.g. land reform to break up large holdings or to consolidate fragmented holdings.

THE PLANTATION ECONOMIES AND AGRICULTURAL ADJUSTMENT

The plantation system has dominated agricultural organisation in many small island states. This is the case in many Caribbean islands, in Mauritius and in some Pacific islands. Although the system has lost some of its early features, it remains substantially a large farm organisation concentrating on export crops. Where abundant land existed outside the system, or where plantations failed, a dualistic agricultural structure developed. However, in many cases, especially in the 'sugar islands', the family farms became satellite producers of the plantation crops. This was because of the established production and marketing infrastructure for the plantation crops, and the failure of agricultural policy to encourage a more diversified production structure.

The plantation system has not led to successful agricultural development in small states, especially those with high man:land ratios, because of its failure to adjust to the changing requirements for agricultural progress. The distortion in agricultural development was particularly severe in those islands where all or most of the cultivable land came under the plantation system. The rigidity of the system, in terms of the size of production units and the types of crop grown, meant that the agricultural sector could not adjust to a more intensive system which could absorb increases in the rural population and provide increasing incomes. This encouraged early rural emigration. Barbados is a good example of a small country which, with a persistent large-scale farm organisation concentrating on one export, generated not only a rural exodus but also emigration because of the limited economic opportunities outside agriculture. From the early part of this century, Barbadians moved in large numbers to other parts of the world. In other islands of the Caribbean and in Mauritius, the availability of land led to the substantial development of small-scale farming, but many of the farms became producers of plantation crops. Under the system, plantation crops were exported, and much of the domestic food consumed was imported.

The consequence is an agricultural sector which is making little contribution to economic development. The lack of buoyancy in export markets for traditional crops such as sugar, and the lack of response of the agricultural sector to an expanding domestic market for food, lead to an unfavourable trade balance in food. Small countries which have been net exporters are becoming net importers. In the early 1970s, the Commonwealth Caribbean, as a group, became a net importer of food. While traditional exports of sugar and bananas are not expanding, imports of food are increasing steeply and the unfavourable balance is growing at a fast rate. Thus the large agricultural sector has become less significant as a net contributor to foreign exchange earnings. Moreover, it is not a large contributor to employment. The capital intensive and crop extensive types of agriculture, encouraged by the large-scale farm organisation, have forced migration from the countryside to the towns and to other countries. It is significant to note, in this connection, that agricultural employment and the proportion of the employed population in agriculture declined earlier in the Caribbean than in countries like Taiwan where economic development is more advanced. Land reform, where land was scarce, and trade and agricultural policies which did not give undue priority to plantation crops, would have helped greatly to bring about: the needed agricultural adjustment to new high value crops for both the export and domestic markets; the extension of family farming, which would have been more labour absorptive; and a more science-based agriculture, which would have provided higher productivity, less capital intensiveness and more attractive incomes. These policies emphasise the importance of an appropriate strategy for agricultural adjustment and development, and indicate the importance of programme financing in agriculture as opposed to concentration on narrowly conceived 'bankable' projects for expanding the production of individual crops.

Such an agricultural strategy would also have provided greater support for the tourism and manufacturing sectors. Efficient domestic food production would have helped to reduce pressure on manufacturing wage rates and would thus have contributed to making manufacturing more competitive. Tourism would have had greater interaction with the agricultural sector, to their mutual benefit. The different demand structure of family farms, compared to large commercial farms and plantations, would also have helped manufacturing development. Large-scale farming tends to result in a large proportion of farm receipts being spent on capital equipment and other sophisticated farm inputs which are not readily produced locally. Family farms, on the other hand, spend a higher proportion of their receipts on consumption expenditure because of a more intensive use of labour. Their non-labour inputs also tend to be more easily produced by local industries, e.g. simple farm implements which could be produced by local metal-working industries.

The failure of the agricultural strategy in many small and large developing countries has been compounded by inefficient price and trade policies. Price control for farm products has helped to worsen the terms of trade of agricultural producers. Trade policies have emphasised securing and maintaining preferential access for traditional crops, and this has served to reinforce the rigidity of the agricultural system rather than encourage adjustment to products with better demand and price prospects.

The failure of agriculture has not been due to agricultural policies alone. The emphasis given to import-substitution in manufacturing has helped to worsen the agricultural terms of trade. Both consumption and intermediate goods are obtained by the agricultural sector at inflated prices, and this in turn tends to raise costs of agricultural production and to affect its competitiveness. Thus, a combination of an inappropriate agricultural strategy, and a manufacturing sector which is too import-substitution oriented, leads to production costs in both the agricultural and manufacturing sectors which are out of line with world prices. And this is sometimes sustained by an over-valued currency. Rising new protectionism now constrains reliance on an export-oriented strategy, but it remains the case that small states have little choice. They have to continue to stress export orientation and adopt strategies which strive to minimise the adverse effects of protectionism on their industrial and agricultural exports.

Early adoption of a policy of land reform to provide more land for family farms, emphasis on new export lines in agriculture and greater response to rising local demand for food, would all have led to a better evolution of agricultural development in small countries which have been dominated by the plantation system. Responding to the expanding domestic market for food should not mean less emphasis on exports, especially where small countries are well endowed with land. The slow emergence of export-oriented manufacturing in many small states gives foreign exchange earnings from agriculture special importance, especially where a buoyant services sector is absent. This means that, if dependence on low value plantation crops were to be reduced, greater attention would have to be given to developing new export lines in agriculture.

Although Taiwan is not a small country according to the classification used in this paper, it is not a very large country and the evolution of its agricultural development provides lessons which seem to have great significance for small countries. A characteristic it shares with many small countries is a high man:land ratio. In the early years of this century, under Japanese colonial administration, there was a heavy emphasis on sugar and rice production for the Japanese market. Land was very unequally distributed. After the Second World War, land reform helped to change the cropping pattern. More intensive agriculture resulted in the form of high value crops both for export and to meet domestic food needs. Some current high value agricultural exports are bananas, canned pineapples, canned mushrooms and canned asparagus. The new emphasis on small-scale intensive farming not only provided cheap food to the industrial sector, but also prevented an exodus from the countryside. It also increased the demand for industrial products and provided a surplus for investment in the industrial sector. In 1955 agricultural exports were responsible for 92 per cent of Taiwan's exports, of which 76 per cent were sugar and rice. By 1970 industrial exports were 78 per cent of total exports, and of the 20 per cent agricultural exports, sugar and rice were responsible for only three per cent. The farm labour force continued to increase in Taiwan until the end of the 1960s.[2]

Taiwan's agricultural development, however, can only be an indicative model. Some small states are too remote to have similar export opportunities. Others, well endowed with land, can support a high level of development based on less intensive agriculture, and the example of New Zealand may be more appropriate in such cases than that of Taiwan. In some small countries, because of high emigration and small populations, labour is beginning to be short in the countryside. This situation points to the need for a mechanised and science-based agriculture. If capital is available, mechanisation can be adopted quickly, but the development and adoption of technology for a highly productive agriculture take time. An appropriate strategy seems to be to give greater emphasis to mechanisation and improved farm practices if agriculture is to survive and assist development. The situation may require increased farm size, which may be particularly necessary where emigration is causing farms to be left idle. In the latter case, a policy of land consolidation may also be necessary. The need for land redistribution at an early stage and land consolidation at a later stage emphasises the importance in agriculture of policies concerned with removing rigidities in basic economic organisation.

For small countries at a low level of development, the problem is often not adjustment from plantation agriculture, but movement from susbsistence farming to commercial farming. Slow adjustment from subsistence farming, when food has to be imported for urban residents and tourists, has led to the advocacy of large-scale state farms as a remedy to agricultural problems. State farms are also being tried in other situations of sluggish agricultural growth. The results from this policy have not been encouraging. The experience of countries where agriculture has adjusted to changing demand patterns and has made a great contribution to economic development, such as Japan, Taiwan and South Korea, would seem to indicate the need for persistence with support for the encouragement of family farming, except where land is adequate for the encouragement of a more dualistic agricultural structure. In Guyana, for instance, land is relatively abundant. Sugar, the traditional export crop, is produced on a large-scale mechanised basis. Rice is produced for the domestic and regional market on small, large and medium-sized farms. Other crops are also produced on small and medium-sized family farms. Although there is a low man:land ratio, much expenditure is required to make unutilised land cultivable. In spite of the abundance of land, there is much underemployment. The availability of land, however, seems to point to a future in mechanised larger-scale farming. The solution to underemployment appears, therefore, to point to making more land available rather than discouraging cost-effective mechanisation. Belize is another example of a developing country with a very small population and abundant land. Agriculture there is supporting high growth rates on the basis of a dualistic agricultural structure.

AGRICULTURE AND OTHER SECTORS

Having considered small countries in various agricultural circumstances, we now look at the implications for agriculture of favourable resource endowments for other sectors. Many tropical and sub-tropical islands have very suitable resources for tourism development, and the large relative size of the services sector in many small countries indicates the importance of tourism in these countries. Tourism adds to the local demand for food, especially high value foods such as vegetables, fruits, dairy products, poultry, pork and other meat. Nearly all of these involve intensive production methods which are suitable for small states with high man:land ratios. The food needs of the tourist sector are demanding in quality and marketing, and in spite of the natural advantage provided by nearness to the market, domestic agriculture has not in many cases been very responsive to these needs. Some small countries have already developed the intensive agriculture required, either because they are already involved in exporting the relevant food products or because there is already susbstantial local demand. Cyprus and Israel are examples of such countries. Where the tourist sector is large, it could have adverse effects on agriculture by attracting people away from the land, and sometimes land away from agriculture. Policies must be geared to avoiding such effects. An agricultural sector is required which is geared to meeting the challenge of higher wages in other industries by becoming increasingly science-based and mechanised. Strict land-zoning policies could prevent land speculation from diverting agricultural land from optimum use. In the absence of appropriate agricultural adjustment to the tourist sector, tourism's contribution to economic development is reduced, and increased dependence on tourism leads to less stable and balanced economic development.

When small states are well endowed with oil and other minerals, similar policies are required to prevent adverse effects on the agricultural sector. The energy and other mineral sectors do not interact with the agricultural sector at the level of demand as much as manufacturing and tourism. Employment generation in them tends not to be high, and is usually of a high income kind with a low demand for food products, especially local food products.

Island states are well located for endowment with fishery resources. The 200 mile Exclusive Economic Zone (EEZ) adds substantially to the resources available to them because of the very large additional sea area which comes under their economic control. Small states do not often have the capital resources and skills to protect and exploit the great potential added to their economic development by the EEZ. This points to the need for the pooling of resources in regional co-operation and for entering into joint ventures with foreign enterprises with the necessary capital and skills. The effect on agriculture of fisheries development is similar to that of other sectors such as oil and other mineral production. An additional factor is that fish is a food which is a substitute for other foods, such as meat, which are produced by the agricultural sector.

LOCATION PROBLEMS

Small countries have great need of foreign trade for their development. However, some island small states are in remote locations. The Pacific islands are examples of such states. Where transportation problems inhibit export development, economic development could be severely inhibited. Regional shipping is normally poorly developed. The problem is usually to break the vicious circle between low volumes of cargo and the infrequency of service. It is being aggravated by technological change which is increasing the size of vessels and cargo handling units. Small tropical or sub-tropical countries, favourably located in relation to major industrialised countries, have been able to use their warm climate to produce vegetables for the winter market in temperate industrialised countries. This type of agriculture is suited to the land endowment and the advanced level of economic development of some small states. Small countries, such as Israel and Cyprus, have been able to make use of these opportunities, which would have been greater but for the protection adopted by the importing countries to assist local producers in the summer trade. The Caribbean countries do not have the same advantage in the North American market, since the climate is suitable in the southern United States for growing winter vegetables. Some market opportunities exist, but the Caribbean islands face competition from countries such as Mexico which are well endowed with resources for the products required. There are opportunities in these large markets, however, for selected high value tropical crops, which specially designed agricultural policies could help to develop. Some trade is already taking place in high quality crops from small countries, e.g. quality coffee produced in Jamaica, and pimento and other spices produced in Jamaica and other Caribbean islands.

Adding to the transportation problems faced by the Pacific islands is the fact that the developed countries nearest to them do not have large populations, and the one with the largest - Australia - can itself produce tropical crops. New Zealand has a market for winter vegetables which is being supplied by the Pacific islands, but protection offered to local glasshouse production has constrained its size. Rising energy costs are making glasshouse production less competitive, and this should give producers in the Pacific islands, as well as in the Mediterranean small countries, an increased comparative advantage in the horticultural trade.

CONCLUSION

The approach adopted in considering the implications of small size for the role and problems of agricultural development is to look at the land endowment of countries with small populations, their resources for the development of other sectors, their location and their existing levels of development. A priority aspect of the problem is the role and problems of agricultural development in the poorest small countries, but it has not been possible to give special attention to this in the paper.

Large countries do not tend to have larger farms. They do not necessarily provide opportunities, therefore, for scale economies at the farm level. However, external economies are possible through scale economies in research, extension, training, the procurement and distribution of inputs, and the transportation and marketing of output. Regional co-operation by neighbouring small states in procurement, marketing and research offers some scope for alleviating scale problems.

Because of its large size and its interactions with other

sectors, agriculture has a crucial role to play in economic development, although its growth is usually much lower than that of other sectors. It has the same role in small states, although where geographical size is very small, it is possible for a country to by-pass the initial primary role of an agricultural sector.

Small countries must have a strong dependence on foreign trade for their economic development. The difficulties in making a breakthrough in export-oriented manufacturing prolong a dependence on the export of agricultural and other primary products. Where small states are well endowed with land, it may be possible to achieve and sustain high levels of income from agricultural development. The example of New Zealand indicates this possibility. There are also better prospects for mineral resources where the land area is large, which would extend the development possibilities.

Many small countries are not so well endowed. They must undergo an early transformation to a high dependence on the industrial and other sectors. Agriculture has a very important role in helping this process. It must, however, undergo adjustment to play this role. Crucial for this is the farm size structure. Many island small states started out as plantation economies. While providing the advantage of early involvement in international trade, the plantation system tends to have a rigidity which prevents transformation to land-use and farm size structures appropriate to the population and the land resources of the country. Where a small country has a high man:land ratio, land reform to transform a plantation or large holdings system to family farms is crucial. Where man:land ratios are low, a more dualistic agricultural structure is possible.

In the absence of land reform, the adjustment to high value crops and more intensive methods of cropping, which are suitable for densely populated small countries, would not take place. Premature emigration from agriculture would be encouraged, and the country would remain stuck with an agricultural sector which made little or no contribution to employment or economic development because of its capital intensiveness and crop extensiveness. An inappropriate agricultural sector could frustrate the whole development process.

Where land reform leads to a more appropriate farm size structure, adjustment to a more appropriate intensive agriculture is facilitated. Exports shift to more high value crops, and increasing productivity helps to provide attractive incomes and labour absorption. Agricultural adjustment facilitates economic transformation. Increasing productivity and product switching provide the economy with its food needs at low cost. Increasing agricultural incomes and employment generate a pattern of demand which assists the expansion of the industrial sector, and the surpluses of the agricultural sector provide investment capital for industry. Product switching in exports provides the foreign exchange which must come largely from the agricultural sector in the early stages of development.

Agriculture would then assist industrial development which, with an appropriate strategy (i.e. one which is not strongly oriented towards import substitution), would be more able to make the breakthrough into export-oriented manufacturing. An efficient manufacturing sector would, in turn, because of its demand for food and other agricultural products and raw materials, and because of its low cost supply of agricultural inputs, assist the development of the agricultural sector. Policies which are strongly oriented towards import-substitution in industry and keep food prices artificially low, aggravate the declining terms of trade of agriculture and frustrate agricultural and economic development. Japan, Taiwan and South Korea are examples of countries in which industrialisation was facilitated by appropriate agricultural adjustment. The man:land ratio of Taiwan is similar to that of many small countries, and the course of agricultural development there offers useful lessons for these countries.

The emphasis on an appropriate strategy for agricultural adjustment and development highlights the need for sector planning, and for development financing which is based on programmes and is not overly concerned with individual 'bankable' projects. Financing for land distribution, land consolidation and research might be as important as that for the direct expansion of production of individual crops.

Island small states tend to have favourable resources for tourism development. Good prospects for tourism can help to avoid the developmental problems posed by the size constraints on the development of the manufacturing sector. Tourism increases the demand for food, and can therefore increase its contribution to economic development. The agricultural sector must adjust to meeting this demand and prevent tourism from prematurely withdrawing labour and land from the agricultural sector.

Agriculture has strong interactions not only with industry and tourism, but also with the transport and distribution sectors. Oil and other mineral industries tend not to have a strong positive effect on agricultural demand, but can have adverse effects on the agricultural labour supply because of the aspirations they create. Unrealistic aspirations are a general problem in small countries which have a large tourism sector and are near to industrialised countries.

The location of small countries can influence agricultural development prospects. The transportation problems of remote islands affect their export trade in agricultural products, many of which are perishable. Nearness to large industrialised countries provides market opportunities for market-garden and other high value crops, which tend to be suitable for the resource endowments and development levels of small states.

NOTES

1.   Demas (1965) used a usable land area of 10-20 thousand square miles or less as one of the criteria in defining small countries.

2. The source for data on Taiwan used in this paper is Johnston and Kilby (1978).

REFERENCES

Commonwealth Secretariat, 1980, "Basic Statistical Data on Selected Countries (with populations of less than five millions)", London.

Demas, William G., 1965, "The Economics of Development in Small Countries, with Special Reference to the Caribbean", Montreal: McGill University Press.

Food and Agriculture Organization, 1978, "Production Yearbook", Vol.32, New York: United Nations.

Johnston, B.S. and Kilby, P., 1978, "Agricultural and Structural Adjustment: Economic Strategies in Late Developing Countries", London: Oxford University Press.

The World Bank, 1980, "World Bank Atlas", Washington, D.C.
_____, 1980, "World Development Report", Washington, D.C.

United Nations Conference on Trade and Development, 1979, "Handbook of International Trade and Development Statistics", New York: United Nations.

Ward, R.G., 1979, 'Agricultural Options for the Pacific Islands'. Paper presented to a Seminar entitled "The Island States of the Pacific and Indian Oceans: Anatomy of Development",Canberra: Australian National University, Development Studies Centre.

8. The Role of Foreign Investment and Exports in Industrialisation

Sanjaya Lall and Surojit Ghosh*

It is perhaps one of the more curious paradoxes that economists - theoretical and empirical - have had very little to say about how size may affect the "Nature and Causes of the Wealth of Nations". If one looks at the literature it is necessary to go back to the 1957 International Economic Association conference as the first and perhaps only attempt to deal exclusively with this issue.[1] In recent years, with a large number of new nations emerging from colonial rule, the great majority of which would be classified as 'small' by any index, it has become even more important that this issue be properly analysed. But in the 1980s the problems that analysts face have a further twist: nearly all of these countries are poor; they are generally dependent on an agrarian economy, have an inadequate infrastructure and are lacking in vital developmental resources such as entrepreneurship and technical skills.

It seems fairly generally accepted by economists that small economies will be heavily dependent on the international economy, on factors, that is, outside their control and influence, for their development. Thus, trade, access to foreign technology and foreign direct investment would seem to offer the only means by which small economies can diversify their exports, industrialise and establish a viable base for long-term growth. But is this really so? Or is is one of the hoary bits of conventional wisdom that are based on faulty reasoning and incorrect information? This paper addresses itself to these questions.

The first section starts by defining a 'small' economy. The second section discusses the problems for small economies in international trade, and section three deals with technology transfer and foreign direct investment. This paper concludes with some qualifying remarks. Inevitably, there is a certain amount of repetition. The multinational corporation (MNC) is almost ubiquitous in the discussion because of its large potential role in all aspects of the international involvement of small economies. We try, however, to keep the issues as distinct as possible.

*We are grateful to Bimal Jalan, Ed Dommen and Steven Britton for their comments on an earlier draft. Needless to say, we retain full responsibility for the views expressed in this paper.

DEFINITION OF A 'SMALL' ECONOMY

In economic theory, and more particularly in international economics, a 'small' economy is a precise concept. Area, population or size of GNP are, if at all, only incidentally relevant characteristics. As has been argued (Prachowny, 1975, p.1), a small economy "... possesses no physical dimensions; it has only economic properties". These economic properties are precisely posited in economic theory: relative to the total supply of goods and assets, a small country supplies such a small proportion that it cannot influence their price, i.e. it is a price taker and its terms of trade are outside its control. At the macroeconomic level, smallness implies that domestic expansion or contraction will have no significant effect on economic activity in the rest of the world.

Unfortunately, such a definition is of limited use for us. Note, first of all, that the definition requires an open economy. A country is defined as small not by its internal economic characteristics, but by its relationship with its trading partners. Although, as we shall see, the countries of interest to us may have to pursue 'open' economy policies, the above definition includes many nations in the Third World that cannot be considered small. Few developing countries have a sufficient share of the market for any product of significance to be able to exercise any form of international monopoly power.

Clearly then, we have to judge an economy to be small by some other dimensions: what ought they to be? When they hear the phrase 'small economy' most people have a fairly good intuitive idea of what is meant. They tend to select countries not only by their economic properties but also by their geographical and demographic characteristics. Examples immediately spring to mind: Hong Kong, Singapore, Bhutan or a number of the newly independent South Pacific islands, the various independent states in the West Indies or Central America and countries in Africa such as Burundi, Rwanda or Lesotho.[2] Each is characterised by its small geographical size, small absolute size of population and narrow resource base.[3]

For the purposes of economic analysis, <u>area</u> by itself does not seem to be a very useful distinguishing characteristic. The development problems of a resource-scarce, poor economy with a small population but a large surface area (e.g. Chad or Niger) are probably not very different from those of similar poor country with a small area (e.g. Bhutan or various island states). There may be special circumstances where area by itself does become a significant factor, but in general - and in present conditions - it is more meaningful to rely on population size and incomes (or, together, simply GNP) as the main parameters to define 'smallness'.[4]

Does smallness in this sense raise special problems of development? If we look at most of the features that mark poor countries, there appears to be no particular difference between them according to their size. The lack of shelter, nutrition, education and employment that characterises large poor countries is equally characteristic of small ones. Does size then affect avenues that are open to them for future development? Does a small internal market, given the lack of a valuable natural resource, compel a country to adopt a different set of policies from a country which has a large market? At first sight, it would appear to. In so far as economies of scale pervade economic (particularly manufacturing) activity, the options open to large and small countries are bound to be different. A large economy can do practically everything that a small one can, but not vice versa. We may proceed usefully by using this contrast as far as their international economic relations are concerned.

It would, however, also be useful to contrast small poor economies with those small economies which also lack a natural resource base, but are now relatively well off. The experience of such 'small' economies as Hong Kong or Singapore, which, despite the handicaps of their size, have managed to achieve high incomes and impressive growth rates, has an obvious bearing on the policies poorer small countries may adopt. This is not say that every small economy can 'do a Hong Kong'. Clearly, the special location, historical background and educational endowments of Hong Kong and Singapore have been vital to their success: but the identification of these factors itself may help us to understand what the others lack, and so what they must strive to attain.

SMALL ECONOMIES AND INTERNATIONAL TRADE

Even a cursory examination of the current trading patterns of small poor economies reveals the following four features:

- a high ratio of foreign trade to national income,
- a high degree of concentration on a few products in exports,
- a high degree of concentration on a few countries to which exports are sold, and
- a low degree of concentration by commodity in imports.

These features can be attributed to a number of factors: geographical concentration caused by historical ties with particular metropolitan powers; the lack of broad-based industrial development coupled with a narrow natural resource base; the inability to achieve economies of scale in many lines of industrial production directed at internal markets; and the underdeveloped nature of social and economic infrastructure. Of these, the third would appear to be the critical feature of small as opposed to large developing economies, and it is on this that we concentrate our discussion.

While an elementary knowledge of industrial economics and some basic common sense would establish the importance of scale factors in the determination of comparative advantage, 'pure' trade theory has tended to ignore this reality. As Chipman (1965, p.737) notes in a survey of trade theory:

"It is probably correct to say that economies of scale tend to be ignored in theoretical models not so much on empirical grounds as for the simple reason that the theoretical difficulties are considerable, and it is not generally agreed how they can be incorporated into a model of general equilibrium or whether they are at all compatible with the assumptions of perfect competition. That this is a poor reason for excluding them from consideration is evident, especially if it is true that they constitute one of the principal sources of international trade."

Though a few neoclassical theorists have tackled 'special cases' where the economic size of a trading country does influence its comparative advantage, the treatment has been highly abstract, simplified and static (Meade,1955;Ohlin,1933). The main result seems to have been that the existence of scale economies introduces the possibility of multiple equilibria and thus renders a unique solution on specialisation impossible - a theoretically interesting but practically irrelevant result. Interestingly, even earlier attempts explicitly to marry trade theory to development policy[5] ignored the special problems raised by scale economies for small economies trying to find their due place in the international economy.

A simple explanation for this neglect may be found. The size of the domestic economy is irrelevant in pure trade theory because of the assumptions on which this theory is based; given universally identical production functions (i.e. no technological lags), no economies of scale, perfect market information (no uncertainty) and homogeneous products and factors, only relative factor prices (determined by relative physical abundance or scarcity) are relevant to the determination of comparative advantage. A small economy need suffer no handicap relative to a large one.

This theoretical result has to be modified to accommodate three possible sources of divergence in export performance between large and small economies: economies of scale, technology and marketing. Let us take them in turn.

Scale economies. Abstracting for the moment from the problems of being underdeveloped, a small economy should be able to reap all scale economies as easily as a large one (and thus, given the right knowledge and factor endowments, be equally efficient in exporting all industrial products) if it is assumed that there is no difference between selling domestically and internationally. The large economy can only have an advantage in reaping scale economies if it is admitted that there exist significant costs in learning about, cultivating, winning and servicing foreign as compared to local markets. This involves, in turn, admitting that market knowledge (as concerns foreign and local markets) is not perfect, that products are differentiated (and so brand loyalty, familiarity, promotion and the like, and not just price competition, are important), that selling involves risks and costs (and that these increase when a seller steps into foreign territory), and that after-sales service has additional costs which rise with distance.

In the real world, of course, all these factors do exist. There are differences in cost in servicing domestic and international markets, which make it easier for a large economy to reach economic levels of production in capital-intensive activities than a small one (we are ignoring the alternative of exporting via MNCs, which by definition reduces the extra costs of learning about and reaching foreign markets, but shall return to it later). The handicap facing small economies in exporting capital-intensive products on their own is not insuperable, as the example of developed countries like Switzerland or the Netherlands shows, but historically it has been overcome only when the economy has built up extensive trading banks and a considerable technological potential.

As far as developing countries are concerned, however, scale factors combined with the extra costs of exporting would (in the absence of MNC entry) give large economies a clear advantage in the production and export of capital-intensive products. A recent paper by Chenery and Keesing[6] differentiates developing countries by size and external orientation, and traces different emerging patterns of export specialisation inter alia to differences in size and the ability to reap scale economies domestically. This does not, of course, mean that large economies need have a superior export performance to small ones: the possession of a wider range of options is a very different matter from how successfully those options are exploited. However, the static advantage of small economies lies more in products not amenable to scale economies, while that of large ones is not restricted in this way.

Technology. Technology is not a universal or free good, and much of modern trade in manufactured products depends on the fact that different countries operate at different technological levels, enjoy different technological specialisation and are able to generate different rates of technological progress. This is not merely a matter which concerns exports of the industrialised countries. Developing countries, while starting exports of manufactures from 'traditional' products that use simple, well-diffused technologies, are starting to move rapidly into a diverse range of complex and high-skill technologies. The dynamism they are evincing in shifting their comparative advantage is due (again, abstracting from MNCs) to their ability to assimilate, adapt and improve upon new manufacturing technologies. This process of 'minor innovation' on the part of developing country enterprises involves costs, risk and effort (Nelson and Winter, 1977, pp.36-76; Kay, 1977), since firms possess only limited, localised knowledge of technologies they use or import (in contrast to the theoretical world where the whole production function is fully known and where firms can costlessly shift technologies in response to changes in factor prices). We shall return to technology later, but the point to note here is that technical progress is an essential ingredient in establishing a dynamic export potential in manufactured products, and that even when the technology is not new in international terms, its use by a developing country entails a species of 'innovative' effort based primarily on production experience.

Why should such innovative effort differ between small and large developing economies? The answer again lies in differences in the scale of activities which the economies can efficiently support. If the argument of the previous section has validity, large economies can efficiently foster a much broader industrial base than small ones, and can thus provide the learning base for a wider range of manufacturing technologies.[7] Thus, scale will affect not only the static pattern of commodities which economies of different size can economically export but also the dynamic changes in these patterns as a result of domestic learning and innovation. Large economies will be able to develop new advantages in a broader range of products, and, over the long run, to inject a much greater innovative effort of their own into the products which they share with small economies, simply because they produce more of the intermediate and capital goods that are used to manufacture those products.

The experience of Hong Kong and Singapore, the most advanced and dynamic of the small economies, illustrates this point.[8] If we ignore exports that take place under the aegis of MNCs (which come to some 90 per cent of the total for Singapore but very much less, around 11 per cent, for Hong Kong if selling arrangements with foreign buyers are ignored), the areas of competitive strength of local enterprises are exactly those in which small developing markets can be expected to foster local technological capability: textiles, garments, plastic products, and footwear. For Hong Kong, these product groups accounted for nearly 58 per cent of total exports (excluding re-exports) in 1977 (Chen, 1980, p.25): they are produced by industries with few economies of scale, having well-diffused technologies with a high labour cost content and amenable to upgrading by the 'learning' of production and managerial skills that do not require local capital goods industries. If we add other 'simple' products which now account for increasing shares of Hong Kong's exports, like toys, cutlery and consumer electronics, we can see a clear pattern of highly successful diversification by local enterprises into new manufactured products where the size of the domestic economy channels local innovative efforts into activities that require skill and not scale to be competitive.

The entry of MNCs can, of course, cut across this evolutionary pattern quite sharply. Since MNCs possess internationally integrated production systems and a ready supply of transferable technology and skills, the size of a potential host country is irrelevant to their location decision. If other factors are favourable (and we return to this later), a small country like Singapore can attract very 'heavy' and high-technology activities as successfully as a large one.

To return, however, to the technological basis of dynamic comparative advantage in domestic enterprises in large and small economies, two points stand out. First, local firms in countries like India, Brazil or Argentina, with large and diversified 'heavy' industrial sectors, show export advantages in a much wider range of products than their counterparts in small economies. While to some extent this reflects the deliberate strategy of the governments concerned to force the pace of import-substituting industrialisation, it also shows a natural realisation of comparative advantage based on scale and learning. In theory, these large economies could also have established powerful export industries in the light consumer goods in which Hong Kong and, later, larger economies like Taiwan and South Korea have shown such dramatic successes. In practice, however, the interventionist policies which led to the building up of 'heavy' industries were imposed too broadly and ham-fistedly to differentiate between industries which had to be geared to international markets from the start ('light' consumer goods) and those which needed a period of protected learning before they became competitive.

The second point worth noting is that while Hong Kong and Singapore illustrate the possibilities of technological dynamism in small economies, it is not clear how easily their experience can be replicated by the mass of 'small' or 'tiny' economies which do not enjoy their peculiar locational and historical advantages. Both Hong Kong and Singapore started their industrialisation process with relatively high incomes, a stock of entrepreneurial and commercial talent, well established international contacts, a trading infrastructure based upon entrepot trade, and an inflow of skilled and/or cheap labour. Insofar as technical progress is based on 'learning' various skills, therefore, these economies moved into manufacturing from a large and well established base of skills which could be readily applied to industry. These skills were not acquired by import-substituting activity but by historical accident which inserted them into the hub of the world trading system.

Does this mean that other small economies, less well-located and endowed, are caught in a vicious circle which they cannot break? That, in other words, they cannot enter world markets for manufactured products because they lack the skills and infrastructure which Hong Kong and Singapore had, and they cannot acquire them without a domestic base for industrial activity?

As far as the development of purely local manufacturing capabilities is concerned, there clearly is a serious problem here. But the vicious circle may not be an unbreakable one. The attraction of foreign enterprises, if it were possible, would clearly provide a viable solution: not only would these enterprises provide a direct injection of the skills which are lacking, but their entry would enable an industrial and communication infrastructure to be built up, and, in the longer term, their presence would stimulate local suppliers and sub-contractors to set up with technologies which spilt over (by trained workers striking out on their own) or were imitated by potential entrepreneurs.[9] It may even be possible to foster an independent indigenous manufacturing sector drawing on traditional handicrafts and manufacturing skills. Here, however, we would need to distinguish between the 'small' and the 'tiny' economies: the latter may not even be able to sustain the scale of manufacturing which is required for the simplest of modern (i.e. exportable) products. The former, the larger of the small economies, may be able to build up skills and techniques based on temporary protection, and so enter export markets for simple manufactured products, especially if they can overcome the marketing handicap by entering into international subcontracting arrangements with foreign buyers (Sharpston, 1975; Watanabe, 1972). Once a base of industrial skills and infrastructure exists, of course, further diversification need not require a protected learning period: the foreign buyers can directly provide the knowhow and designs needed.[10] However, even international sub-contracting cannot take root in a completely unindustrialised economy - a universal base of manufacturing experience and skills has to be present.

What of the 'tiny' economies? It is difficult to believe, on the scanty evidence at hand, that they can achieve anything substantial by way of an independent exporting capability in manufacturing industry. The main hope here would seem to be in direct investment in export industries by foreign enterprises. The attraction of such investment would itself require the building up of skills and infrastructure - this raises problems to which we return later.

Marketing. So far we have deliberately concentrated on skills related to production: let us now turn to an activity which is equally skill-intensive and perhaps in even greater need in developing countries wishing to export: marketing.[11] Orthodox theory assumes away too easily the significant barriers to entry into international trade arising from the need to market products effectively: given competitive markets and homogeneous products, price is the only factor assumed relevant. The real world is, unfortunately, far more complex. Any new entrant into the world of international trade in manufactures faces a variety of handicaps even if its products are of good quality and of low price (we are assuming away all barriers deliberately imposed by foreign governments). For consumer goods, these arise from the existence of strong product differentiation based on brand-name promotion and (for durables) the need to provide an effective after-sales service network. For capital goods, an element of brand-name preference is certainly present, but more effective barriers are posed by the need to tailor large items to individual needs (and so to meet different national standards, to keep in contact with all important customers, to have a continuous flow of technical information to and from users, and so on), to provide a 'package' of equipment and services for turnkey projects, to provide after-sales service, spares and modifications, and to be able to supply credit (usually in large sums and at concessional terms) to buyers.

These problems face any new exporter, large or small. Do small countries face a particular disadvantage? Two opposing answers are possible. First, that enterprises from small economies, by facing international markets from the start, will be more adept at 'marketing' in the broad sense than those from larger economies, to the extent that they are likely to be more sheltered. The growth in exports of 'high fashion' consumer goods from Hong Kong may be cited to support this argument. Second, however, it may be argued that in the absence of a large, sheltered domestic market, enterprises would not be able to try out design modifications in more familiar and less risky conditions, to learn how to set up sales/service organisations or to develop special products with the benefits of economies of scale. After all, much (but by no means all) of the 'high fashion' end of Hong Kong's exports is handled by foreign fashion groups which either set new trends or act as a direct conduit between rapidly changing market needs and the producers.

The answer is not clear cut, and much depends on the nature

of product technology and the 'openness' of the economy. A large economy with fairly liberal trading policies can enjoy the benefits of both large domestic markets and exposure to foreign markets, while one with protectionist policies may end up with poor quality products which have no foreign market potential. Similarly, a small economy with a strong entrepot tradition may be highly attuned to developed country consumer tastes, while one which is relatively isolated may find it impossible to reach the requisite level of awareness and sophistication. For goods (especially capital goods) requiring more complex technology, greater engineering ability and large minimum scales, the existence of large internal markets may be essential for gaining marketing expertise. In this, marketing factors would reinforce technical factors in confining small economies to particular types of 'mature' goods. However, experience suggests that, within these confines, small open economies, by virtue of their exposure, build up marketing skills more rapidly and effectively than large economies which are necessarily more inward looking (and often become more so by seeking to realise their potential for 'heavy' industrialisation behind protective barriers). The value of marketing experience and skills cannot be overstressed in the field of international trade: the building-up of such skills for new entrants to manufacturing industry and trade faces the same sort of problems as for manufacturing technology. Perhaps the difficulties for small economies are greater here, and recourse to foreign assistance more imperative.

To sum up, the dynamic comparative advantage of domestic enterprises in small economies is bound to be different from that in large ones (though, as will be seen below, the free entry of foreign enterprises may modify this considerably) because of the different possibilities of absorbing new technology and developing an internationally viable base for production and marketing. This need not imply that a small developing economy will do worse in trade than a large one - clearly, this depends on a host of historical, geographical, social and political factors apart from sheer size. However, for relatively isolated, unindustrialised and technically backward economies, smallness may indeed pose a distinct handicap in comparison to a similarly unindustrialised but large economy. If these initial handicaps can be overcome, a small economy can efficiently establish a trading pattern which will have different characteristics from those of larger countries. The small economy will tend to have a 'natural' comparative advantage in the production and export of products which are amenable to relatively small-scale production; the large economy may produce these as well as other commodities. Both large and small economies will have a comparative advantage in manufactured products which are relatively 'mature' in their technology, and both will be able to diversify over time into more skill-intensive activities, but given the different opportunities open for 'learning' domestically, the sorts of activity undertaken by both will reflect the influence of size. Comparable large economies will tend to be more diverse and more capital-intensive in their exports; they will, at the same time, tend to be less adept at sophisticated international marketing.

Within the constraints imposed by size, the sorts of international trade policy option open to small, backward economies may be grouped into three (which are not mutually exclusive).

First, to seek to develop domestic enterprises as the main vehicle for expanding manufactured exports to the world at large. As noted previously, this would involve, for countries without previous manufacturing, trading or financial experience, some sort of import-substituting strategy - a policy which has rather severe limitations.

Second, to seek to rely mainly on foreign enterprises to provide capital, technology and marketing (i.e. multinational manufacturing firms) or only product design and marketing (i.e. foreign retailing firms). This alternative, while not simple, holds much more promise, and is discussed in the next part.

Third, to seek to develop within a regional customs union, an alternative much praised in the theoretical literature and often attempted in practice. We have not touched upon this so far, and it will be useful to dwell on it briefly.

The core of the theory of customs unions as developed in the context of the Western European experience is not particularly useful for the analysis of economic integration schemes in most of the developing countries because of its focus on the static allocation effects within flexible industrialised economies.

The essence of the case for economic integration in developing areas is the need to take advantage of economies of scale in industries that are just beginning or not as yet established (Helleiner,1972). For the small economy it is probably the only way to carry out a reasonably efficient and widespread policy of import-substitution. Integration schemes in developing countries are best thought of as co-operative protection schemes against non-members within which industrial markets are swapped in such a manner that the aggregate import substitution scheme is attained at lower total cost, and with a greater degree of specialisation, than if each member had proceeded with its own programme independently. In terms of static customs union theory, this market-swapping constitutes 'trade-diversion' which is not in the world interest or in that of member countries, because it diverts trade from a low-cost source outside the membership to a higher-cost source within it; but if the diversion were to occur anyway, through protection by each national industrial sector, or if the time horizon envisaged were long enough to ensure the development and efficient functioning of the industry, it is a desirable policy decision.

There exist other reasons for economic integration, but they are all of secondary importance. For instance, if the bloc of states forming an agreement is large enough, it may extract improvements in terms of trade with respect to non-members. In the same vein, a large bloc can presumably carry greater weight in international negotiations. It is also frequently claimed that the creation of large industrial markets will generate more external economies and attract more foreign investment. Both of these claims may be correct, but they are the outcome of the emergence of the opportunity for realising scale economies in the industrialisation process rather than separate arguments for economic integration.

The advantages of economic integration agreements among small developing nations are so obvious that one wonders why there are no successful functioning unions.

In the first place, an agreement to remove tariffs against the products of a partner, while continuing them jointly with respect to non-members, will result in the same high import price but less revenue collected by the tariff. A nation will presumably only agree to the increase in costs this way if it receives better prices for its exports to the partner or some other form of compensation. If there exists one member with a relatively well developed industrial sector, it may be difficult to avoid imposing worsened terms of trade upon the less developed members through their participation. Apart from this, there may also be a tendency for all the industrial activity to concentrate around the original industrial base, since that is where the industrial infrastructure and other benefits thrown off by the pole can best be realised. The polarisation of industrial activity in one country can create 'backwash' effects for others, with capital, skilled labour and entrepreneurship in other parts of the tariff-free area all gravitating to the growth pole.

Finally, as the recent experience of the Caribbean, East Africa and the Andean Group shows, there are numerous political, ideological and administrative problems in successfully implementing integration schemes, for large as well as small countries. When different economies start with different levels of industrial development, and sometimes different political systems, achieving a similar structure in each of them, and a sharing of benefits regarded as equitable by each, is an extremely difficult task. It is for these reasons, rather than any intrinsic defect in the theory of integration, that this option seems of limited promise to the small developing countries.

SMALL ECONOMIES, TECHNOLOGY TRANSFER AND MULTINATIONALS

This section deals with the special problems faced by small economies in tackling technology transfer and MNCs. The two are placed together: despite the fact that the MNC is only one avenue for technology transfer, it is probably the single most important one, and for small economies without a strong indigenous industrial class, it is likely to be overwhelmingly important.

The debate about the costs and benefits of MNCs for developing countries is a passionate but inconclusive one,[12] and we do not intend to enter into it here. We take for granted that the main function to be served by the import of technology and the attraction of foreign capital will be to build up an export capability: import-substituting activity is, for reasons given above, not considered.

For export-orientated activities, the contribution of foreign capital may be considered under the following three headings, which constitute the main 'monopolistic advantages' of multinational firms:[13] technology, marketing, and achievement of economies of scale.

Technology. The provision of modern technology is of prime importance to the industrialisation of every developing economy, large or small. While for large economies legitimate questions may be raised about the use of modern techniques to produce 'inappropriate' products for the domestic market, for small economies their inherent export orientation leaves little room for advocating that a different set of techniques, for producing a set of products geared to low income markets, be employed. This is the first major difference between large and small economies: their different degrees of trade dependence permit them differing degrees of freedom to choose techniques and products for their industries.

There is another important difference: large economies are able to sustain a much broader and deeper indigenous technological capability than small ones. The reasons for this have been touched on already, but to reiterate: large economies can economically set up a much more diverse range of activities and so absorb a much greater range of knowledge and experience; they are more likely to be able to set up local capital goods industries, where most new manufacturing 'knowhow' is created or (if it originates elsewhere) is embodied in new equipment; they are more likely to be able to set up an indigenous entrepreneurial class which 'internalises' the knowledge of production techniques, and to be able to set up local enterprises of a size able to generate innovative activity; and they are more likely to have peculiar market conditions, raw materials and local supplier capabilities which necessitate local technological effort. They can, therefore, build up export capability in a broader range of technologies, and even enter international markets to export technology itself in a diverse range of forms and industries.[14]

This is not to argue that small economies will have no local technological capability. On the contrary, their advantage in small-scale production and their very exposure to international markets is likely to give the more advanced ones a strong competitive ability in setting up, managing and marketing the products of small, 'mature' technology enterprises. The evidence shows that a number of firms from Hong Kong and Singapore are technologically competent enough to have become 'mini multinationals' in their own right. They are setting up affiliates in countries with lower wages or easier access to the markets of the rich countries to produce garments, umbrellas and simple consumer electronics. Their 'knowhow' does not lie in the ability to design and manufacture the capital goods required - they buy the machines abroad for the well-diffused techniques - but in mastery over production engineering and selling.[15]

This being said, however, it must be stressed that large economies can absorb and generate such 'knowhow' plus that related to more complex industries. The implication for dealing with MNCs are as follows.

First, small economies cannot 'unpackage' MNCs (i.e. buy

technology, brand-names, skills etc. in separate forms as needed by local enterprises) as well, or to the same extent, as large economies. The only instances for which this does not apply are for the small-scale, relatively mature industries in which they have built up production expertise.

Second, since small economies cannot offer MNCs the benefits of a profitable internal market, they must offer them inducements to locate their export activities in these countries. Such inducements generally include a well-developed infrastructure, fiscal incentives, skilled or semi-skilled labour at competitive rates, a stable and low risk (of government intervention or trade union action) 'profile', and liberal trading, investing and repatriation conditions. Thus, their bargaining power to extract concessions from MNCs is relatively low, though it rises over time: Singapore has, with rising real wages, persuaded MNCs to move into higher skill activities, and is now introducing corporate income tax on its export-orientated guests (Lall,1978). If the tax rates are reasonably attractive, there is little reason to fear that MNCs will pull up stakes and leave a well-established base, or that they will use transfer prices on their trade with other affiliates to switch profits away.

Third, small developing economies are less likely to enjoy the benefits of backward linkages created by foreign firms, both because local supplier capabilities are bound to be limited and because an export orientation will give little margin to protect 'learning' by suppliers. However, two sorts of linkage are still possible: first, even MNCs manufacturing for export give rise to some technological spillover in relatively simple component manufacture, as has happened in electronics in Hong Kong and Singapore.[16] Second, foreign buying enterprises can set up international subcontracting linkages (this is considered again below).

Finally, the technological 'upgrading' of small economies is likely to follow the initiative of MNCs, while that in large economies may to some extent be independent, derived from indigenous R & D and the growth of the industrial/engineering infrastructure. It would not make much sense for a small economy to set up science and technology institutions to produce new production knowledge: it will do much better to rely on a continuous supply of such knowledge from abroad by attracting foreign manufacturing activity.

Marketing. The provision of marketing 'knowhow' and assets has been one of the most important contributions of MNCs to the export growth of developing economies (Helleiner,1973; de la Torre, 1974). Here the main thrust has come not so much from multinational manufacturers as from foreign buying/retailing firms which are increasingly scouting the developing world for suitable production sources. The buyer is far more than a passive agent comparing relative prices: he is often active in providing product design, materials, specifications and even finance, apart from the main function of supplying market outlets and an established brand-name (Westphal et al., 1979; Watanabe, 1972). The provision of tariff-duty drawbacks on the overseas processing of components supplied by developed countries (especially the US) has accelerated this tendency; in fact, manufactured imports under this particular category have grown much faster in recent years than total manufactured imports from developing countries (Finger, 1975).

Do small developing economies derive any special benefits from the provision of marketing 'knowhow' and assistance by foreign enterprises? Both large and small countries lack the expertise to market new products in developed countries; and they certainly do not have the established names and outlets that MNCs possess. However, a number of enterprises in developing countries are building up their own trade-names and retail networks for sophisticated products abroad: e.g. India's TELCO sells commercial vehicles under Tata brand-name, and the Korean Hyundai is launching its passenger car (the 'Pony') in various developing countries. These are relatively large enterprises with considerable manufacturing and retailing experience which new enterprises in small countries may find difficult to duplicate. It is clear that the large size of the domestic market, has contributed to their success by allowing them to become large and cut their teeth on complex marketing problems at home. As far as some complex industrial products are concerned, therefore, small economies are at a relative disadvantage. They may also be at a disadvantage in building up a brand image for simpler products which they export, if only because they do not have a home market on which to recoup the costs of the heavy promotion required. Thus, the corresponding benefits that small economies may gain from MNC marketing are larger.

As for the costs, the greatest potential danger of relying on foreign marketing enterprises is that they may turn out to be 'footloose', i.e. they may switch sources as costs rise, or may run down activity in developing countries to a much greater extent than at home. There is little evidence to substantiate these fears on economic grounds[17] though there is a clear risk that non-economic factors (political instability in particular) may adversely affect a particular host country.

Economies of Scale. We earlier identified the scale factor as a major determinant of the long-term pattern of comparative advantage to which a small economy could aspire. We also noted that the entry of MNCs could effectively relieve the constraint imposed by the small size of the domestic market. Subject to transport and labour costs and the availability of local skills, MNCs with established international markets could use small economies as staging posts for export-based manufacturing either for complete products or for specialised processes requiring large amounts of labour (and even, as with petrochemicals in Singapore, for highly capital-intensive processes to service neighbouring markets). There is considerable evidence that small economies have managed to break into world markets in both ways: Singapore and Hong Kong are used by MNCs to manufacture a range of products, and they are also used as assembly locations for high-technology industries (mainly electronics). US firms are continuously diversifying their offshore assembly activity into new areas in the Caribbean and Central America. The foreign contribution is fairly obvious, and need not be laboured.

CONSTRAINTS ON SMALL ECONOMIES

The preceding discussion has suggested that export-based industrialisation under the aegis of MNCs is a desirable, even essential, strategy for small economies that wish to develop. Apart from the fortunate few that are endowed with a valuable natural resource, there seem few other options available. Perhaps a decade or two ago even this option would have seemed highly unrealistic. With the expansion of MNC operations and the growth of international subcontracting, however, the possibility that even small economies can benefit from the international 'restructuring' of industry does not seem so remote. And the experience of a few successful economies shows that it has actually been done.

But this brings us to a basic problem which we have touched on but not tackled squarely: given the theoretical benefits of a successful export-led strategy, how plausible is it to suggest that all small economies can actually undertake it? Can they all emulate Hong Kong and Singapore? Can they compete with their larger developing cousins for the scarce financial, technical and managerial resources that are available? The progress that has occurred so far has been highly unevenly distributed: countries with some past experience of industrial, commercial or financial activity have established a long lead, and such factors as political stability, favourable location and a period of exceptionally auspicious trade conditions have all contributed to their success. What does the current international environment hold for new entrants?

It is clearly very difficult to provide definite answers. We may, however, proceed in small steps, by considering each of the handicaps that backward small economies may face: their 'given' location and factor endowments; political factors; new trends in world trade; and the evolution of MNCs.

Let us start with the 'given' location and endowments. Many small economies lack the rudimentary infrastructure and skills to attract even the simplest of export-orientated activities, and their low wages cannot compensate for this lack in a world where several countries have low wages and the larger ones can offer something more (internal markets). Even if they had the skills and infrastructure, some are so remote that transport cost considerations rule out 'sourcing' activity for them. And, even for the suitably located candidates, the number of aspirants is so large that foreign investors and buyers can pick and choose, bargain for the maximum concessions, and play one country off against the others. This does not contradict the fact that those countries which have established theselves as attractive locations for MNCs have succeeded in attracting other MNCs and retaining them despite rising wages. It does raise problems for newcomers whose political and social credentials are not well established.

The policy implications for the aspirants are not very clear. Those small economies which are located in likely areas for the attraction of export-orientated investments should try to get other conditions right, i.e. stable regimes for manufacturing, good infrastructure, competitive wages and attractive fiscal policies.[18] They should also provide a modicum of skills to their work force and impose conditions on foreign enterprises to prevent the worse kinds of exploitation. However, this leaves out the economies which are outside the possible 'catchment area'. Here the problems are acute, and foreign investment or buying does not seem to offer much of a solution.

Without a detailed examination, we cannot assess how many small economies fall outside the 'catchment area' in the foreseeable future, either for reasons of location or because of their extreme underdevelopment. There must be a fair number in Africa south of the Sahara and in the remote parts of Asia and the Pacific. Despite the possibility that technological changes might turn transport costs in their favour, the trickling of international production down the wage scale is bound to take a long, perhaps impossibly long, time. Even if the small economies offered exceptionally attractive terms, they have far too many equally eager competitors to hope that they will all enjoy a sudden influx of activity. Perhaps one new development holds out more hope: the number of growth poles in the world economy is increasing, as fast growing developing countries themselves become exporters of capital and technology. Thus, even areas remote from the metropolitan powers may be able to attract activity from neighbouring developing countries. How far this will fuel their overall economic growth is a matter for conjecture, but the possibility should be noted.

Second, political factors may render some economies unable to adopt, or benefit from, export-based strategies. In part this may be deliberate: socialist economies may not wish to participate in the emerging international division of labour according to capitalist market forces (though there are few socialist countries today which do not have policies to attract foreign export-orientated activity). In part, it may be uncontrolled: social and political instability may scare off sensitive investors. The implications of this are fairly obvious and need not be further discussed.

Third, new trends in world trade may block the entry of new competitors in the simpler activities in which they have a comparative advantage (particularly clothing and footwear). While the market for a large number of more sophisticated products is relatively open, and the more active developing countries are diversifying into them (Donges and Reidel, 1972), these are not activities which newcomers can hope to undertake. This still leaves scope for export growth in components and processes which are part of integrated MNC networks, where protectionism is much lower and where the MNCs themselves constitute a powerful force to keep trade relatively unrestricted (Helleiner, forthcoming). Thus, offshore assembly of electronics, office machines, and other light consumer goods (excepting garments and shoes) may be feasible paths of expansion for the newcomers.

Finally, the evolution of international investment itself will affect their prospects directly. There are two opposing factors at work. First, the pressures of internal and international competition, and the rise of new MNCs, are continually forcing firms in the industrialised countries to relocate production in cheaper areas, not

158

only for products at the 'mature' stage of the product cycle but also some at the early stages (Vernon, 1979). Second, however, the continuing recession and the growth of unemployment has evoked strong trade-union reaction against the 'export of jobs'. To a large extent this reaction has not been successful in halting the process of relocation, particularly in industries with 'light', high-value components and high labour requirements. Indeed, some countries (Japan and West Germany in particular) have not placed any hinderances in the way of this relocation, and have even facilitated it. The United States has officially promoted relocation via its tariff concessions to US components processed abroad, but its unions have been clamouring for restrictions on such job exports. Similar pressures are being felt in the United Kingdom, but little is known about the extent of overseas processing done by British MNCs.

While there may be some artificial barriers raised to the relocation of processing in developing countries, they are not likely to be crippling or permanent. The more important factor, and one outside the direct control of governments, is likely to be the pace of the worldwide economic growth itself, and few would now dare to prognosticate on this score.

In sum, the benefits that incorporation into the international economy offers to small developing countries are mainly a function of the latter's 'given' economic and political conditions. The international economy itself, while suffering from recession and its associated protectionist effects, still offers considerable scope for the growth of well-located economies which offer cheap, efficient and stable environments for the basing of export-orientated activity. For such economies, a liberal trading and foreign investment strategy - coupled perhaps with some judiciously applied measures to stimulate indigenous entrepreneurial development hitched, as it were, to the main engine provided by foreign enterprises - can be effective and successful. For others, a substantial number of small and tiny economies, the international economy does not afford such rewards in the foreseeable future. Until such time as they have themselves created an attractive investment climate and an adequate infrastructure of skills and communications, a liberal strategy may prove inadequate and frustrating.

NOTES

1. See Robinson (1960).

2. For a complete list, see, for instance, Commonwealth Secretariat (1979).

3. Kuznets (1960, pp. 14-32) defined a small economy as one with a population of under ten million. Of these there were 30-odd nations in the late 1950s. The Commonwealth Secretariat's cut-off of five million yields a universe of 59 'small' economies, of which 18 have per capita incomes of under $250 (in 1977).

4. According to the Commonwealth Secretariat's compilation, of the 59 'small' economies, only twelve had total GNPs of over US$1 billion, and eight of over US$2 billion. One country (the Dominican Republic) had a total GNP of over US$4 billion. If this were excluded, we could place a cut-off point at around US$2.5 billion, and further classify small economies into three groups: 'tiny', with total GNPs of under US$100 million (16 in number); 'medium', with GNPs of US$100-700 million (28); and 'relatively large', with GNPs of over US$700 million (14).

5. For instance, Chenery (1965). However, in Chenery's later work with Syrquin (1975) explicit account is taken of small 'primary-oriented' economies and small 'industry-oriented' economies. Since the purpose was to analyse different patterns of growth, little attention is unfortunately paid to the issues that concern us here.

6. Chenery and Keesing (1979) extended and refined the country classifications used by Chenery and Syrquin (1975).

7. On the importance of the initial period of learning, see Hirsch (1977).

8. On Singapore, see Wong (1979); on Hong Kong, see papers by Chen and Hung (1980).

9. For such linkages in the electronics industry in Singapore, see Pang and Lim´ (1977). For a more general analysis of linkages, together with a case study of automotive firms in India, see Lall (1980a).

10. On the significance of technology and skill transfer by foreign buyers in Korea, see Westphal, Rhee and Pursell (1979).

11. Chenery and Keesing (1970) lay great stress on this determinant of export performance, and provide illuminating examples.

12. For a review, see Lall and Streeten (1979).

13. See Kindleberger (1968), Caves (1971) and Lall (1980b).

14. For a general discussion of these factors and their relation to the 'revealed comparative advantage' of developing countries in technology markets, see Lall (1979).

15. See papers by Lecrew and Wells (forthcoming); and Lall (forthcoming).

16. See Lall (1978) and Watanabe (1978). On the Irish experience with MNC linkage creation, see McAleese and McDonald (1978).

17. For an examination of the behaviour of MNCs in Ireland during the recent recession, see McAleese and Counahan (1979) and the reference in note 16 above.

18. We are accepting the sad fact here that developing countries will continue to compete with each other in offering fiscal incentives to foreign investors. There are perfectly good theoretical arguments for their banding together to tax MNCs, but the number of countries is so large, and their political interests so diverse, that in practice it seems wiser to accept the inevitable conflict.

REFERENCES

Caves, R.E., 1971, 'International Corporations: the Industrial Economics of Foreign Investment'. In "Economica", Vol.38, No.149.

Chen, E.K., and Hung, C.L., 1980, 'Foreign Investments'. In D. Lethbridge, ed., "The Business Environment in Hong Kong", Hong Kong: Oxford University Press.

Chenery, H.B., 1965, 'Comparative Advantage and Development Policy'. In "Surveys of Economic Theory", Vol.II, Survey VI, London: Macmillan.

_____ , and Keesing, D.B., 1979, "The Changing Composition of Development Country Exports", The World Bank Staff Working Paper, No.314, Washington, D.C.

_____ , and Syrquin, M., 1975, "Patterns of Development", London: Oxford University Press.

Chipamn, J.S., 1965, 'A Survey of the Theory of International Trade: Part II, The Neo-Classical Theory'. In "Econometrica", Vol.3, No.4.

Commonwealth Secretariat, 1979, "Basic Statistical Data on Selected Countries (with populations of less than 5 million)", London.

Donges, J.B., and Reidel, J., 1972, "The Expansion of Manufactured Exports in Developing Countries: An Empirical Assessment of Demand and Supply Issues", Weltwirtschaftliches Archiv.

Finger, J.M., 1975, 'Tariff Provision for Offshore Assembly and the Exports of Developing Countries'. In "Economic Journal", Vol.85, No.338.

Heath, D.C., and Lall, S., forthcoming, 'The Export of Capital from Developing Countries: India'. In J.H. Dunning and J. Black, ed., "Interntional Investment and Capital Movements", London: Macmillan.

Helleiner, G.K., 1972, "International Trade and Economic Development", Harmondsworth: Penguin.

_____ , 1973, 'Manufactured Exports from Less Developed Countries and Multinational Firms'. In "Economic Journal", Vol.83, No.329.

_____ , forthcoming, 'Structural Aspects of Third World Trade:

Some Trends and Some Prospects'. In "Journal of Development Studies".

Hirsch, S., 1977, "Rich Man's Poor Man's and Every Man's Goods", Tubingen: J.C.B. Mohr.

Kay, R., 1977, "The Innovating Firm", London: Macmillan.

Kindleberger, C.P., 1968, "American Business Abroad", New Haven: Yale University Press.

Kuznets, S., 'Economic Growth of Small Nations'. In E.A.G. Robinson, "Economic Consequences of the Size of Nations". London: Macmillan.

Lall, S., 1978, 'Transfer Pricing in Assembly Industries'. In "Industrial Co-operation", Commonwealth Economic Papers, No.11, Commonwealth Secretariat, London.

_____ , 1978, 'Transnationals, Domestic Enterprises and Industrial Structure in Host LDCs: A Survey'. In "Oxford Economic Papers", Vol.30, No.2.

_____ , 1979, 'Developing Countries as Exporters of Technology'. In H. Giersch, ed., "International Economic Development and Resource Transfer", Tubingen: J.C.B. Mohr.

_____ , 1980a, 'Vertical Inter-firm Linkages in LDCs: An Empirical Study'. In "Oxford Bulletin of Economics and Statistics", Vol.42, No.3.

_____ , 1980b, 'Monopolistic Advantages and Foreign Investment by US Industry'. In "Oxford Economic Papers", Vol.32, No.1.

_____ , and Streeten, P., 1977, "Foreign Investment, Transnationals and Developing Countries", London: Macmillan.

Lecraw, D.J., forthcoming, 'Internationalisation of Firms from LDCs: Evidence from the Asian Region'. In K. Kumar and M.G. McLeod, ed., "Multinationals from Third World Countries", Lexington: Lexington Books.

McAleese, D., and Counahan, M., 1979, 'Stickers' or 'Snatchers'? Employment in Multinational Corporations during the Recession'. In "Oxford Bulletin of Economics and Statistics", Vol.41, No.4.

_____ ,and McDonald,D.,1978, 'Employment Growth and the Development of Linkages in Foreign-Owned and Domestic Manufacturing Enterprises'. In "Oxford Bulletin of Economics and Statistics", Vol.40, No.4.

Meade, J., 1955, "Trade and Welfare", London: Oxford University Press.

Nelson, R.R., and Winter, S.C., 1977. 'In Search of Useful Theory of Innovation'. In "Research Policy".

Ohlin, B., 1933, "Interregional and International Trade", Cambridge (Mass.): Harvard University Press.

Pang, EngFong, and Lim, Linda, 1977, "The Electronics Industry in Singapore: Structure, Technology and Linkages", Singapore: Economic Research Centre Research Monograph Series.

Prachowny, M.F.,1975, "Small Open Economies", Lexington:

Lexington Books.

Robinson, E.A.G.,ed., 1960, "Economic Consequences of the Size of Nations", London: Macmillan.

Sharpston, M.,1975, 'International Sub-Contracting'. In "Oxford Economic Papers", Vol.27, No.1.

Torre, J. de la, 1974, 'Foreign Investment and Export Dependency'. In "Economic Development and Cultural Change", Vol.23, No.1.

Vernon, R., 1979, 'The Product Cycle in a New International Environment'. In "Oxford Bulletin of Economics and Statistics", Vol.41, No.4.

Watanabe, S., 1972, 'International Sub-contracting, Employment and Skill Promotion'. In "International Labour Review", Vol.105, No.5.

_____ , 1978, "International Sub-contracting: A Tool of Technology Transfer", Tokyo: Asian Productivity Organisation.

Wells, L.T., forthcoming, 'Foreign Investors from the Third World'. In K. Kumar and M.G. McLeod, ed., op. cit.

Westphal, L.E., Rhee, Y.W., and Pursell, G., 'Foreign Influences on Korean Industrial Development'. In "Oxford Bulletin of Economics and Statistics", Vol. 41, No.4.

Wong, J., 1979, "Asean Economies in Perspective", London: Macmillan.

9. Balance of Payments Problems and Macro-economic Policy in Small Economies

G.K. Helleiner*

This paper cannot hope to deal in detail with all of the many issues surrounding balance of payments problems and macro-economic management in small countries. What is attempted is a general survey of the state of current knowledge regarding the main elements of small countries' recent experience with external 'shocks'. The following section considers the role of external trade and its instability in small economies. In the second section capital flows to small developing countries and some of their attendant risks are discussed. The third section addresses some of the major aspects of macro-economic policy in the face of external 'shocks', including, in particular, exchange rate policy. A brief summary and conclusion can be found in the final section.

EXTERNAL TRADE AND ITS INSTABILITY IN SMALL ECONOMIES

One of the best established of the 'stylised facts' about small countries is the relative 'openness' of their economies.[1] 'Openness' has many dimensions - it relates to goods markets, factor markets and financial markets, not to speak of cultural, social and political dimensions. In the literature of small country economies, since domestic financial 'markets' are frequently non-existent (indeed they are sometimes wholly internalised within foreign productive and financial firms), and international factor movements (particularly inward flows of labour and outward flows of capital) are usually stringently controlled, what is usually meant by 'openness' relates to production and trade. Capital inflows do possess certain small country characteristics, as will be seen later, but in this section the focus will be on the more familiar trade questions.

The most systematic study of international patterns of development which has so far been undertaken (Chenery and Syrquin, 1975, p.75) found that, regardless of per capita incomes, small countries - defined (liberally) as those with populations of

* The author is grateful to Valerie Bencivenga for computational assistance.

under 15 million - on average have over twice the export/GNP ratio of larger countries.

Openness to international trade is typically even greater in the very smallest economies - the so-called 'mini states'. In the words of a recent study, "the economic characteristics of a mini state are that goods which are produced tend to be exported, goods which are sold in the mini state tend to be imported, and the commodities which are both produced and consumed within the mini state tend to be services. Even a substantial amount of these services may be purchased by foreigners in a mini state which specialises in tourism, offshore banking, offshore insurance or tax avoidance facilities". (Khatkhate and Short, 1980, p.1018.) A sample of countries with populations of 1.2 million and under, reported in this paper, had exports in 1978 accounting for an average of 57 per cent of their GDP and imports averaging 60 per cent of total domestic spending.[2] Moreover, as growth proceeds in very small countries there is every indication that this degree of openness will become even greater: "... the process of growth inevitably requires that the ratio of exports to GDP increases because the domestic market is too small for domestic production to achieve economies of scale, and because efficient utilization of the domestic resource base requires a larger market than just the domestic one" (ibid.,p.1018).[3]

The unusual degree of this type of openness in small countries renders them peculiarly vulnerable to 'external shocks'. They are therefore likely to be disproportionate gainers, other things being equal, in terms either of proportions of GNP or per capita, from reforms in the international trading order. The contribution of the export sector to national income is frequently much less, however, than the value of exports as recorded in the trade statistics; particularly is this so in export sectors which are foreign-owned or which utilise large volumes of imported goods and services. The 'retained value' can be both much less significant in national income and much more stable than the export statistics suggest (Brodsky and Sampson, 1980). In the Bahamas, Netherlands Antilles, and the US Virgin Islands, exports (and imports) are several times as large as GDP (ibid., p.43). Particularly in small countries is it important to work with retained value estimates in the export sector rather than with the more readily available export statistics; unfortunately, the more appropriate data, which would make it possible to generalise about 'net' export instability in these and other countries, are not available in international sources. The discussion which follows is therefore forced to rely on gross export data.

Export instability (gross) is the type of 'external shock' which has received the most detailed research attention. At least as valuable as analyses of nominal export instability, as indicative of trade-related shocks, would be analyses of instability in the commodity and income terms of trade which take fluctuations in import prices into account as well; but these are not readily available either. Since ultimately it is the quantity of imports which should be the object of stability policies on external account, the most appropriate focus for empirical analysis should be net exports plus net capital flows, the whole deflated by an import price index.

The evidence on export instability fairly consistently demonstrates that small countries experience more of it. Sometimes increased stability of export receipts is associated with larger absolute size of the exports themselves (Massell, 1970; Naya, 1973; Knudsen and Parnes, 1975), and sometimes with the economic size (GNP) of countries (Erb and Schiavo-Campo, 1969). There is a general presumption, supported by some empirical work, that small countries have exports which are more concentrated both geographically and in terms of commodities (Kuznets, 1964; Michaely, 1972); and high concentration is itself associated with greater instability (Knudsen and Parnes, 1975; Massell, 1970). Thus (although this may be only of academic interest) the high export instability of small countries appears in substantial degree to be the product of structural characteristics associated with size, rather than of size per se; when these characteristics were allowed for, Knudsen and Parnes (1975, p.78) actually found large countries to have greater export instability than small.[4]

It would be useful to know the recent and prospective instability of different kinds of export and combinations of exports.[5] There is little recent empirical support, for instance, for the still common presumption that primary products are more unstable components of an export account than are manufactured ones (Naya, 1973; Askari and Weil, 1974; Massell, 1970). But we still do not know too much about optimal commodity 'baskets'. In the Chenery-Syrquin subclassification of 'small' countries - 'primary-oriented' versus 'industry-oriented' - which has been more unstable? Can this type of research at last focus on retained value from exports, at least in the case of the small countries for which this measure is most obviously the only meaningful one? Can one offer any generalisations as to prospective markets and likely degrees of instability on the basis of income-elasticities of demand, and growth forecasts, in major markets or the likelihood of protectionist barriers?

High (gross nominal) export instability may or may not inhibit economic growth. Controversy has raged over this relationship for some years (MacBean, 1966; Knudsen and Parnes, 1975; Glezakos, 1973; Voivodas, 1974). What cannot be disputed, however, is the fact that fluctuations in net real export proceeds in highly export-dependent economies create major difficulties of macro-economic management.

CAPITAL FLOWS TO SMALL ECONOMIES AND THEIR RISKS

Perhaps only slightly less well known than the 'openness' of small countries on trade account is the 'small country effect' in official development assistance. Per capita aid receipts have long been significantly higher in small countries than in larger ones; it is possible to interpret aid allocations in terms of a fixed amount for each country (an intercept) plus a further allocation based on population.[6]

TABLE 1

CAPITAL FLOWS AND STOCKS IN DEVELOPING COUNTRIES, 1978, AND THEIR
RELATION TO POPULATION AND PER CAPITA INCOME: REGRESSION RESULTS

Independent variable — Dependent variable	Constant	Population	Per Capita Income	N	R^2
(1.1) Official development assistance (ODA)-net					
(a)	94.98 (18.87)***	2.30 (0.32)***		142	.27
(b)	112.91 (21.92)***	2.26 (0.32)***	-0.11 (0.01)	142	.28
(1.2) Non-ODA resource flow-net					
(a)	195.31 (53.10)***	1.75 (0.90)*		142	.03
(b)	168.55 (62.08)***	1.83 (0.91)**	0.02 (0.02)	142	.03
(1.3) Total (net) resource flow: (1) + (2)					
(a)	290.29 (55.24)***	4.06 (0.94)***		142	.12
(b)	281.46 (64.73)***	4.08 (0.95)***	0.01 (0.02)	142	.12
(1.4) Stock of direct foreign investment					
(a)	641.11 (158.80)***	7.95 (2.37)***		109	.10
(b)	547.14 (186.66)***	8.21 (2.39)***	0.05 (0.05)	109	.10
(1.5) Stock of external public debt					
(a)	2043.25 (543.98)***	33.67 (6.88)***		78	.24
(b)	558.80 (744.96)	35.38 (6.62)***	1.91 (0.68)***	78	.31

Notes: Standard errors are recorded in parentheses. Asterisks indicate statistical significance using a two-tail test: *** significant at the 1% confidence level, ** significant at the 5% confidence level and * significant at the 10% confidence level. The countries included in the analysis are all those for which both population and per capita income are reported in the OECD source, but China and European less developed countries are excluded.

Sources: Population and per capita GNP data are from OECD, 'Development Co-operation', 1980, pp. 238-40; total resource flows from ibid, pp. 214-15; official development assistance from ibid, pp. 212-213; non-ODA resource flow from ibid, p.165; and stock of external public debt from The World Bank, World Development Report 1980, Washington D.C., pp. 138-39.

For the purposes of this paper I have analysed the most recent complete OECD data (those for 1978) on resource flows - both official development assistance (ODA) and other types - to see whether traditional 'small country effects' are still to be found. To my knowledge, this is the first attempt to uncover such effects in non-ODA capital flows. Table 1 records the results of the regression exercise relating total capital receipts to population and per capita income in 1978. Despite much rhetoric about the changing purposes and patterns of official development assistance, the traditional pattern is still to be found in aid flows. The usual 'small country effect' is visible in the positive (and significant) intercept in equation (1.1).

TABLE 2

AVERAGE PER CAPITA CAPITAL FLOWS AND STOCKS IN DEVELOPING
COUNTRIES OF DIFFERENT POPULATION SIZE, 1978*

Population size	Under 5 million	Over 5 million	Under 10 million	Over 10 million
Flows				
1) Official development assistance (ODA)-net	161.38 (85)	13.42 (57)	131.42 (108)	8.50 (34)
2) Non-ODA resource flow-net	294.67 (85)	19.13 (57)	235.07 (108)	22.05 (34)
3) Total (net) resource flow: (1) + (2)	456.05 (85)	32.56 (57)	366.49 (108)	30.56 (34)
Stocks				
4) Stock of direct foreign investment	3011.80 (57)	43.56 (52)	2267.66 (76)	48.32 (33)
5) Stock of external public debt	529.55 (29)	166.97 (49)	399.72 (45)	168.20 (33)

* The number of countries in the sample is recorded in brackets.

Sources: See Table 1.

Not previously noticed is the fact that there is also a similar - indeed even larger - bias in favour of small countries in non-aid capital flows to developing countries; this is shown in equation (1.2). In consequence, the small country effect is even larger for total (net) resource flows than it is for official development assistance (equation (1.3)). This can also be seen in the data on stocks of direct foreign investment and external public debt, which are also shown in equations (1.4) and (1.5); in these presentations, however,

169

the data exclude many countries in which the absolute size of these stocks is small, so that they must be more carefully interpreted.

Table 2 records average per capita capital flows and (with the same caveats as before) capital stocks of various kinds for small countries and for large ones, with the divisions between 'small' and 'large' taken alternatively as five million and ten million of population. Again, the evidence is clear. Per capita receipts of every kind are substantially larger for small countries than for large ones.

Why should non-concessional capital flows demonstrate the same bias towards small countries as aid flows? Capital flows which originate with or are influenced by official sources - such as non-concessional loans, export credits or guarantees - may be influenced by some of the same diplomatic factors as aid flows, and therefore may be expected to demonstrate some of the same inter-country distribution characteristics. It is more difficult to see why Buggins' turn should play much of a role in private capital flows. But perhaps it does; and perhaps bankers and businessmen also like to 'show the flag' in as many national markets as possible even if doing so involves a little sacrifice of return. It may also be that these capital flows are related to export performance; since exports per capita are unusually high in small countries, so are private capital flows per capita. Another possibility is that risk considerations lead individual private decision-makers to a wider geographic spread of their activities than strict profit maximisation would require.

In the case of borrowing rights in the International Monetary Fund (whether conventional or special), I have not been able explicitly to test for 'small country effects'. The original formula determining the size of IMF members' quotas was based, with some fuzziness about the edges, on a combination of national income, gold and foreign exchange holdings, trade, export variability, and the degree of openness (Aufricht, p.35). In the mid-fifties, the Fund took special account of the needs of small countries whose quotas "were found to be particularly inadequate ... requests for increases in small quotas would be sympathetically considered by the Fund, if so requested by the members concerned, in accordance with a formula which involved higher percentage increases for smaller quotas" (ibid., p.37). Several countries availed themselves of this opportunity and one may assume that the many small countries that have since become IMF members have benefited from comparable special consideration in the determination of their quota sizes. It may be worth noting the disproportion in the quotas awarded to new IMF members in 1979-80; tiny St. Lucia (population 120,000) was given a quota amounting to SDRs 30 per capita, whereas Zimbabwe (population 6.9 million) received 14.5, and China received 0.58 SDRs per capita.[7] Thus it seems that borrowing rights in the IMF are characterised by the same kind of 'small country effect' as official development assistance; no doubt this is primarily for the same sort of reason as in the case of aid flows, but there is some evidence to suggest that it is also because of the recognised balance of payments needs of small countries.

Balance of payments assistance (grants or loans) offered by the

STABEX programme within the Lome Convention is based on a formula relating to the absolute value of particular commodity exports to the EEC. Thus ACP countries with high such export values relative to population or GNP, other things being equal, can expect greater STABEX funding relative to population or GNP than can other ACP countries. Again, while I have not conducted a systematic analysis of the matter, this seems likely to generate a bias - in terms of per capita receipts - in favour of the smaller (more open) economies.

I am unaware of studies of the instability of various kinds of capital flows to developing countries. In any case, it is difficult to think of a priori reasons for expecting them to be more unstable or less unstable in the case of small countries. A high degree of 'openness' on capital account, such as the above tables reveal, however, does leave small countries unusually vulnerable to fluctuations in capital receipts. Where there are high debt servicing obligations implied by these high capital inflows, it also leaves them exceptionally vulnerable to short-term liquidity crises in the management of the balance of payments. Conventional debt servicing ratios (relating service obligations to the value of exports) do not show small countries as nearly so exceptional, however, since exports per capita or as a proportion of GNP are also, as has been seen, exceptionally high.

The risks associated with different kinds of foreign capital inflow obviously vary. Those associated with official development assistance are 'non-economic' and have to do with the regularity of expected receipts; uncertainties flow from the vagaries and mysteries of foreign donor decisions. Fixed-interest portfolio capital, such as may be obtained on bond markets or from supplier credits or from the World or Regional Development Banks, involves the borrower in a rigid and inflexible commitment in the balance of payments which, barring rescheduling or default, may create increased pressure on other important imports in periods of export difficulty. Private bank borrowing has now emerged as a particularly risky enterprise, since not only are borrowers bound to the regular payment of future servicing obligations but now, with the introduction of floating interest rates, they cannot even know in advance how large the interest payments will be; interest payment obligations vary with monetary events abroad which have nothing whatever to do with domestic capacity to repay. Once begun, there may also be uncertainties about the capacity to roll loans over as they mature. Direct investment is the least likely of the various forms of foreign borrowing to generate liquidity (balance of payments) problems on account of servicing obligations, in that at least dividend payments may be related to domestic circumstances and capacity to pay. Obviously, however, dividend payments in respect of particular investments may be unrelated with the state of the overall balance of payments; moreover, direct foreign investment is frequently accompanied by fixed payments (and often over-payments) for technology, management, overheads and items other than dividends.

MACRO-ECONOMIC POLICIES IN
SMALL ECONOMIES

The costs of instability can include (i) those of social disruption in consequence of wide fluctuations in the fortunes of individuals and groups and, probably, in the distribution of income; (ii) those of distorted investment patterns as decision-makers evade the activities which seem most vulnerable to periodic 'shocks' and resulting uncertainties; and (iii) unnecessary frictional costs in consequence of periodic overshooting in allocative decision-making. Some believe that instability is also inflationary and/or likely to lower overall savings rates, but these consequences are rather more speculative, and have not been firmly verified in empirical analysis.

Since it is always possible for governments to offset the consequences of external fluctuations through the use of reserves and borrowing, their maximum cost must be that of carrying sufficient foreign exchange reserves and/or borrowing enough to permit the economy to ride smoothly through them. That said, it can be assumed that the governments of economies subject to 'external shocks' will do their best to minimise their costs - through external insulation devices where possible and various domestic stabilisation policies where they are not. In order to develop the most appropriate macro-economic policies one requires a detailed and accurate understanding of how the economy in question functions and, in particular, how it is affected by external events.

It has quite accurately been said that "until recently short-run LDC macro-economics was a relatively neglected topic. The past few years, however, have seen a remarkable upsurge in analytical work in LDC macro-economics." (Leff and Sato, 1980, p.170.) This upsurge has been concentrated, in the main, on the semi-industrialised and larger of the developing countries. Detailed econometric modelling of the small developing economy, where it exists at all, is typically still extremely crude. On the one hand, there are simple monetarist models of the traditional Polak type (1957), in which income velocity of money and the import coefficient are assumed constant and no distinction is made between real and nominal changes in national product. On the other hand, presumably (though published versions are hard to find), there are the usual models from the general theoretical literature (on 'small countries') with only minimal modification for the peculiar characteristics of particular small developing countries. As has been seen, there are frequently not even data on the extent of retained value in the export account.

A high propensity to import, such as is found in small developing countries, reduces the domestic multiplier effect of disturbances of whatever origin. The more open to trade is an economy, the greater is both its vulnerability to external shocks and the extent to which its domestic shocks are shared with the rest of the world. Thus Mathieson and McKinnon (1973) even purport to have shown that greater openness is associated, in at least one sample of countries and one time period, with greater stability of real investment; and Iyoha (1973) has similarly found that greater openness is significantly associated with lower rates of price inflation. These matters clearly deserve more research exploration through careful macro-economic modelling of individual small economies' experiences. In this paper I can do no more than offer some generalisations as to small economies' macro-economic policy choices.

Exchange Rate Policies

Small 'open' economies, although highly vulnerable to external shocks, cannot as easily insulate themselves from some of their macro-economic effects through adoption of flexible exchange rates as can (at least in principle) larger countries. Thin foreign exchange markets and structural rigidities imply the risk of extreme volatility for a 'free' foreign exchange rate; and the small, open character of the economy would translate wide exchange rate fluctuations into equally great internal price and cost disturbances, quite possibly leading to declining use of the local currency for the denomination of contracts. These countries are therefore likely to be forced to peg their currencies to some external standard - in practice, the US dollar, French franc, pound sterling, increasingly the SDR, and occasionally other currencies like the South African rand and the Spanish peseta. Some small countries even continue to use foreign currency as the domestic circulating medium, e.g. the US dollar in Panama and Liberia, the New Zealand dollar in the Cook Islands and Niue, and the Australian dollar in Nauru, the New Hebrides, Kiribati and Tuvalu (Khatkhate and Short, p.1022).

The great majority of developing countries, not all of which are small at least in terms of population, do now formally peg the value of their currencies. Of the only 25 developing countries listed by the International Monetary Fund as pursuing exchange rate policies other than pegging (on 31 January 1981), 15 were countries with populations of over ten million; of the remaining ten (small) unpegged developing countries, five could be considered 'special cases' (Bahrain, Lebanon, Qatar, Saudi Arabia and United Arab Emirates). Thus only Bolivia, Costa Rica, the Maldives, Uruguay and Western Samoa are left as 'unusual' small and unpegged exchange rate cases.[8]

In research undertaken for the Group of Twenty-four, and summarised in Table 3, calculations were made of the exchange rate peg which would, under certain assumptions as to trade flows, have minimised short-term effective exchange rate instability in the post-1973 (global floating) period for each of the developing countries for which the IMF had data. The vast majority of them would have done so by pegging to the SDR (assumed a basket of 16 major currencies, throughout the period) or by retaining their actual practices. Of the 44 developing countries which would have done best, in this respect, by pegging to national currencies (the US dollar, French franc, pound sterling, and ECU, considered for this

TABLE 3

PEG THAT WOULD HAVE MINIMISED 'EXTERNALLY CAUSED' NOMINAL
EFFECTIVE EXCHANGE RATE INSTABILITY IN 1973-79 PERIOD,
DEVELOPING COUNTRIES (TRADE WEIGHTS)

Hypothetical SDR*	79
US dollar	14[1]
French franc	11[2]
Pound sterling	4[3]
ECU	15[4]
Actual (other basket, float etc.)	8[5]
Total	131

[1]The Bahamas, Costa Rica, Dominican Republic, Haiti, Honduras, Mexico, Netherlands Antilles,Panama, Panama CZ, Sao Tome and Principe, St. Pierre and Miquelon, Trinidad and Tobago, US Virgin Is., Venezuela.

[2]Central African Republic, Chad, Comoros, French Guiana, Guadeloupe, Mali, Martinique, Niger, Reunion, Senegal, Upper Volta.

[3]Bolivia, Paraguay, St. Helena, Tonga.

[4]Benin, Brunei, Cameroon, Cyprus, Falkland Is., The Gambia, Gibraltar, Malawi, Malta, Mauritania, Mauritius, Seychelles, Sierra Leone, Swaziland, Togo.

[5]Faroe Is., Fiji, Guinea-Bissau, Greenland, Grenada, Kiribati, Morocco, Nauru.

*Basket assumed in force throughout the period, rather than only beginning in July 1974; changed in July 1978.

Source: Helleiner, G.K., 1981, The Impact of the Exchange Rate System on the Developing Countries: Report to the Group of Twenty-four, UNDP/UNCTAD project INT/75/015, p.105.

purpose as a 'national' currency), 42 of them have populations of under ten million and 34 of them under five million. (Mexico and Venezuela were the only large countries which would have done best pegged to a national currency, the US dollar).

More systematic attempts to explain econometrically the determinants of exchange rate pegging or flexibility all confirm the importance of country size: small countries are more likely to peg the values of their currencies in terms of some foreign standard and are more likely to intervene in foreign exchange markets (Heller, 1978; Dreyer, 1978; Holden et al., 1979). The influence of size on exchange rate policy is additional to the influences of other variables frequently associated with size: in particular, openness in trade, and concentration in trade both in terms of direction and of commodities.

Pegging to a foreign currency has the disadvantage that the country doing so thereby subjects itself to effective currency fluctuations which are purely the product of fluctuations in the value of the currency to which it is pegged vis-a-vis third currencies. A further source of external shocks - foreign currency fluctuations - is therefore added to all of the others already faced by the typical small country. Moreover, there has been a significant increase in the importance of this kind of external shock with the introduction of the key currencies' floating regime early in 1973. A vigorous literature has emerged in recent years on the elements of the decision as to the optimum currency (or basket of currencies) to which to peg.[9] Clearly, a major input to this decision must be the currency composition of international trading and financial ties; a country which has close economic links with France, for instance, will find it convenient (and risk-minimising for most of both its private and public transactors) to peg to the French franc.[10]

Equally clearly, once such a peg is chosen there are incentives created for the continuation of transactions in the currency of peg. Thus small countries are subject to continuing pressure to remain within their current (currency-related) spheres of foreign influence. Diseconomies of scale associated with the creation of trade infrastructure[11] also seem likely to encourage concentration of trade and financial flows along traditional geographic channels. There appears to be a clear cost to the pursuit of diversification, whatever may be its possible benefits.

While a pegged exchange rate results in the transmission of external shocks directly to the domestic economy - through direct effects on aggregate demand, the price level and the money supply - it also reduces the domestic impact of internally generated disturbances or policy errors by distributing some of their effects to the rest of the world. Where the exchange rate is truly fixed, as in cases in which foreign currencies are employed as domestic money, national macro-economic policy-makers are constrained in their range of policy options. To some degree, this is also true of those whose national currencies' exchange rates are changed only infrequently. While cause and effect are always difficult to discern, there is no doubt that most of those countries which maintained strictly unchanged pegs throughout the 1973-79 period experienced relatively modest rates of inflation.

Table 4 lists all of the countries (for which the IMF has data) which actually retained unchanged nominal pegs in terms of the US dollar, the French franc or the pound sterling during the entire 1973-79 period; all but five are small in the sense that their population is under ten million. Table 5 records inflation rates and per capita GDP growth rates for all of the small, pegging countries from Table 4 for which the World Development Report presents data. Growth rates in these countries are, on average, below those of the countries to which they have pegged, and they are also below those of other comparable developing countries. In the case of franc peggers, however, their inflation rate is also lower, on average, than those of other developing countries and is, indeed, exactly equal to that of France. The peculiar conditions under which the former French colonial possessions in Africa make their macro-economic policy are probably more important to this result than any subtle arguments about the impact of alternative exchange rate policies. While these data suggest that pegging is associated with slower growth and less inflationary pressure, the direction of causality must remain a matter for debate.

Macro-Economic Policy Response to External Shocks

As has been seen, the level of economic activity and the rate of inflation in small open economies are obviously highly influenced by events in the world economy. These countries' typically pegged (though sometimes adjustable) exchange rates mean that global growth, recession and inflation are transmitted directly and immediately to the domestic economy. This vulnerability to 'shocks' from the world economy is found both in respect of longer-run macro-economic experience and of short-term performance. The typical external 'shock' experienced by small developing economies takes the form of sharp change in their external (commodity) terms of trade. In recent years, the main such 'shock' has, of course, been a sharp deterioration in the terms of trade, and it will be convenient to consider policy response in terms of that type of shock.

The policy responses to (negative) external shocks must involve some combination of the following:

(i)   domestic deflation-reduced rates of growth of total consumption or investment or both, probably achieved to a substantial extent by reduced governmental expenditure but also through other fiscal and monetary measures;

(ii)   domestic restructuring of production and consumption - increasing the prices of tradeable goods relative to nontradeables so as to encourage increased import substitution and exporting, through tariffs and other controls, export subsidies, currency devaluation, etc; and

176

TABLE 4

COUNTRIES MAINTAINING UNALTERED PEG, APRIL 1973 - JUNE 1979

US dollar Small[1]	French franc (All small)	Pound sterling (All small)
The Bahamas	Benin	Falkland Is.
Bahrain	Cameroon	The Gambia
Bermuda	Central Af. Rep.	Gibraltar
Bolivia	Comoros	Seychelles
Yemen PDR	Congo	St. Helena
Dominican Rep.	Fr. Guiana	
Ecuador	Fr. Polynesia	
El Salvador	Gabon	
Guatemala	Guadeloupe	
Haiti	Ivory Coast	
Honduras	Madagascar	
Liberia	Mali	
Libya	Martinique	
Neth. Antilles	New Caledonia	
Oman	New Hebrides	
Panama	Niger	
Paraguay	Reunion	
Somalia	Senegal	
Surinam	St. Pierre & Miq.	
U.A.E.	Togo	
Yemen A.R.	Upper Volta	

Large[2]

Afghanistan
Ethiopia
Iraq
Pakistan
Venezuela

[1]Under 10 million population. [2]Over 10 million population.

Source: UNDP/UNCTAD Project INT/75/015 (unpublished).

TABLE 5

ECONOMIC PERFORMANCE OF UNALTERED PEGGERS FOR
WHICH THE WORLD BANK REPORTS BASIC DATA

	Inflation Rate (1970-78)	Rate of Growth in GDP per capita (1960-78)
Small dollar-peggers		
Bolivia[m]	22.7	2.2
Dominican Rep.[m]	8.6	3.5
Ecuador[m]	14.8	4.3
El Salvador[m]	10.3	1.8
Guatemala[m]	10.8	2.9
Haiti[l]	12.2	0.2
Honduras[m]	8.0	1.1
Liberia[m]	9.7	2.0
Libya[o]	20.7	6.2
Panama[m]	7.5	2.9
Paraguay[m]	12.3	2.6
Somalia[l]	10.7	-0.5
Average[d] (excluding Libya)	11.6	2.1
United States	6.8	2.4
Small franc-peggers		
Benin[l]	7.4	0.4
Cameroon[m]	9.8	2.9
Central Af. Rep.[l]	9.0	0.7
Chad[l]	7.4	-1.0
Congo[m]	10.6	1.0
Ivory Coast[m]	13.9	2.5
Madagascar[l]	9.6	-0.3
Mali[l]	7.8	1.0
Niger[l]	10.7	-1.4
Senegal[l]	8.0	-0.4
Togo[l]	7.4	5.0
Upper Volta[l]	9.6	1.3
Average[a]	9.3	1.0
France	9.3	4.0
Average for all developing countries		
Low-income(l)	10.6	1.6
Middle-income (m)	13.1	3.7

[l]Low income, $360 per capita GNP in 1978 prices, and below.

[m]Middle income, from $361 to $3,500 per capita GNP in 1978 prices.

[o]Capital surplus oil exporter.

[a]Simple average.

Source: World Bank, World Development Report, pp.110-111.

178

(iii) external financing of import requirements and/or the running down of foreign exchange reserves .

There are limits to the possibilities of financing continued imports in the face of a decline in the purchasing power of exports, either through the use of reserves[12] or increased external borrowing; indeed much external financing must be considered by the policy-maker as totally exogenous. Unless new sources of stabilisation finance materialise, small countries subject to large external shocks will regularly therefore have to consider the alternatives of deflation and restructuring. Since there are inevitable lags in the responses of both producers and consumers to altered market incentives, real restructuring of output may take some time; controls over imports and other foreign payments, however, can take immediate effect. Also fairly quick to take effect, though not as quick as controls, are deflationary macro-economic (monetary and fiscal) policies.

Immediate policy response to external shock is therefore likely most frequently to take the forms of macro-economic policy 'tightening' and increased controls over external payments. The main policy issues have to do with whether investment or consumption will be cut, whether the cuts will be imposed on the private or the public sectors, and which particular groups, sectors or departments will bear the greatest cuts in real expenditure. Uncertainty as to the duration of the deterioration in the balance of external payments is also likely to delay somewhat the application of real restructuring policy (as opposed to 'temporary' controls or deflationary policies), except in circumstances - such as those of the oil price increases of 1979-80 - where its 'permanence' cannot be doubted.

There are obviously analogous policy issues associated with the upswings in the external account. 'Stop-go' phenomena therefore are typical of small economies' macro-economic experience. These could, in principle, be alleviated by the holding of adequate reserves, but in the case of most poor small countries this involves a price that policy-makers are unwilling or unable to pay.

Macro-economic Financial Management in Small Economies

Small size involves certain scale diseconomies in financial management. There is frequently 'lumpiness' about information systems and the managerial function, in that there is a minimum expenditure on these inputs below which the quality of such systems or management is likely to be severely deficient. Without up-to-the-minute information or the experience and expertise to know how best to respond to it, it is easy for local managers of foreign exchange reserves to experience unnecessary losses, or to forego available gains in what have become highly volatile foreign exchange and short-term money markets. If managerial or informational services are purchased from specialists there are again diseconomies of scale in the typical schedules of their charges. When cover is

179

sought by small countries' monetary managers against foreign exchange risks, they also face higher bid-ask spreads (charges) than those enjoyed by larger market participants. In general, transaction costs rise as a proportion of the value of transactions with declines in the absolute value of transactions.

Small size also renders it more difficult and/or costly to diversify one's financial portfolio. Particularly is this so in respect of external debt, in that small developing countries typically have limited control over its currency composition or therefore that of their current debt servicing obligations. Limited in their creditworthiness, they usually are able neither to choose the currencies in which they borrow nor to refinance their existing debt into different currencies. Single externally financed projects can leave small countries dangerously exposed to foreign exchange risk, since they do not have the advantages of the 'natural pooling' that derives from larger size. Recent reforms in the World Bank's financial management practices explicitly recognise this small-country problem: in 1980 the Bank introduced a currency-pooling system in which all Bank borrowers henceforth receive the same currency 'basket' instead of, as before, receiving currencies according to the chance circumstance of the Bank's recent borrowings and the decisions of its portfolio managers. Similar moves to reduce the potential currency exposure of small countries can shortly be expected in the Regional Development Banks as well.

For those small countries with diversified international transactions (by currency) but with difficulties or extra costs in acquiring and/or managing diversified financial portfolios, the use of 'basket' currencies in the denomination of contracts would be particularly helpful as a defence against currency fluctuations. The SDR is by no means the only possible such 'basket', and is clearly not optimal for all or even superior to existing national currencies for some, but it is the obvious candidate for increased use at the global level; IMF borrowing and lending is already denominated in SDRs, and there is no reason why many other trade and financial contracts could not also be so denominated. A recent report (Helleiner,1981) to the Group of Twenty-four put it as follows:

"The denomination of more trade and financial contracts in SDRs would reduce the degree of short-term exchange risk incurred by those developing countries with the least capacity to protect themselves against it. For those countries that already peg the value of their own currencies to that of the SDR, the use of SDR-denominated contracts would significantly reduce the short-term exchange risks of all private traders as well as of the country as a whole, and return individual and sectoral-specific exchange rates to the control of the monetary authorities. Increased availability of SDR-denominated contracts might thus also offer further impetus toward the pegging of national currencies to the SDR. As more developing countries pegged to the SDR, the short-term stability of their exchange rates vis-a-vis one another would also be stabilised".

SUMMARY AND CONCLUSIONS

To the extent that there are real social costs to instability and that small countries are disproportionately vulnerable to externally created shocks, regardless of their other characteristics, there is a special need for balance of payments financing in their case. In the absence of adequate balance of payments finance, small countries are particularly susceptible to 'stop-go' macro-economic policies and experiences. The holding of adequate external reserves and/or resort to commercial borrowing facilities can offset, to some degree, these characteristics; but, as has been seen, small countries face extra costs and risks in the employment of these options, where they are open to them at all.

On the other hand, significant 'small country effects' are still to be found in the flow of net resources to developing countries - in non-aid flows as well as aid flows - generating larger flows per capita to small developing countries than to large ones. For many small countries these regular extra capital flows probably more than compensate for the special costs of 'extra' macro-economic disturbances from external sources. For instance, the average difference in total annual resource receipts per capita between countries with a population under five millions and larger countries (seen in Table 2) translates, on reasonable assumptions, into extra capital flows as large as, or larger than, the former countries' average total annual imports. In addition, virtually all of the reforms of the international economic order which the Group of Seventy-seven pushes in the various arenas of the North-South dialogue are, in per capita terms, and other things being equal, of disproportionate value to the small countries.

International policies could be devised in recognition of the peculiar susceptibility of small countries to external shocks: e.g. by increasing their access to low-conditionality balance of payments financing facilities; providing them with more stable access to official development assistance via longer-term aid commitments; reducing their exposure to foreign exchange risk by denominating their financial and commercial contracts (where appropriate and desired) in terms of 'basket' currencies like the SDR; and assisting them to pool their financial information, skills and, in some cases, resources, to achieve scale economies in their utilisation. Since these countries already receive disproportionate help from abroad in some areas, such special forms of assistance are unlikely to be forthcoming purely in consequence of their 'smallness'. In those cases, however, where the need for special assistance is acknowledged on the basis of other criteria, notably that of poverty, 'smallness' might well constitute grounds for further special measures - which would be of relatively miniscule cost to foreign donors, but conceivably of quite significant assistance to poor small countries' national monetary authorities. Economic co-operation among small countries, particularly those with similar traditions, common language, geographic proximity, etc., can also be achieved - in macro-economic management (reserve and debt management, information pooling, research, etc.) as in all other fields -with or without external assistance.

NOTES

1. For a useful list of the usual characteristics of small countries, see Selwyn (1980, p. 946).

2. Calculated from Khatkhate and Short (1980, p. 1018).

3. In Luxembourg, the above ratios are over 80 per cent!

4. See also Erb and Schiavo-Campo (1969, pp. 272-5).

5. For example Brainard and Cooper (1968).

6. See OECD (1969, pp. 178-9); see also, in particular, Isenman (1976).

7. Calculated from IMF (1980, p. 83).

8. See IMF (IFS, March 1981).

9. See, for example, Lipschitz (1979); Helleiner (1981); and references cited therein.

10. Needless to say, the selection of any paticular peg does not preclude periodic readjustments of the value of one's currency in terms of the peg currency if the pursuit of macro-economic policy objectives seems to require it.

11. The trade infrastructures referred to are credit systems, information and marketing networks, shipping arrangements, etc.

12. The holding of reserves involves opportunity costs which are generally considered to be politically, if not economically, high.

REFERENCES

Askari, Hossain and Weil, Gordon, 1974, 'Stability of Export Earnings of Developing Countries'. In "Journal of Development Studies", Vol.II, No.1.

Aufricht, Hans, 1964, "The International Monetary Fund, Legal Bases, Structure, Functions", New York: Praeger.

Brodsky, David A. and Sampson, Gary P., 1980, 'Retained Value and the Export Performance of Developing Countries'. In "Journal of Development Studies", Vol.17, No.1.

Brainard, W.C. and Cooper, R.N., 1968, 'Uncertainty and Diversification in International Trade'. In "Food Research Institute Studies", (Stanford), Vol.8, No.3.

Chenery, Hollis and Syrquin, Moises, 1975, "Patterns of Development, 1950-1970", London: Oxford University Press.

Coppock, Joseph D., 1962, "International Economic Instability", New York: McGraw-Hill.

Dreyer, Jacob S., 1978, 'Determinants of Exchange-Rate Regimes for Currencies of Developing Countries: Some Preliminary Results'. In "World Development", Vol.6, No.4.

Erb, Guy F. and Schiavo-Campo, Salvatore, 1969, 'Export Instability, Level of Development and Economic Size of Less Developed Countries'. In "Oxford Bulletin of Economics and Statistics", Vol.31, No.4.

Glezakos, C., 1973, 'Export Instability and Economic Growth: A Statistical Verification'. In "Economic Development and Cultural Change", Vol. XXI, No.4.

Helleiner, G.K., 1981, "The Impact of the Exchange Rate System on the Developing Countries: Report to the Group of Twenty-four", UNDP/UNCTAD Project INT/75/015, UNCTAD/MFD/TA/13.

Heller, H. Robert, 1978, 'Determinants of Exchange Rate Practices'. In "Journal of Money, Credit and Banking", Vol.10, No.3.

International Monetary Fund, 1981, "International Financial Statistics", Vol.XXIV, No.3, Washington, D.C.
International Monetary Fund, 1980, "Annual Report", Washington, D.C.

Isenman, Paul, 1976, 'Biases in Aid Allocations Against Poorer and Larger Countries'. In "World Development", Vol.4, No.8.

Iyoha, Milton A., 1973, 'Inflation and 'Openness' in Less Developed Countries: A Cross-Country Analysis'. In "Economic Development and Cultural Change", Vol.22, No.1.

Khatkhate, Deena R. and Short, Brock K., 1980, 'Monetary and Central Banking Problems of Mini States'. In "World Development", Vol.8, No.12.

Knudsen, Odin and Parnes, Andrew, 1975, "Trade Instability and Economic Development", Lexington: D.C. Heath.

Kuznets, Simon, 1964, 'Quantitative Aspects of the Economic Growth of Nations: IX, Level and Structure of Foreign Trade: Comparisons for Recent Years'. In "Economic Development and Cultural Change", Vol.76, No.1, Part II.

Leff, Nathaniel and Sato, Kazuo, 1980, 'Macro-economic Adjustment in Developing Countries: Instability, Short-run Growth and External Dependency'. In "The Review of Economics and Statistics", Vol.LXII, No.2.

Lim, 1976, 'Export Instability and Economic Growth: A Return to Fundamentals'. In "Oxford Bulletin of Economics and Statistics", Vol.38, No.4.

Lipschitz, Leslie, 1979, "Exchange Rate Policy for a Small Developing Country, and the Selection of an Appropriate Standard", IMF Staff Papers, Vol.26, No.3, Washington, D.C.

MacBean, Alasdair, I., 1966, "Export Instability and Economic Development", London: George Allen and Unwin.

Massell, B.F., 1970, 'Export Instability and Economic
          Structure'. In "American Economic Review", Vol. LX,
          No.4.
Mathieson, D. and McKinnon, R., 1973, 'Instability in Under-
          developed Countries: The Impact of the International
          Economy'. In M. Reder and P. David, eds. "Essays in
          Honor of Moses Abramovitz", New York: Academic Press.
Michaely, M., 1962, "Concentration in International Trade",
          Amsterdam: North-Holland.
Naya, S., 1973, 'Fluctuations in Export Earnings and Economic
          Patterns of Asian Countries'. In "Economic Development
          and Cultural Change", Vol. XXI, No.4.
Organisation for Economic Co-operation and Development, 1969,
          "Development Assistance, Efforts and Policies of the
          Members of the Development Assistance Committee,
          Review", Paris.
_____, 1980 "Development Assistance, Efforts and Policies of
          the Members of the Development Assistance Committee,
          Review", Paris.
_____, 1980 "Development Co-operation", Paris.
Polak, J.J., 1957, "Monetary Analysis of Income Formation and
          Payments Problems", IMF Staff Papers, Vol.6 No.1.
Selwyn, Percy, 1980, 'Smallness and Islandness'. In "World Deve-
          lopment", Vol. 8, No.12.
Voivodas, C.S., 1974, 'The Effect of Foreign Exchange Insta-
          bility on Growth'. In "Review of Economics and
          Statistics", Vol.LVI, No.3.
The World Bank, 1980, "World Development Report", Washington,
          D.C.
The World Bank, 1980, "Annual Report", Washington, D.C.

10. Financial Sectors in Some Small Island Developing Economies

Maxwell J. Fry*

Size has an important impact on some economies' financial sectors. The financial sectors of 'tiny' economies differ radically from the financial sectors in larger economies. Specifically, they are generally dominated by foreign commercial banks and are invariably uncompetitive. Domestic financial institutions, where they exist in tiny economies, tend to be government-owned or joint ventures between the government and foreign banks. The explanation for all this lies in the fact that strong scale-economies exist in the banking industry.

Economies of scale can be exploited by multinational banks even in the smallest economy, provided only that the economy is large enough to support one bank branch. The minimum economic size is considerably smaller for branch viability than for de novo bank viability. A branch has recourse to head office services abroad, whereas a de novo bank must set these up itself within the economy.

This paper examines the financial sectors in a sample of two 'small' (population between one and five million) and nine 'tiny' (population under one million or 1979 gross national product of less than US$ 2½ billion) island economies. The sample was chosen on the basis of geographical spread - four from the Pacific, three from the Caribbean, two from the Indian Ocean, and two from Southeast Asia - and data availability. Table 1 gives 1979 population, per capita income and gross national product (GNP) for all the sample countries.

Financial sectors in this sample range from one of the most undeveloped monetary systems in the world, that of Maldives, to two of the most advanced, those of Hong Kong and Singapore. In all but these latter two economies (the two 'small' economies) and Papua New Guinea (a 'small' economy on the population criterion, but a 'tiny' economy on the basis of the GNP measure), the financial

---

*My thanks to Warren Coats, Vicente Galbis, Tony Hughes, Deena Khatkhate, Ian McCarthy, Rupert Mullings, Yuzuru Ozeki, Sukhdev Shah and Edward Shaw for their help.

TABLE 1

POPULATION, PER CAPITA GNP AND AGGREGATE GNP IN SAMPLE ECONOMIES
(1979)

Economy	Population (thousands)	Per Capita GNP (US dollars)	GNP (millions of US dollars)
The Bahamas	231	2,780	642
Barbados	253	2,400	607
Fiji	618	1,690	1,044
Hong Kong	4,671	4,000	18,684
Maldives	149	200	30
Papua New Guinea	3,000	650	1,950
St. Lucia	122	780	95
Seychelles	65	1,400	91
Singapore	2,368	3,820	9,046
Solomon Islands	219	440*	96
Western Samoa	158	420*	66
Total	11,854	2,729	32,351

* Estimate from a source other than that quoted.

Source: The World Bank, 1980, "World Bank Atlas", Washington, D.C.

sectors are dominated by branches or subsidiaries of foreign commercial banks. Indeed, five of the 'tiny' economies - The Bahamas, Maldives, Seychelles, Solomon Islands and Western Samoa - possess no purely domestic commercial banks.

A bird's eye view of the financial sectors in all the sample economies is presented in Tables 2 and 3. Of particular note is the fact that only Hong Kong and Singapore have any private joint stock domestic commercial banks. Barbados, Fiji and Papua New Guinea each have one government-owned domestic commercial bank and the governments of Solomon Islands and Western Samoa have both participated with a foreign commercial bank in the establishment of one domestic commercial bank. A government-sponsored co-operative bank exists in St. Lucia. In three of the sample countries - The Bahamas, Maldives and Seychelles - there are no domestic commercial banks and all banking business is undertaken by branches of foreign commercial banks.

Commercial banks dominate the financial sectors of all the sample economies except Hong Kong and, to a lesser extent, Singapore. The Bahamas and Papua New Guinea have a few savings and loan associations (S&Ls), Seychelles has the Government Savings Bank and there is a Post Office Savings Bank in Western Samoa. These are the only non-bank 'depository' institutions outside Hong Kong and Singapore in all the sample economies. Other non-bank financial intermediaries found in the sample economies include pension/provident funds, insurance companies, finance companies (depository institutions found only in Hong Kong), trust companies and stock exchanges (in Fiji, Hong Kong and Singapore). There are also government-owned development banks and/or similar developmental financial intermediaries in all the sample economies except Hong Kong and Maldives. Finally, five economies - The Bahamas, Barbados, Hong Kong, Seychelles and Singapore - have offshore banking. The operations in Barbados and Seychelles are still at an embryonic stage. The big offshore centres are located in The Bahamas, Hong Kong and Singapore.

As pointed out earlier, there is strong correlation between strength and breadth of these financial sectors and economy size. The financial sector in Maldives is rudimentary in the extreme and those in St. Lucia, Seychelles, Solomon Islands and Western Samoa are just one rung further up the ladder. Papua New Guinea has a marginally more extensive financial sector, despite the fact that its per capita income is about half that of Seychelles. Hong Kong and Singapore possess financial sectors comparable to any found in the western industrial countries. The correlation is caused by the economies of scale which exist in financial intermediation.

ROLE OF FINANCIAL INTERMEDIARIES

Financial intermediaries perform two major economic functions in almost all economies. First, they create money and administer the payments mechanism. This incurs social or resource costs. The resource cost of a commodity or full-bodied money equals the total

TABLE 2

FINANCIAL INTERMEDIARIES IN SAMPLE ECONOMIES

Economy	Monetary Authority	Commercial Banks Domestic	Foreign	Non-bank Financial Intermediaries
The Bahamas	Central Bank	0	11	4 S&Ls; 9 trust companies
Barbados	Central Bank	1 (government-owned, universal bank)	6	Trust companies
Fiji	Central Monetary Authority	1 (government-owned)	5	National Provident Fund; insurance companies; Unit Trust of Fiji
Hong Kong	Financial Secretary	32 (universal banks) (all private)	81	265 deposit taking companies; insurance companies; money and commodity brokers
Maldives	Department of Finance	0	2	None
Papua New Guinea	Central Bank	1 (government-owned)	3	S&L societies; 1 merchant bank
St. Lucia	Member of East Caribbean Currency Authority	1 (cooperative bank)	4	None
Seychelles	Monetary Authority	0	6	Government Savings Bank
Singapore	Monetary Authority and Board of Commissioners of Currency	12 (all private)	37	Central Provident Fund; Post Office Savings Bank; insurance companies
Solomon Islands	Monetary Authority	½ (government-owned)	2½	National Provident Fund
Western Samoa	Monetary Board	½ (government-owned)	1½	National Provident Fund; Post Office Savings Bank; Public Trust Office; insurance companies

value of the money supply. The costs of producing and maintaining fiat paper money rarely exceed five per cent annually of the value of notes outstanding. They comprise, in the main, costs of replacing worn notes, adding additional notes and preventing forgery. The costs solely of supplying and maintaining deposit money are far lower. They are only the book-keeping costs. The domestic or national resource cost of using a foreign fiat money, as in the case of Maldives' use of the US dollar as money in its tourist areas, is again the total value of the foreign currency in circulation (Drake, 1980).

The resource costs of administering the payments mechanism include the value of resources used up in the process of providing currency of desired denominations when and where it is wanted and in effecting deposit transfers. The Federal Reserve System, for example, incurs resource costs greater than the GNPs of several of

Economy	Government-owned Development Banks	Institutional Interest Rate Setting Procedure	Offshore Banks	Remarks
The Bahamas	0	No formal controls but bank cartel fixes rates in consultation with central bank	263	
Barbados	1	Minimum deposit rates and maximum weighted-average loan rate set by central bank	1	Some private companies and individuals borrow and lend directly without going through financial intermediaries because of wide spread
Fiji	1	Maximum deposit and loan rates established with approval of Ministry of Finance	0	Stock exchange established in 1979. Eight companies listed by June 1980
Hong Kong	0	Maximum deposit rates fixed by bank cartel led by Hong Kong and Shanghai Bank	378	Hong Kong and Shanghai Bank performs several central bank functions. Currency notes are issued by commercial banks which are universal banks in character
Maldives	0	No controls. Loan rate is based on New York prime plus 1½ per cent. Bank cartel suspected	0	Maldives Monetary Authority is due to be set up
Papua New Guinea	2	Rediscount rate and moral suasion used by central bank to influence deposit and loan rates. Bank cartel suspected	0	
St. Lucia	4	No control. Bank cartel suspected	0	
Seychelles	1	Prime rate fixed by Monetary Authority. Maxima and minima for deposit and loan rates set by bank cartel in consultation with Monetary Authority	1	
Singapore	1	All interest rates are determined competitively in a free market. Bank cartel was abolished in 1975.	70	
Solomon Islands	2	Monetary Authority fixes deposit rates and minimum and maximum loan rates	0	The post office sells 3-year government national savings certificates. 5-year government development bonds are sold through Monetary Authority and commercial banks
Western Samoa	1	Government fixes all institutional interest rates. Highly selective credit policy is pursued	0	The Bank of Western Samoa is owned jointly by the government and a New Zealand commercial bank

the sample countries in running the national cheque clearing system in the United States.

For various reasons, a country may not possess the most efficient money and payments system. The government may be using money issue as a stop-gap, inefficient revenue source. There may be legal and/or regulatory constraints preventing the adoption of such technological innovations as the electronic transfer of funds. A country may choose to produce its currency notes domestically, despite the lower costs of notes printed abroad. Similarly, foreign banks could be excluded in favour of indigenous enterprise, despite the fact that multinational banks might bring in technical know-how at very low marginal cost, stimulate competition and facilitate the inflow of foreign capital (Grubel, 1977). Infant-industry, dependency or nationalistic arguments would be used to justify the deliberate choice of less than maximum possible economic efficiency in such a case.

Inefficiency may also be unintentional. This is likely to occur with respect to the supply and maintenance of deposit money when the deposit industry is not behaving competitively. Uncompetitive behaviour may be the result of economies of scale: in a very small economy, the banking industry may simply be a natural monopoly. More typically, however, uncompetitive behaviour is caused by reserve requirements and/or interest rate controls.

Reserve requirements and binding ceilings on rates impose a private cost on deposit suppliers. They involve no resource cost. Hence, total private costs of supplying deposits will exceed the resource or social costs and the supply of deposit money will be sub-optimal. Even if required reserve ratios are deemed necessary for prudential or monetary policy purposes, the welfare distortions can be removed completely by paying a competitive interest rate on required reserves (Fry, 1979a). The main welfare costs of deposit and loan rate ceilings spring not from their effect on the supply of deposits but rather from their impact on financial intermediation between savers and investors. It is to this second major function of financial intermediaries that this paper now turns.

Intermediating between savers and investors differentiates financial institutions from all other business enterprises. On the one hand, financial intermediaries' assets consist predominantly of financial claims or financial instruments, i.e. claims against other economic units or ownership in them. On the other hand, financial intermediaries offer their own financial instruments to the public and to other economic enterprises. Banks offer deposits - passbook entries or deposit receipts - which represent claims against the bank. Other financial intermediaries offer insurance, pensions, bonds, etc. In each case, a claim is created against the issuer. But the claim may be contingent upon special conditions - death or an accident, reaching retirement age, etc.

Financial intermediaries must attract lenders (depositors or savers) and borrowers (investors) by offering financial claims which are more attractive to savers than those offered directly by investors, and by offering more attractive loan arrangements than investors can get directly from savers. Financial intermediaries can raise the net return to savers and lower the gross cost to investors through specialisation and by reaping the economies of scale in financial transactions, information gathering and portfolio management.

Financial intermediaries emerge and survive if and only if their indirect claims can compete successfully with the market for direct claims. This is dependent, in turn, on their ability to reduce search costs and risk, on the one hand, and the costs of so doing, on the other. It is to the efficiency of financial intermediation that the paper now turns.

RESOURCE MOBILISATION AND ALLOCATION

Various indirect methods exist for evaluating the efficiency of financial intermediation. Ceteris paribus, unit resource costs of intermediation between savers and investors would be associated negatively with efficiency. However, it is crucial here to measure resource costs of transferring funds from original savers to final investors. Unit resource costs per financial intermediary may be very misleading if, as is the case in India, for example, there is much financial layering, i.e. one financial intermediary borrowing from another financial intermediary which, in turn, borrows from yet another. In this case, unit resource costs of each financial intermediary must be summed to produce the total intermediation cost between savers and investors.

Taking financial layering into account, costs of financial intermediation might be measured at the micro level by assessing the resource costs associated with lending for new investment from an increase in available funds, i.e. from saving. In practice, total operating costs - wages, depreciation, intermediate input costs, e.g. computer expenses, advertising, etc. - as a percentage of total earning assets may serve as a reasonably proxy. Ceteris paribus, the lower this percentage, the smaller will be the spread between net returns to savers and gross costs to investors. Higher net returns to savers and lower gross costs to investors may increase both saving and investment and, hence, the rate of economic growth.

Operating resource costs have been high and rising in several of the sample economies. The explanation lies in (i) interest rate ceilings; (ii) an oligopolistic and cartelised industry; (iii) accelerating inflation; and (iv) high and rising reserve requirements. Deposit rates of interest administratively fixed below their market equilibrium levels cause banks to substitute non-price for price competition. As inflation accelerates, the gap between the free competitive market equilibrium deposit rate and the fixed ceilings widens. The result is even higher levels of expenditure on non-price competition.

Expenditure by depository institutions on non-price competition has nowhere been valued by depositors at par with interest payments. The evidence comes from money demand estimates which invariably show that real money demand is associated positively with the real deposit rate of interest, i.e. the nominal deposit rate minus expected inflation. Money is always defined here broadly to include savings, time and post office deposits, as well as currency in circulation and sight deposits.

Non-price competition incurs resource costs while price competition in the form of higher deposit rates does not. Interest is a transfer payment and involves no resource cost. This distinction would not matter from the welfare standpoint were the resource costs of non-price competition valued at par by depositors. Since, clearly, they are not, there is resource misallocation when depository institutions are forced to substitute non-price for price competition.

Deposit rate ceilings tend to encourage and condone bank cartels. Overt banking cartels for interest rate setting exist in The Bahamas, Hong Kong and Seychelles, among the sample countries, as shown in Table 3. Cartels tend to raise operating resource costs, so reducing the efficiency of financial intermediation.

Accelerating inflation combined with fixed or sticky nominal deposit rates of interest reduces real money demand and, hence, the real volume of resources at the disposal of the financial intermediaries. The nominal volume of deposits fails to increase in step with nominal GNP, perhaps not even in step with inflation itself, as inflation accelerates. Bank operating costs, on the other hand, do tend to rise in step with nominal GNP. Hence, as a percentage of earning assets, operating resource costs increase.

Higher reserve requirements raise bank operating costs. Ignoring bank capital and excess reserves, earning assets equal deposit liabilities when required reserves are zero. Suppose resource costs of maintaining deposits are two per cent of total deposits and costs of servicing the asset portfolio are three per cent. In this case, the overall bank operating cost ratio is simply five per cent. Now consider what happens when a required reserve ratio of 50 per cent is imposed. For the same deposit volume, the earning assets are halved. The calculated overall bank operating cost ratio is now three per cent for earning assets, but resource costs for maintaining a volume of deposits twice the size of the earning asset portfolio are four per cent of earning assets. Hence, the overall bank operating cost ratio is now seven per cent.

In addition to operating resource costs which drive a wedge between financial intermediaries' lending and borrowing rates, discriminatory taxation of financial intermediation must be considered. Required reserves are themselves a form of taxation on financial intermediation. Suppose earning assets yield an average return of twelve per cent. Again ignoring excess reserves and capital, financial intermediaries could just offer seven per cent on deposit liabilities and break even, given resource costs of two per cent for deposits and three per cent for earning assets, as in the example above, when the required reserve ratio is zero.

Now introduce a 50 per cent reserve requirement. The resource costs rise to seven per cent of earning assets and the net yield on earning assets of five per cent has to be spread over deposits twice the size of these assets. Hence, the average deposit rate is reduced from seven to $2\frac{1}{2}$ per cent. The spread between lending and borrowing rates has widened from five per cent (the operating cost ratio), with zero required reserves, to $9\frac{1}{2}$ per cent. The 50 per cent reserve requirement effectively imposes a tax on deposits of $2\frac{1}{2}$ per cent.

The reserve requirement tax increases as inflation accelerates. Suppose inflation rises from zero to ten per cent and earning assets now yield an average return of 22 per cent (twelve per cent plus the ten per cent inflation adjustment). Ceteris paribus, financial intermediaries will be able to offer a maximum deposit rate of $7\frac{1}{2}$ per cent - 22 minus 7, the result divided by two. The 50 per cent reserve requirement now imposes an effective tax on deposits of $7\frac{1}{2}$ per cent. And it has reduced the real return on deposits from +$2\frac{1}{2}$ per cent to -$2\frac{1}{2}$ per cent. Naturally, savers are deterred by the substantial decline in their real return. Real money demand and, hence, the real volume of financial intermediation will fall. This, in turn, raises the operating resource cost ratio, since financial intermediation is subject to economies of scale.

Conventional taxes - interest withholding taxes, stamp duties, transactions taxes, value-added taxes, profit taxes, licence fees, etc. - all widen the competitive spread between financial intermediaries' borrowing and lending rates. They, therefore, have exactly the same effect on the real volume of financial intermediation, saving and investment as do higher operating resource costs.

If one of the objectives of an economic development plan is to encourage domestic resource mobilisation, then discriminatory taxes - conventional as well as reserve requirements - on financial intermediation should be removed. At the same time, bank cartels must be destroyed and financial intermediaries made to behave competitively. The optimal competitive solution might have to be forced upon some of the sample countries' cartelised and/or oligopolistic financial systems by fixing minimum deposit rates of interest and obliging depository institutions to satisfy all deposit demand at these rates. This would be the only control needed to produce the competitive result, provided loan demand were elastic at rates above the competitive loan rates of interest (Fry, 1980b). Minimum deposit rates are clearly preferred to licence fees as a means of tapping monopoly profit. Barbados is the only economy in the sample in which minimum deposit rates are set.

The easiest way to establish and then maintain a real deposit rate approximating to the competitive rate is deposit indexation. Depository institutions could be directed to adjust nominal deposit values by the change in an appropriate index at regular intervals. For most of the sample economies, the best index might be calculated from trade-weighted average government bond yields in industrialised countries adjusted for any change in the value of the domestic currency vis-a-vis this currency basket. For example, the exchange rate might start at Rs5 to B1, where Rs represents the domestic currency and B is the trade-weighted currency basket. Over the subsequent month, foreign government bond yields average 0.75 per cent (as a monthly rate). In this case, the index moves from 100.00 to 100.75. If the exchange rate had depreciated from Rs5 to B1 to Rs5.10 to B1, then the index becomes 102.765, i.e. 5.10 divided by five, the result multiplied by 100.75.

Now financial intermediaries would adjust all deposit values by the change in the index every month. A balance of Rs.10,000 is adjusted automatically to Rs.10,276.50. Any nominal interest offered, say, on longer-term deposits would be paid on the adjusted deposit value. Depositors know in advance that they will be compensated for subsequent price changes. Hence, their own expectations regarding the future inflation rate are now irrelevant to their deposit holding decisions. And the real deposit rate equals whatever nominal rate is paid on the adjusted deposit value plus the trade-weighted average real government bond yield abroad. The latter has tended to remain remarkably stable over the long-run in most industrial countries.

Efficiency of financial intermediation is affected positively by economy size for two reasons. First, a large economy can support a large financial intermediary and there are economies of scale to financial intermediation (Baltensperger, 1972). Secondly, there is more potential for competition in a larger than in a smaller economy. Whether or not that potential is realised depends on the legal and regulatory environment in which the financial intermediaries operate. All one can conclude here is that it is probably impossible under any circumstances for Maldives to attain as great an efficiency of financial intermediation as, say, Hong Kong or Singapore.

Apart from constraints imposed by economy size, however, monetary authorities can have considerable influence over financial intermediaries' operating efficiency. No matter how small the economy, competitive conditions can be simulated through minimum deposit rates. All other interest rate regulations can be dismantled.

Domestic inflation in all the sample countries is determined by exchange rate policy. In today's inflationary world, gradual appreciation of the domestic currency vis-a-vis a trade-weighted currency basket is needed to ensure price stability. Papua New Guinea, Singapore, Solomon Islands and Western Samoa have all opted for below-average inflation rates over the past quinquennium by means of domestic currency appreciation. Aside from other benefits of price stability, there is, ceteris paribus, greater efficiency of financial intermediation.

Reserve requirements do not constitute an instrument of monetary control in any of the sample countries. The nominal money supply is an endogenous variable determined inter alia by exchange rate policy. However, reserve requirements can and do extract seigniorage from financial intermediaries subject to them. They are a discriminatory tax which increases the spread between financial intermediaries' lending and borrowing rates. In turn, this greater spread reduces the aggregate size of the financial sector and so may raise operating resource cost ratios. In addition, of course, reserve requirements ensure a divergence between private and social or resource costs and, hence, produce a sub-optimal level of financial intermediation. If required reserves are deemed essential on prudential grounds, they should receive a competitive market return (Fry, 1979a).

Maldives and Solomon Islands have no regulations pertaining to financial intermediaries' asset portfolios. Hong Kong and Papua New Guinea set no required reserve ratios but do impose minimum liquid asset ratios. In effect, this is almost the same as paying a competitive interest rate on required reserves. Liquid assets are defined broadly in Hong Kong and the regulation has several loopholes which render it ineffective, while financial intermediaries in Papua New Guinea typically hold liquid assets far in excess of the requirements.

Of the remaining economies in the sample, all of which do impose cash reserve requirements on their financial intermediaries, only Fiji pays any interest - $3\frac{1}{2}$ per cent - on required but not excess reserves held on deposit with the Central Monetary Authority. However, the reserve requirement in Western Samoa imposes no net tax on the financial intermediaries as a group because the reserves deposited with the Monetary Board are redeposited with one of the two commercial banks. Hence, its sole impact is to redistribute income from the newer bank - the Pacific

Commercial Bank - to the commercial bank which actually issues Western Samoa's currency - the Bank of Western Samoa, in which the government has 50 per cent ownership.

The remaining five economies in the sample could raise the efficiency as well as the quantity of financial intermediation from sub-optimal towards optimal levels by paying a market rate of interest on required reserves, substituting a liberally-defined liquid asset ratio for the required reserve ratio, or simply abolishing reserve requirements altogether.

Only intra-marginal taxes tapping purely consumer or producer surpluses, e.g. a poll tax, produce no economic distortions. And it turns out that several of the sample economies effectively impose intra-marginal taxes on money holders. Table 4 gives the current structure of deposit rates of interest and the average inflation rate, as measured by the consumer price index over the period 1978-1980, for eight of the sample economies. In only one of these - Singapore - were deposit rates determined competitively in a free market. And in only one of these economies - Singapore - were real deposit rates of interest positive on average over the period 1978-1980.

Of significance here is the fact that the term structures of deposit rates in Fiji, Papua New Guinea, Seychelles and Western Samoa are steeply rising. This indicates neither strong liquidity preference nor high marginal rates of time preference - these structures are imposed solely from the supply side. What they do approximate, however, is a monopolist's profit-maximising strategy through product differentiation (Fry, 1981d).

The problem can be viewed as one of minimising the cost of generating a given real money demand (Fry, 1978a). Given the inflation rate and the real money demand target, interest costs will be minimised by paying zero or low nominal rates on sight and short-term deposits, for which there are no close substitutes, and higher rates on longer-term deposits, for which closer substitutes in the form of tangible inflation hedges do exist. To stabilise the aggregate real money demand in the face of volatile inflation, the nominal rates of longer-term time deposits must be adjusted continuously in step with changes in inflationary expectations. In other words, the real deposit rate on long-term deposits has to be held constant. Therefore, the term structure has to be tilted more, the higher is the expected rate of inflation.

Whether the appropriate real rate on long-term deposits is negative, positive or zero depends on the volume of real money demand to be generated. In a growing or potentially growing economy, the basic objective of accelerating economic growth would necessitate positive real long-term time deposit rates in order to maximise the real supply of domestic credit, one of the main assets backing deposit liabilities of the financial intermediaries. Positive real long-term deposit rates also deter socially inefficient currency substitution and excessive foreign borrowing, both of which may well involve unnecessary resource costs borne entirely by the small island developing economy (Fry, 1980d).

TABLE 4

TABLE 4

DEPOSIT RATES OF INTEREST AND INFLATION

(per cent)

Economy (Date Introduced)	Deposit Maturity					Inflation (1978-80)
	Savings	3 mth	6 mth	12 mth	2-3 yr	
The Bahamas (1980 IV)	6.39	7.74	7.98	8.11	8.56	9.1
Barbados (3/1980)	3.0-5.0	3.5-4.5	3.8-5.0	4.0-5.5	-	13.5
Fiji (9/1980)	4.5	5.5	6.25	7.0	8.0-8.5	9.2
Papua New Guinea (12/1979)	3.75	4.75-7.2	-	5.5-7.5	-	7.6
Seychelles (5/1980)	6.5-8.0	8.0	8.5	9.0	10.0	12.6
Singapore (3/1980)	7.52	8.79	8.80	8.56	-	5.8
Solomon Islands (9/1980)	4.0	5.75-6.0	6.5	-	-	9.1
Western Samoa (6/1979)	4.0	6.5	7.0	8.0	8.5	13.8

Sources: The Central Bank of The Bahamas, 1980, "Quarterly Review", Vol.7, No.4
Nassau, The Bahamas; Central Bank of Barbados, 1980, "Economic and
Financial Statistics", Bridgetown, Barbados; and International
Monetary Fund, "International Financial Statistics", various issues,
Washington, D.C.

From another viewpoint, a greater inflation tax is levied on current and short-term deposits, for which there are no close substitutes, while a smaller tax is extracted from deposits for which closer substitutes do exist. Monopolistic product differentiation is designed to tap consumer surplus, in this case from savers. The tax is used in some of the sample economies as one source of credit subsidy for priority sectors. It is also absorbed in the high administrative costs of the uncompetitive financial sectors found in all these economies, with the exception of Singapore.

Governments of most of the sample economies appear to behave as if they were subject to two conflicting objectives. On the one hand, they are anxious to mobilise domestic resources by offering attractive returns to savers. On the other hand, they wish to finance their own sometimes considerable borrowing requirements as cheaply as possible. Furthermore, some of these governments - excluding those of The Bahamas, Hong Kong, Maldives and Singapore - clearly believe that priority groups, sectors and regions need cheap credit.

These objectives may indeed conflict when the subsidies for government and other priority borrowers are paid by deposit holders. A proportional tax on all deposits to be spread proportionally among borrowers would have no effect at all, provided that interest rates were adjusted upwards by exactly the amount of the tax/subsidy; free-market interest rates would make this adjustment automatically. Were rates not adjusted, the quantity of deposits demanded, i.e. lending, would decline.

The two objectives need not conflict, however, were the tax on deposit holders levied as a poll tax or in the form of any alternative intra-marginal tax which tapped only consumer surplus. The monopolistic price discrimination in terms of the present structures of deposit yields in Fiji, Papua New Guinea, Seychelles and Western Samoa do seem, in principle, capable of tapping consumer surplus without reducing aggregate real money demand. Unfortunately, the rigidity of the structure of nominal institutional interest rates produces money demand fluctuations _pari passu_ with changes in inflationary expectations. Indexation of long-term deposits to a price index would introduce the necessary flexibility in effective nominal rates to allow consumer surplus to be tapped without reducing real money demand in the face of rising inflationary expectations.

Concern over the efficiency of financial intermediation might appear unwarranted were saving completely interest-inelastic. If, however, saving is responsive to the net real yield on indirect claims, then reducing the spread between financial intermediaries' lending and borrowing rates will increase saving, investment and the rate of economic growth. The present author has conducted empirical tests on a number of developing countries. In all cases, the results are consistent with the hypothesis that national saving rates are affected positively and significantly by the real deposit rate of interest (Abe et al., 1977; Fry, 1976a; 1978b; 1979b; 1980a; 1981a; 1981b; Fry and Farhi, 1979; Fry and Mason, 1981).

Financial intermediaries can be evaluated not only in terms of their efficiency in mobilising resources but also on the basis of their efficiency in allocating resources. The majority of governments in the sample economies evidently believe that the financial intermediaries cannot and/or do not allocate resources efficiently. In the majority of the sample - the exceptions include The.Bahamas, Hong Kong, Maldives and Singapore - governments intervene by means of selective credit policies, involving credit rationing at low interest rates, aimed at influencing deliberately the allocation of resources by the financial intermediaries.

Selective credit policies invariably involve ceilings applied to institutional loan rates of interest. Loan rate ceilings deter productive risk-taking on the part of financial intermediaries (Fry, 1981c). Hence, a low interest rate policy reduces both the quantity and the average efficiency of investment. In a number of empirical studies (Fry, 1978b; 1978c; 1979b; 1980a; 1981a; 1981b; 1981e; Fry and Farhi, 1979; Fry and Mason, 1981), the present author found that investment efficiency as measured by incremental output/capital ratios was positively and significantly correlated to the real deposit rate of interest. Quantitatively, economic growth seems to be reduced through lower volume and efficiency of investment by about one half of a percentage point for every percentage point by which the deposit rate is set below its competitive, free-market equilibrium level (Fry, 1980a; 1981b). Productive risk-taking may well be doubly deterred in tiny economies where financial intermediaries are unable to diversify optimally their asset portfolios.

In fact, nationalised financial intermediaries are often directed to take risks and to extend small loans which are more expensive than larger loans to administer without regard to compensating returns. For example, the overall costs -including expected delinquency and default costs - of providing credit to small farmers in India averages $2\frac{1}{4}$ percentage points more than the cost of providing credit to large farmers. Consequently, smaller farmers are subsidised to a greater extent than larger ones, even with a uniform loan rate.

The result of disregarding risk completely has been serious levels of delinquency and default in the loan port-folios of many public sector financial intermediaries. For example, about 50 per cent of India's land development banks' loans are del inquent. When the distinction between a loan and a gift becomes blurred, collection of loans by other financial intermediaries is affected. Private money lending in rural areas of India has declined dramatically in recent years, due in part to increasing collection difficulties. Similar problems of unacceptably high delinquency and default rates on priority loans extended by government-owned financial intermediaries exist elsewhere, e.g. in Indonesia, Korea, Nepal and Western Samoa. Half of the Development Bank of Western Samoa's agricultural loans have had to be rescheduled.

Ultimately, the costs of high delinquency and default rates are borne by depositors. Hence, they reduce the aggregate real supply of loanable funds. At the same time, delinquency and default rates of the magnitudes found, for example, in India, Indonesia, Korea, Nepal and Western Samoa reflect adversely on both the administrative and allocative efficiency of the public sector financial intermediaries. Of course, risks are an inherent part of the process of economic development. But performance criteria should promote profitable, productive risk-taking and deter mere indiscriminate lending.

The optimal solution to loan rates is the abolition of ceiling and the abandonment of selective credit policies. If certain economic sectors are to be subsidised, subsidies could be given in fiscal form rather than through low interest rates. Ministries of Finance object that this raises Budget expenditures. In fact, however, the cost of the fiscal subsidy can be identical to that of the interest rate subsidy. The tax which financed the interest rate subsidy, i.e. deposit rates held below their market equilibrium levels, can finance a direct fiscal subsidy or grant instead. Preferably, the tax system would be reformed at the same time so that the implicit deposit tax - a socially inefficient tax on saving - is dropped in favour of another tax which is not so inefficient. Fiscal subsidy has two other advantages. It can be confined more easily to the priority activity itself and it need not distort factor prices. Labour as well as capital can be subsidised.

An appropriate legal framework together with price stability are two basic prerequisites for promoting efficient financial intermediation. The legal framework will determine, in large part, the structure of the financial sector. Khatkhate and Riechel (1980) point out the drawbacks of banking laws which enforce specialisation:

In developing countries, demand for even basic financial services has often not yet been appropriately articulated. In such situations, it appears desirable to generate through official intervention such special sources of supply that can meet socially desirable, albeit partially dormant, private demand. For this purpose, developing countries have often established new specialised financial institutions to satisfy the previously unmet demand. Operations of such institutions are generally insulated from competition by appropriate legislation and are even given substantial subsidies. Such actions are often defended by arguments that resemble those employed in the infant industry advocacy. However, the efficiency gains expected from such specialised and protected institutions are unlikely to be realised, because the necessary competitive conditions are often absent. In fact, a specialised institution created by special statute often assumes a monopoly position. The establishment of a special institution can be justified only if it will expand the overall size of the financial sector, widen its spectrum of financial services, and <u>reduce</u> the degree of concentration. In order to accomplish these goals, the new institution needs to be broadly based and, after the infancy phase is over, needs to be exposed to competitive forces across the board.
(pp.504-505.)
The foregoing analysis suggests that the fragmentation of the financial sector that follows from legislated specialisation tends to produce two undesirable consequences: a decline in overall efficiency and an increase in the degree of concentration.
(Ibid., p.502.)

Khatkhate and Riechel advocate multi-purpose or universal banking, citing the German experience as an object lesson for most developing economies, in particular small ones (ibid.). Legislative and regulatory changes are required in most of the sample economies, with the notable exception of Hong Kong which already has a universal banking system, to permit multi-purpose banking.

Four benefits can be derived by switching from specialised to universal banking: (i) improved economic efficiency; (ii) more long-term capital; (iii) promotion of entrepreneurship; and (iv) greater financial stability. Efficiency can be raised through the adoption of a universal banking system, which can reap greater economies of scale, be more responsive to changing demands and, at the same time, exhibit increased competitiveness and reduced concentration (ibid.).

Universal banks can supply both short- and long-term capital from resources mobilised directly from savers. Specialised development banks - the only suppliers of long-term funds under a specialised system - invariably get most of their resources from other financial intermediaries, e.g. the central bank. Not only does this create inefficient financial layering, it also results almost always in an acute shortage of long-term investible funds.

Universal banks can be expected and encouraged to promote entrepreneurship, as they did during Germany's industrialisation, by offering packages of credit combined with managerial and technical assistance, much as the World Bank does today.

Finally, multi-purpose banks may well be less prone to financial instability than specialised financial intermediaries. Scale-economies enable them to acquire more information cheaper, transform more short-term liabilities into longer-term assets and diversify their portfolios to greater extents than can smaller, specialised banks (ibid.).

A move towards universal banking has already started in the western industrial countries, as well as in a few developing countries:

> ... many other developing countries ... sorely disappointed by a lack of long-term financing for development programmes ... are following the richer world's example. They are going down the path of universal banking.
> (The Economist, 1981, p.96.)

The major potential danger of universal banking, a system under which financial intermediaries are permitted to acquire equity interests in their borrowers, lies in the conflict-of-interest issue. However, appropriate legislation can confront this potential problem in advance:

> ... conflict-of-interest situations and the prevalence of excessive market power require legislation, like antitrust laws, oriented toward tackling these problems directly rather than indirectly through a narrowing of the range of activities a financial institution can cover. The possibility that such unsavory practices may recur should not be taken as a pretext to devise a straightjacket of banking legislation that would destroy the responsiveness, flexibility, versatility, and the dynamism of the financial system.
> (Khatkhate and Riechel, 1980, p.513.)

The case for a legislative framework conducive to the development of universal banking is strong. For small island developing economies the case for encouraging, without discriminatory taxes, large, reputable foreign banks to help develop a universal banking system is even stronger.

A competitive banking system is imperative for financial development. Setting <u>minimum</u> deposit rates of interest has already been suggested as a device which might be used to force uncompetitive banking systems to seek out borrowers in a competitive manner. At the same time, interest rate flexibility has been advocated to prevent falling money demand from exacerbating inflationary pressures created, for example, by monetary accommodation of exogenous supply shocks.

The two proposals could be combined through the introduction of an indexed negotiable certificate of deposit (NCD) of, say, five-year maturity. Banks might be obliged to offer these NCDs, whose principals would be indexed. At redemption, the face value of the NCD would be adjusted by the cumulative change in the price index adopted. Annual interest payments of, say, three per cent would also be adjusted by the same index.

These NCDs may serve three purposes. First, they lengthen the maturity of bank's liability portfolios, so enabling the banks to increase their medium- and long-term lending activities without undue risk. Secondly, trading in NCDs produces a simple market in which experience with a market-determined yield can be gained with minimum risk.

The third function of the NCDs is to stabilise aggregate real money demand in the face of volatile inflation. To understand this point, one might assume that savings can be distributed among four assets - currency in circulation, C, demand deposits, D, negotiable certificates of deposit, T, and unproductive tangible assets held as inflation hedges, A. If C,D,T and A possess just two attributes - return and liquidity - the ranking by return must necessarily be identical to the ranking by illiquidity. In this case, it can be shown that substitution will take place only between adjacent assets (Barrett, Gray and Parkin, 1975). This means that the demand for A is determined only by r_A, the real return on A, and r_T, the real return on T. Hence, aggregate real money demand too is a function only of r_A and r_T. Returns on C and D will affect the composition of the money stock, but not the aggregate real demand for money (Fry, 1978a). Evidently, real money demand can be stabilised by holding just the difference between r_A and r_T constant. This is exactly what the untaxed indexation of NCDs or time deposits achieves (Bhatia, 1974).

Deposit indexation may be a radical reform because it breaches, where they exist, nominal interest rate ceilings. The main benefits of deposit indexation imposed on a non-competitive banking system are: (i) it stabilises real money demand (Simkin, 1978); (ii) it forces financial intermediaries to behave competitively in their search for borrowers; and (iii) it enables long-term lending to continue under conditions of volatile inflation (Bhatia, 1974).

Loan indexation might also be considered, particularly in high inflation countries. The point of indexing medium- and long-term loans is to lengthen their effective maturities. High inflation and concomitant high nominal loan rates reduce effective maturities by requiring borrowers to accelerate repayment of principal. The high nominal loan rates simply compensate for the fall in the real value of the principal outstanding. Hence, they can be viewed in real terms as accelerated principal repayments (Fry, 1980c).

The indexed NCDs might be the first step towards the complete abolition of interest rate ceilings, where they exist. The introduction of indexed NCDs would necessitate the maintenance of positive real rates for <u>all</u> loan rates of interest to prevent 'round-tripping', i.e. borrowing at subsidised rates simply to acquire the attractive-yielding NCDs. The primary beneficiaries of such tandem interest rate reform would be small- and medium-size business enterprises. Indirectly, of course, everyone would gain from the resulting lower rate of inflation and higher rate of economic growth.

FOREIGN BANKS

In unit banking states in the United States, there was one bank for every US$65 million of 1979 GNP. However, these banks can and do share services, such as computer facilities, etc., so enabling them to reap the benefits of scale-economies. Furthermore, they can easily purchase intermediate inputs such as cheque books from specialised firms supplying the US banking industry as a whole. Labour costs of all insured banks in the United States were 1.6 per cent of their earning assets in 1976. The comparable figure for Turkey, for example, was 5.8 per cent. Unit labour costs of banking in the United States cannot, therefore, be presumed to exceed unit labour costs of banking in any of the sample countries.

From all this, one might accept that the minimum economy size needed to support one viable <u>de novo</u> domestic bank would be a 1979 GNP of at least US$100 million. This implies that not even one private domestic bank could survive without government subsidy in Maldives, St. Lucia, Seychelles, Solomon Islands and Western Samoa (the very tiny economies of the sample). On this estimate, The Bahamas and Barbados could support six each, Fiji ten and Papua New Guinea 20 private domestic banks, provided each bank had only one branch.

The estimate for Papua New Guinea brings home the fact that not only is economy size crucial but so also is expertise. Qualified personnel to run 20 private domestic banks in Papua New Guinea is just not available there. Even with adequate economy sizes, Afghanistan and Nepal illustrate well the problems of establishing and maintaining all-domestic financial sectors without a sufficient supply of trained personnel. Specifically, foreign trade financing constituted a serious impediment to foreign trade in these countries. The banks could not be relied upon to execute correctly even such standard operations as opening letters of credit (Fry, 1974a; 1974b; 1976b; 1978c). Foreign banks tend to have strong comparative advantages in terms of expertise and experience in foreign trade finance. For some of the sample economies, size, training and know-how deficiencies leave no room for choice. Either financial inter-mediation is undertaken by foreign banks or there will be none at all.

Grubel (1977) has provided probably the most comprehensive framework with which to assess the benefits and costs of permitting foreign banks to establish branches in countries where a choice is actually possible (also see Drake, 1980). Grubel (1977) suggests that the main advantages to be measured are: (i) increased competition forced on domestic financial intermediaries which would form an oligopolistic if not cartelised industry in the absence of foreign banks; (ii) the importation and use of existing stocks of knowledge, capital or know-how at a very low marginal cost; and (iii) increased efficiency of international capital flows.

The potential disadvantages which should be considered include: (i) inefficiency in resource mobilisation and allocation resulting from unfamiliarity with local conditions; (ii) export of national saving to the country of origin resulting again from unfamiliarity with or unresponsiveness to local conditions; (iii) formation of a foreign bank cartel which dictates or thwarts monetary policy measures; and (iv) increased difficulty of starting a domestic bank when foreign banks are well established and hold all the best accounts.

The four potential disadvantages listed above can be realised and magnified all too easily by inappropriate laws and regulations. Inefficient resource mobilisation and allocation is assured when the monetary authority sets binding deposit and loan rate ceilings. Conversely, permitting and encouraging mobile bank branches, providing partial loan guarantees, ensuring prompt and effective legal redress in cases of loan delinquencies and defaults, contributing towards training costs, etc., can promote efficient resource mobilisation and allocation on the part of both domestic and foreign financial intermediaries.

Charging licence fees, as St. Lucia does for both head offices (EC\$20,000 annually) and branches (EC\$1,000 each), is likely to reduce efficiency of financial intermediation. Setting minimum deposit rates, as Barbados does, may raise efficiency. No matter how small the number of financial intermediaries, whether domestic or foreign, regulations can be designed and implemented to simulate competitive conditions, i.e. by setting minimum deposit rates of interest. Equally important, discriminatory taxation of financial intermediation can and should be avoided in the interests of efficient financial intermediation.

Most measures discussed above in connection with increasing or decreasing financial intermediation efficiency also affect the incentive on the part of foreign financial intermediaries to siphon off national saving to their home countries. Additionally, a rapidly depreciating domestic currency tends to stimulate capital flight, whereas a smoothly appreciating exchange rate may well deter it.

That foreign bank cartels in the sample countries can indeed influence, if not dictate, domestic monetary and/or fiscal policy is illustrated by a recent event in St. Lucia. In 1980, the government proposed, albeit misguidedly, to impose a two per cent tax on banks' deposit liabilities. The proposal was dropped after 'discussions' with the foreign banks. A potential or existing foreign bank cartel may perhaps best be averted or undermined by relatively free entry conditions. However, tiny developing economies could realise substantial savings in information gathering costs from granting licences only to large, reputable foreign banks which would be least likely to risk adverse publicity from sharp, if not illegal, practice. There might also be some advantages, as Seychelles appears to have recognised since 1976, in encouraging foreign banks from several different countries to set up offices.

There seems to be no proven way of solving the problem of subsequent domestic entry into the financial intermediation industry which historically has been the exclusive territory of foreign financial intermediaries. Government-ownership is the only method so far attempted with respect to commercial banking in all the sample countries, except Hong Kong and Singapore. An alternative technique could be to reserve the field of thrift intermediation, i.e. S&Ls, finance companies, trust companies and mutual savings banks, for domestic enterprise. At an appropriate moment, these institutions could be put on an equal footing with commercial banks, as is now happening in the United States. Yet another altérnative might be to issue fixed period, e.g. 15-year, licences to foreign banks with an agreement that the intermediary would be transferred to national ownership at the expiration of the licence.

Three of the sample economies - The Bahamas, Hong Kong and Singapore - host large functional offshore banking centres. Recently two others - Barbados and Seychelles - enacted the legislation necessary to permit offshore banking. Each has so far attracted one offshore bank. Several other economies in the sample are flirting with the idea of opening up offshore centres.

McCarthy (1979, p.48) concludes his analysis of the benefits and costs of hosting offshore banking centres as follows:

While the benefit-cost equation appears favourable for existing centres, it seems possible, indeed probable, that there is little unsatisfied demand for new offshore centres. There are even some signs at present of an excess supply. If one looks at the existing geographical coverage provided by offshore centres, virtually every area of the world has a selection of offshore centres readily accessible. In addition, improved telecommunications render it easier than before to route paper business through a limited number of centres rather than setting up operations in several widely dispersed centres. In general, therefore, new paper centres are not likely to succeed. In addition, even existing centres might become less important and less profitable if moves to impose controls on the Euro-currency markets are successful, and/or if New York establishes an International Banking Zone.

The probability of New York's International Banking Zone getting launched was increased considerably at the end of 1980 by the submission of the Federal Reserve Board's proposal to permit US banks to establish International Banking Facilities within the United States (Cheng, 1981). The acceptance of this proposal would be a crippling blow to some of the existing offshore banking centres, particularly those located in the Caribbean.

POLICY ISSUES

The importance of 'appropriate' policies has been stressed throughout this paper and in a number of other contributions to this volume. Most of these policies are as relevant to large as they are to small economies. However, the special characteristics of tiny economies' financial sectors raise a number of policy issues which warrant further study:

(i)   What particular financing lacunae, specific to tiny economies, e.g. for small industry, exist?

(ii)   Is there a noticeable lack of risk-taking by tiny economies' financial sectors due, in part, to their inability to diversify asset portfolios sufficiently?

(iii)   What are the most appropriate financial intermediaries, e.g. universal banks, etc., for tiny economies?

(iv)   What are the advantages and disadvantages of alternative methods, e.g. foreign banks, joint ventures, regional commercial banks, etc., of overcoming scale-economy problems?

(v)   What financial innovations from larger economies, e.g. NCDs, index-linked financial claims, finance companies, credit unions, etc., are adaptable for tiny economies?

(vi)   How might a socially optimal amount of <u>productive</u> risk-taking by tiny economies' financial sectors, e.g. through government-sponsored loan guarantee funds, etc., best be encouraged?

(vii)   Is there a case for subsidising financial intermediation in tiny economies and, if so, what would be the most appropriate method?

(viii) Is there any role for a special Commonwealth Bank which might be established with a particular responsibility towards tiny economies?

REFERENCES

Abe, S., Fry, M.J., Min, B.K., Vongvipanond P., and Yu, T.-P.,
    1977, 'Financial Liberalisation and Domestic Saving in
    Economic Development: An Empirical Test for Six
    Countries'. In "Pakistan Development Review", Vol.16,
    No.3.
Baltensperger, E., 1972, 'Economies of Scale, Firm Size, and
    Concentration in Banking'. In "Journal of Money,
    Credit and Banking", Vol.4, No.3.
Barrett, R.J., Gray, M.R., and Parkin, J.M., 1975, 'The Demand
    for Financial Assets by the Personal Sector of the UK
    Economy'. In G.A. Benton, ed., "Modelling the Economy",
    London: Heinemann.
Bhatia, K.B., 1974, "Index-Linking of Financial Contracts: A Survey
    of the State-of-the-Arts", Washington, D.C: World Bank
    Staff Working Paper No. 192, mimeo.
Central Bank of Barbados, 1980, "Economic and Financial Statistics",
    Bridgetown, Barbados.
The Central Bank of the Bahamas, 1980, "Quarterly Review", Vol.7,
    No.4, Nassau, The Bahamas.
Cheng, H.S., 1981, 'From the Caymans'. In "Federal Reserve
    Bank of San Francisco Weekly Letter", 13 February.
Drake, P.J., 1980, "Money, Finance and Development", Oxford:
    Martin Robertson.
Economist The, 1981, 'A Survey of International Banking',
    Vol.278, No.7176.
Fry, M.J., 1974a, "The Afghan Economy: Money, Finance and the
    Critical Constraints to Economic Development", Leiden:
    E.J. Brill.
_____, 1974b, "Resource Mobilisation and Financial Development
    in Nepal", Kathmandu: Centre for Economic Development and
    Administration.
_____, 1976a, "Portuguese Monetary Problems", Lisbon: Banco de
    Portugal.
_____, 1976b, 'A Purchasing-Power-Parity Application to Demand
    for Money in Afghanistan'. In "Journal of Political
    Economy", Vol.84, No.5.
_____, 1978a, 'Deposits and Deposit Rates of Interest'. In
    "Economica", Vol.2, No.2.
_____, 1978b, 'Money and Capital or Financial Deepening in
    Economic Development?' In "Journal of Money, Credit and
    Banking", Vol.10, No.4.
_____, 1978c, 'Pitfalls in Partial Adoption of the McKinnon-Shaw
    Development Strategy: The Nepalese Experience'. In
    "Bangladesh Development Studies", Vol.6, No.3.
_____, 1979a, 'Monetary Control when Demand for Cash is
    Unpredictable: A Proposal for Stabilising the Money
    Multiplier in Portugal'. In "Economic Journal", Vol.89,
    No.355.
_____, 1979b, 'The Cost of Financial Repression in Turkey'. In
    "Savings and Development", Vol.3, No.2.
_____, 1980a, 'Saving, Investment, Growth and the Cost of Financial

Repression'. In "World Development", Vol.8, No.4.
_____, 1980b, 'Money, Interest, Inflation and Growth in Turkey'.
    In "Journal of Monetary Economics", Vol.6, No.4.
_____, 1980c, 'Mortgage Innovation?' In "Federal Reserve Bank
    of San Francisco Weekly Letter", 11 July.
_____, 1980d, 'Money, Interest and Growth'. In German Marshall
    Fund of the United States and the Fundacao Calouste
    Gulbenkian ed., "Il Conferencia Internacional sobre
    Economica Portuguesa", 26 a 28 Setembro de 1979, Lisbon:
    Fundacao Calouste Gulbenkian.
_____, 1981a, 'Interest Rate Policy in India', Honolulu:
    University of Hawaii, Department of Economics. Study
    prepared for the Asian Department of the International
    Monetary Fund, mimeo.
_____, 1981b, 'Interest Rates in Asia: An Examination of
    Interest Rate Policies in Burma, India, Indonesia,
    Korea, Malaysia, Nepal, Pakistan, the Philippines,
    Singapore, Sri Lanka, Taiwan and Thailand', Honolulu:
    University of Hawaii, Department of Economics. Study
    prepared for the Asian Department of the International
    Monetary Fund, mimeo.
_____, 1981c, 'Financial Intermediation in Small Island
    Developing Economies', Honolulu: University of Hawaii,
    Department of Economics. Study prepared for the Common-
    wealth Secretariat, mimeo.
_____, 1981d, 'Government Revenue from Monopoly Supply of
    Currency and Deposits'. In "Journal of Monetary Econo-
    mics", Vol.7, No.4.
_____, 1981e, 'Stabilisation and Growth Strategies for Pacific
    Basin Developing Economies'. In "Federal Reserve Bank
    of San Francisco Economic Review".
_____, forthcoming, 'Financial Development and Stabilisation
    Models for Financially Repressed Developing Economies'.
    In "World Development".
_____ and Farhi, M.R., 1979, "Money and Banking in Turkey",
    Istanbul: Bogazici University Press.
_____, and Mason, A., 1981, 'Children, Capital Inflows,
    Interest and Growth in the Life Cycle Saving Function',
    Honolulu: University of Hawaii, Department of Economics,
    mimeo.
Grubel, H.G., 1977, 'A Theory of Multinational Banking'. In
    "Banca Nazionale del Lavoro Quarterly Review",
    Vol.123.
International Monetary Fund, "International Financial
    Statistics", various issues, Washington, D.C.
Khatkhate, D.R. and Riechel, K.-W., 1980, 'Multi-purpose
    Banking: Its Nature, Scope, and Relevance for Less
    Developed Countries'. In "International Monetary Fund
    Staff Papers", Vol. 27, No.3.
McCarthy, I., 1979, 'Offshore Banking Centers: Benefits and
    Costs'. In "Finance & Development", Vol. 16, No.4.
Simkin, C.G.F., 1978, 'Hyperinflation and Nationalist China'.
    In A.R. Bergstrom, A.J.L. Catt, M.H. Peston and
    B.D.J. Silverstone, ed., "Stability and Inflation",
    Chichester: John Wiley.
The World Bank, 1980, "World Bank Atlas", Washington, D.C.

11. A Note on Transport Issues in Small Economies

Esra Bennathan

In 1979, there were 78 developing countries or territories with a population of five million or less, 49 of them having one million or less (The World Bank, 1980). In this discussion the upper limit of 'smallness' has been taken as five million.

The only general consequence which smallness of population possesses for a country's transport sector and national transport policy arises from economies of scale in transport. Even these scale effects, where they exist, cannot be related simply to size of population: the extent to which they operate depends also on the spatial dispersion of the population. The simplest density statistic (people per square kilometre) is no guide to this dispersion. It is an average constructed with the wrong weights.[1] If the distribution of people by density has the shape J the scale economies of some forms of transport can be obtained even in countries with very small populations.

FEATURES OF SMALLNESS

Economies of scale are the most general characteristic of transport provision for small and dispersed populations. Beyond this, it is not easy to discover characteristics relevant to transport or factors relevant to transport policy which can be confidently associated with population size. Smallness normally appears to be a secondary determinant. It nevertheless gives its own twist to conditions dominated by other factors. One may therefore concentrate the discussion on conditions or features which are to be found in relatively many small economies.

Land-locked, small and least-developed. Of the 20 land-locked countries listed by the United Nations (UNDP, 1980), eleven are 'small' countries. 'Small' countries also account for 19 out of 30 countries defined by the United Nations on a variety of indicators as 'least-developed' (UN, 1980). There is also a significant overlap between the classes of land-locked, least-developed and small: nine of the 19 small least-developed are also land-locked.

Dependence on foreign trade (and transport). The ratio of export value to national product tends to vary inversely with population. If one is willing to ignore the incongruity affecting the usual calculation of this ratio (comparing export value gross of import content with national product which is net of imports), one may think in terms of the share of exports (or imports) in national product. Economists have often considered this relation to be a major consequence of size (Kuznets, 1960). Statistically, the relation is certainly significant. Its quantitative importance, however, is limited: population explains very little of the variation in national export shares.[2]

Commodity concentration of exports. Much the same is true of the relation between population and the commodity concentration of exports: the relation is negative and well defined but lacks great quantitative importance (in the sense of explaining much of what makes for different concentration ratios in the exports of countries).[3]

Direction of trade. Further, the 'hard core least-developed' send on average a substantially larger proportion of their exports (again by value) to other developing countries than do developing countries in general. This dependence of exports on what are normally neighbouring countries is also characteristic of the small countries which make up two-thirds of the group, and particularly of the land-locked countries (UNCTAD, February 1977).

Competition in trade. Lastly, and notwithstanding the relatively high degree of commodity concentration in their exports, the majority of the small countries (and a substantial majority of the small poor countries) appear to be small economies according to the jargon of economics: price-takers in both their exports and their imports. National exports of specific commodities usually form but a small proportion of world supply.

Small size thus often occurs together with one or more of several factors of importance to transport: economies of scale, inability to affect external prices, export concentration, high shares of exports to neighbouring countries, land-lock and also relatively short internal distances for the movement of people and goods. The mere recitation shows that small size alone could lead nobody to predict that any one of these factors will be of importance in the transport economy of any particular small country. But inasmuch as one or more of these conditions are to be observed in a fair number of small economies, they serve to define problems of sufficiently great relevance to be considered.

ECONOMIES OF SCALE

Economies of scale operate in most modes of transport, over certain ranges of traffic. They characterise railways (see, for instance, Heflebower, 1965). One line of rail can take more than one train per day with little additional cost; a locomotive can pull two wagons at hardly more cost than just one. They exist in roads where they arise partly on account of indivisibilities and partly from road quality and capacity being joint-products, their proportions being only variable to a limited extent (Walters, 1968). They characterise ports and other terminals (Bennathan and Walters,

1969). They exist in pipelines and in ships (Cookenboo, 1955; Goss and Jones, 1977).

In all these cases, over the range of traffic subject to economies of scale, if outlay on the facility or service is increased by, say, ten per cent (adding wagons to the train; asphalting an earth road; adding cranes to the port), feasible output rises in greater proportion and unit cost accordingly declines. (In all cases where the costs of transport are distributed over different parties - road authority and lorry operator - cost has to be counted inclusively.) Such economies are rightly considered a major engine of economic growth. But the engine does not start itself. Comparing countries at a given time (or with different rates of growth) the one with the lower demand will have the higher unit cost and thus be at a disadvantage.

Over the range of diminishing cost, moreover, any attempt to charge full cost to the user will discourage traffic which would be prepared to pay the cost which it occasions (marginal cost), but not the full cost. The result of diminishing cost is therefore often either inefficient pricing, which wastes national resources, or deficits. Deficits strain the poor country's fiscal capacity, frequently distribute income from the poor to the rich and sometimes even lead to taxation which defeats the pricing object (taxes and tolls on the use of transport facilities per transit). Often the deficits are not traceable in the books. Ports, for example, usually do not know the economic value of the assets they use. Railway deficits, again, can be lessened or covered by suppressing ('regulating') competition from the roads. The deficit of the railways is then shifted to the roads; often at great cost to users. The roads, however, do not keep books like the railways because they are built, maintained and owned by an authority which does not contemplate charging for use.

The retarding effect of economies of scale in transport can only be attenuated or overcome by increasing demand or by minimising investment which leads to excess capacity. The most obvious policy in this sense is to share transport facilities and services with other countries. While the tradition for doing so exists in railways it does not always survive.[4]

If geography and pattern of settlement and direction of traffic suggest it, one may use the road or port facilities of adjoining countries to the largest possible extent. This may be encouraged by feeder roads and, above all, by the removal of administrative or fiscal impediments. Left to itself, aided perhaps by the minor investment activities of local communities, one finds that transport naturally takes these routes. It is frequently only barriers erected by the state which rechannel the flow. Economic sense must, of course, prevail on either side of the frontier. If State A finds that B's traffic flows on its roads, it may wish to charge for this use of its facilities which, being uncongested, are made free to its own citizens. It will not, with sense, charge more than maximizes income from this source (over and above the cost of road damage) and the corresponding charge will measure the value of the facility to the marginal foreign users. If State A's road becomes congested and there are roads in B leading to the desired destination (to an uncongested stretch of A's road) traffic will flow in the opposite direction, the more amply if A prices its roads. B may then charge on the same principle as did A before its roads became full. If there is no substitute road in B, it may now be built. This picture of shared transport facilities grossly simplifies the mechanism and procedures required to allow the result to emerge. But it indicates the principles of economic evaluation of transport projects which will minimise waste of resources on either side of the frontier. It indicates also the superiority of prices which are flexible and result in revenues over administrative rules and procedures to regulate traffic flows which cause an uncounted cost and no counted revenue (at least not in the public pocket). If the small country is also a small economy in the technical sense, any increase of transport costs in external trade will have to be absorbed by its own citizens while any reduction in those costs will enhance their incomes (and thus taxable capacity). The pursuit of rational use of transport facilities across borders is particularly important for small countries, the more so if much of their foreign trade is conducted with their neighbours. One is led on from here to the matter of foreign investment in transport facilities which will be taken up in connection with land-locked countries (see next section).

If smallness makes for a relatively high cost of transport there is every reason for not making it even higher by policy. Not surprisingly, it may be raised by attempts to compensate for smallness: as by railway freight equalisation rules which protect remote small settlements at the expense of denser populations (the case of Mali and many others). The suppression of competition between modes (or between operators in the same mode) is widely practised and therefore widely raises costs to users. It is particularly dangerous when it results in the suppression of projects which appear profitable by all the standard criteria but would, if adopted, prevent recovery of sunk costs in existing facilities. Costs are raised by numerous procedural obstacles and also by ill-judged impositions and tolls (which drive the cattle driver off the public highway, leaving it empty).

SMALL LAND-LOCKED COUNTRIES

Land-lock adds the quality of remoteness to the transport position of the small country. Land-locked, it lacks direct access to the major mode of transport in international trade (and a mode of importance for internal transport by way of coastal shipping). The specific cost of being land-locked has never been adequately estimated and an estimate would necessarily be rather speculative. It would not be enough to compare the cost of transporting similar goods of the land-locked and the transit country, over similar distances to the ship's side: procedures (and importers) of the transit country are free of the territorial constraint facing those in the land-locked country and can locate themselves at the optimum distance from the port. Fortunately, this difficult question is of little importance to the real economic issues associated with land-locked countries, except when it is proposed to compensate these countries with international aid for the disadvantage from which they suffer. (Proposals formulated in the United Nations in the early 1970s (UNCTAD,1974) were aimed at giving international aid by way of compensating subsidies to the transport sector of land-locked countries: an idea abhorrent to economists.)

For access to the sea, land-locked countries depend on the transport facilities of their transit countries. Small land-locked countries are likely to be at a disadvantage in the cost of developing access to alternative transit countries, even where geography permits. They may further be at a disadvantage in bargaining power or just in economic effect. If their traffic is relatively small there will be little incentive for the transit country to build and develop facilities according to their value to the land-locked country. Even where traffic is not insignificant (and where services are priced and users charged) the transit country may have no reason to adopt a project which the land-locked country would undertake at its own cost if it could take a hand in the neighbour's transport sector. As an example, one may think of the transit country having a higher rate of discount than the land-locked country: a project which the land-locked country would wish to adopt may be rejected by the transit country even if it has the certain prospect of capturing the entire benefit (accruing to the land-locked country) through discriminatory pricing. To overcome the impediment one has to find ways of allowing one country to invest in the transport sector of another: it would be natural for the country with the lower rate of interest to invest in that with the higher rate, if only the right legal, commercial and administrative basis existed for such investments. Real precedents exist: in jointly owned and operated railways and airlines, and in port facilities dedicated to land-locked neighbours (such as exist in Calcutta for Nepal, in Bangkok for Laos, or in Chile and Peru for Bolivia). The most promising form for such investments appears to be joint ventures, which would allow joint control, establish a common economic interest and insulate the activity somewhat from the politics and rigidities of inter-governmental dealings. Existing examples are confined, as one would expect, to modes or facilities which are in the habit of charging prices to users: railways, ports, airlines and ferries. But there is no reason why the principle might not be extended to roads, whether to construction, improvement or maintenance.

We have so far glossed over what many regard (perhaps with not very much reason) as a major problem of transit: the exercise of sheer monopoly power by the transit country. Monopoly power undoubtedly exists and is exercised by transit states (and, independently, by their officials). If exercised, it may be particularly burdensome on small land-locked countries. All dealings between land-locked and transit country hinge on bargaining power, but there are ways of narrowing the area of bargaining and of softening the effect of monopoly. The creation of joint ventures would be one such method. A question of major interest is how monopoly is to be countered, and what is the real effect of some counter-measures. There are taxes, restrictions and regulations but many of these may be looked at as just taxes intended to deny to the transit country some part of its monopoly rent. It is obvious that these may badly misfire. The problem is illustrated in starkly simplified form in Figure 1.

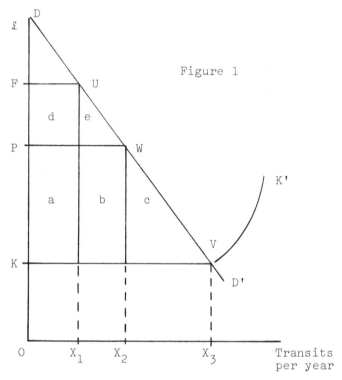

Figure 1

DD' is the demand for transit by the land-locked country's shippers on the single transit road; KK' is user cost per transit. Without any toll, shippers undertake X_3 (uniform) transits per year. The authorities of the land-locked country expect that the transit country will impose a toll simply to appropriate the surpluses of land-locked shippers. (For simplicity, assume that governments cannot discriminate between shippers except according to their nationality.) The land-locked country may then decide to strike first. It imposes a pre-emptive toll at the rate of £KP per transit, to deny the transit country its prey. Let this pre-emptive toll be set for maximum revenue (at W, the elasticity of DV = -1). The transit country thereupon sets a maximum revenue toll of £PF per transit.[5] Transits decline from X_3 to X_2 and then to X_1. As the case is presented in the diagram, it appears that if the area (d + e) exceeds (a), the pre-emptive tax was a mistake: less harm would have come to the land-locked country had it abstained from pre-emptive taxing (or equivalent restrictions or regulations) and allowed

214

the transit country to do its worst (tax at the rate £PK).[6] Now assume that the countries know how to get together for bargaining. In the case when (d + e) exceeds (a), the transit country's tariff revenue is just (d) and it may be willing to suspend the tax in return for an annual amount equal to (d). Alternatively, it may know its total nuisance value, which amounts to (d + e + b). Since (d + e) exceeds (a), the land-locked country could not pay this ransom but it could go some way towards it and still be better off (assuming that money in government coffers is counted as equal to money earned or saved by shippers). In the opposite case, (a) exceeds (d + e) and it appears as though the pre-emptive strike was justified. Now, however, with bargaining, the land-locked country should certainly be able to buy off the transit country.

Alternatively, the transit country strikes first. But after imposing its toll of £PK per transit it finds that half the revenue disappears (in our example) when the land-locked country superimposes a countervailing toll of £FP. The transit country may then lower its toll to regain revenue but its reaction will depend on what it conjectures to be the strategy of the land-locked country. But surely there is room here for a treaty. The land-locked country can bind itself not to levy tolls in exchange for an undertaking by the transit country to reduce its toll and whatever the size of the cut it is bound to benefit the land-locked country. The lower limit to which the transit country will allow itself to be pushed is the toll which will give it just as much revenue as it collected when the countervailing toll was in operation. Needless to add, such bargains can be made in a great variety of ways and in many disguises; but sometimes they cannot be made for want of skill or for lack of a state's control over its own officials and procedures.

This simple and traditional argument shows that where monopoly has to be accepted there are ways, not necessarily very conventional, of limiting its impact. It shows furthermore that collaboration pays: the largest joint revenue for both countries is obtained by setting a toll of £PK. Its distribution is a question of bargaining power, given and unaltered by these and similar manoeuvres.

OCEAN TRANSPORT AND SHIPPING

Commodity concentration in foreign trade acts generally as a cost reducing factor in ocean transport if the cargoes can be shipped in bulk on ocean carriers which offer their services competitively. Even where liner services are preferred, the existence of alternatives tends to hold down the freight rates: liners are generally cartelised and practise price discrimination by criteria of cargo quantity as well as cargo value (Bennathan and Walters, 1969). But this desirable result will only follow if the cargo flows are of adequate absolute size. Moreover, some of the crucial _ceteris paribus_ assumptions fail to hold for many small countries. Absolutely small cargo flows tend to display relatively large imbalances between inbound and outbound movements. These raise freight rates in so far as costs enter into the determination of ocean transport prices. Moreover, the absolute size of cargo flows matters more to freight rates and quality (frequency and transit times) of service, the further a country's ports are placed from the dense international cargo flows (such as Australia-Japan; Europe-Far East; USA-Far East; North Atlantic). Such remoteness entails empty hauls for tramps and bulk carriers and thereby reduces the level of competition which constrains liner pricing; it raises the cost of liner calls and is reflected very clearly in the present pattern of container services and freight rates for containerised cargo (ESCAP, 1980).

The objects of national shipping policy include quite generally the protection of national exporters against monopolistic pricing of shipping services and the promotion of national shipping enterprises. The emphasis differs. Importers usually receive less consideration than exporters (even though the effect of cartel pricing on trade in either direction is the same for the small country). Also, not many of the smallest countries seek to build up an ocean shipping industry. Where both purposes are being pursued the methods are often no more consistent than in other activities in which the state seeks to protect or advance producers. The conflicts arise quite particularly when countries seek to develop their shipping enterprises within the international liner sector. The most common policy to this end is to seek to insert one's liners into the relevant international cartels (conferences) to shield them from the competition of the cartels and also to obtain from them the protection of assured cargo quotas, sailing rights or revenue pool shares. From then on, the temptation for the state is to discourage independent competition with the national conference member, irrespective of the fact that whatever protection is thus afforded to the national company is also given to all foreign members of the cartel (Bennathan, 1981; Vanags, 1977).

The conflicts are, however, not just avoidable but usually stem from the pursuit of a policy which is wrong from both points of view: freight rates and entry of national operators into the international industry. The small country may indeed be in a particularly good position to pursue the most rewarding policy if its small size leads the conference to accept passively the independent (competitive) entry of national liner enterprises into its province. Independent entry combined with passive conferences will exert a downward pressure on monopoly prices (prices in excess of cost) if they are charged in the trade. Monopoly pricing (where it exists) will, on the other hand, afford its own protection to the new entrant unless his costs are so high that he cannot benefit from the effects of foreign monopoly. In that case, however, the only reason for entry would be strategic: that would then be the only economic argument for buying and operating ships. A strategic case for entry exists even if the entrant's costs are so high that he would not obtain any cargo (unless he is subsidised). The only effect of independent entry would then be to contain the prices charged by the cartel. Nobody is likely to argue very strongly for investing in ships that have no prospect of getting cargo. The argument points then not to the development of national shipping but to the encouragement of alternatives to cartelised liner services or to collaboration between countries in the same maritime region. Regional lines, working independently, would be in a position to minimise excess capacity on the tonnage required to assure a credible competitive threat against monopolistic (and discriminatory) pricing of services.

NOTES

1. If average density is calculated as the ratio of the country's population to its area this is equivalent to a weighted average of regional densities with the relative areas of different regions serving as weights. But for most economic problems the appropriate weights would be the proportion of the population living under specified densities.

2. The simplest test of the proposition is performed by regressing the ratio of export (value) to GNP on population size (1973 or 1974, data from UNCTAD, 1977). Estimating across 75 developing countries for which the data are available the result (with t-values in brackets) is:

$$\underline{\text{Export ratio}} = \frac{33.2 - 0.00863 \ \underline{\text{Population}}}{(13.8) \quad (2.1) \quad \text{in '00,000}} \quad (N = 75; \ \bar{R}^2 = 0.053)$$

In this experiment, population size appears as the sole explanatory variable. But it is obvious that there must be other determinants of the export share besides population, and in larger countries one would not expect economies of scale which are related to population size to act as an important constraint in the selection and diversification of economic activities. Unless other variables are to be introduced it would therefore seem a fairer test of the proposition if the sample were restricted to countries below a certain size. One might of course proceed thus in several steps by way of trawling for a critical size. Here we merely select a population of 40 million as the upper limit below which we would expect population to prove its effect on the export share. The restriction of the sample leads us in the expected direction, but not very far: while the t-value of the estimated coefficient on population rises by one-half and the size of the coefficient of determination doubles, it only reaches 11 per cent.

$$\underline{\text{Export ratio}} = \frac{39.19 - 0.0782 \ \underline{\text{Population}}}{(13) \quad (3.1) \quad \text{in '00,000}} \quad (N = 68; \ \bar{R}^2 = 0.11)$$

3.　　The concentration ratio is measured by a form of Hirschman's index, normalised to yield values from 0 to 1 for maximum concentration (UNCTAD, 1977, table 4.5, notes). When regressed on population (omitting once again countries with populations of over 40 million) the result (with t-values in brackets) is:

Export concentration index =

$$0.5698 - 0.00077 \underline{\text{Population}} \quad (N = 62; \bar{R}^2 = 0.11)$$
$$(1.7) \qquad (2.96) \quad \text{in '00,000}$$

4.　　Witness the breaking up of the Regie Dakar-Niger, in the early 1970s, succeeded by two national railway administrations, 660 km in the Senegal and 640 km in Mali, with a change of locomotives at the frontier and taxes levied on foreign wagons staying in Mali beyond a certain time.

5.　　At U_1 the elasticity of the stretch WD = -1.

6.　　Loss if transit country taxes pre-emptively:　a + b + c.
　　Loss if land-locked country taxes pre-emptively:　d + e + b + c.

REFERENCES

Bennathan, Esra, forthcoming, "The International Liner Industry: Structure and Effects on Developing Countries, with Special Reference to India, Malaysia and Thailand".
_____, and Walters, A.A., 1969, "The Economics of Ocean Freight Rates", New York: Praeger.
Cookenboo, L., Jr., 1955, 'Cost of Operation of Crude Oil Trunk Lines'. In L.Cookenboo, ed., "Crude Oil Pipelines and Competition in the Oil Industry", Mass: Harvard University Press.
Goss, R.O. and Jones, C.D., 1977, 'The Economies of Size in Dry Bulk Carriers'. In R.O. Goss, ed., "Advances in Maritime Economics", Cambridge: Cambridge University Press.
Heflebower, Richard B., 1965, 'Characteristics of Transport Modes'. In Gary Fromm, ed., "Transport Investment and Economic Development", Washington, D.C: The Brookings Institution.
Kuznets, S., 1960, 'Economic Growth of Small Nations'. In E.A.G. Robinson, ed., "Economic Consequences of the Size of Nations", London: Macmillan.
United Nations Conference on Trade and Development, 1974, "A Transport Strategy for Land-Locked Developing Countries", New York: United Nations.
_____, February 1977, "Basic Data on the Least-Developed Countries", New York: United Nations.
_____, 1977, "Handbook of International Trade and Development Statistics, Supplement", New York: United Nations.

United Nations Development Programme, 1980, "Development Issue
        Paper for the 1980s", No.15. 'The Most Seriously
        Affected, the Land-Locked, and Island Developing
        Countries', New York: United Nations.
United Nations Economic and Social Commission for Asia and the
        Pacific, 1980, "Report on a Reconnaissance Study of
        Containerisation in India, Malaysia, Philippines and
        Thailand", New York: United Nations.
United Nations General Assembly, 1980, "Basic Data on the Least
        Developed Countries: Report by the Conference
        Secretariat, New York: United Nations.
Vanags, A.H., 1977, "Flag Discrimination: an Economic Analysis".
        In R.O. Goss, ed., op.cit.
Walters, A.A., 1968, "The Economics of Road User Charges", World
        Bank Staff Occasional Papers, No.5, Baltimore: Johns
        Hopkins Press.
The World Bank, 1980, "World Bank Atlas", Washington, D.C.

12. Tourism in the Economic Development of Small Economies: Jamaica's Experience

Paul Chen-Young

Reliance on tourism as a strategy for the development of small economies has its proponents and opponents. Those supporting a tourism-led growth strategy argue that, given the market size and the paucity of natural resources in small economies, the services sector, and especially tourism, is the key area which offers good prospects for economic progress. On the other hand, those who are critical of a tourism-led development strategy usually draw attention to the disruptive effects of tourism on culture and on the environment, the heavy dependence of tourism on imports, the dominance of transnational corporations, and the instability of the industry.

This paper draws on the experience of Jamaica and relates this experience to some of the issues posed by tourism. The issues to be discussed are: (a) instability of earnings; (b) role of transnationals; (c) conflict between national carriers and charters; (d) economic contribution of tourism and dependency on imports; and (e) socio-cultural effect of tourism.

INSTABILITY OF TOURISM EARNINGS

Tourism ranks second after bauxite and alumina in terms of the amount of foreign exchange earned for Jamaica, as Table 1 shows.

TABLE 1
JAMAICAN FOREIGN EXCHANGE EARNINGS BY SECTOR
(1979)

Sector	Earnings (US$ million)	Share (%)
Bauxite and alumina	277.96	45.47
Tourism	141.57	23.13
Sugar	52.26	8.55
Bananas	15.82	2.59
Other exports	123.70	20.23
Total	611.31	100.0

Data in Table 2 show that there was a steady increase in expenditure by tourists from 1967 through 1974, following which there was a decline, with the 1977 figure only 54 per cent of the 1974 total. Expressed in expenditure per room, the decline was from US$13,187 in 1974 to US$7,144 in 1977. The effect on the balance of payments of the declining expenditure by tourists was exacerbated by the higher debt servicing on overseas loans to finance the doubling of room capacity between 1969 and 1976.

The question arises: were the declines in room occupancy and expenditure by tourists peculiar only to Jamaica and, if not, what were the causes? Table 2 shows that the sharp decline in tourist arrivals in Jamaica was not the overall experience of the Caribbean and that Jamaica's share of the total was almost halved between its peak in 1972 and its trough in 1977.

TABLE 2
SELECTED DATA ON TOURISM IN JAMAICA

| | Visitors to | | Jamaican | Hotel | Occupancy | Touri: |
	Caribbean (000)	Jamaica (000)	Share (%)	Rooms (000)	Rates (%)	Expen∙ (U$mn
1967	n.a.	333	n.a.	4.6	65.0	63.6
1968	n.a.	396	n.a.	4.9	66.8	80.5
1969	n.a.	407	n.a.	5.7	62.1	85.7
1970	3,882	309	8.0	7.0	50.1	87.6
1971	4,220	359	8.5	8.1	51.5	99.9
1972	4,670	408	8.7	9.1	48.9	118.7
1973	5,021	418	8.3	10.1	48.1	133.3
1974	5,015	433	8.6	11.1	43.8	146.5
1975	4,878	360	7.4	11.1	43.5	141.4
1976	5,360	328	6.1	12.1	33.2	116.3
1977	5,752	265	4.6	11.0	28.9	78.9
1978	6,689	382	5.7	10.5	40.0	98.1
1979	n.a.	427	n.a.	10.5	48.0	160.0

Source: "European Tourism Demand Study", Steigenberger Consulting, Gmbh, and Caribbean Tourism Research and Development Centre, Barbados, 1980.

The decline in Jamaica's tourism industry came about despite major initiatives by the Government to increase the number of visitors. One approach was to increase promotional expenditure. Table 3 shows that, in the Caribbean, Jamaica had the highest promotional expenditure per visitor in 1978/79.

But evidence from a study (Hines, 1975) of the relationship between promotional expenditure and visitor arrivals over the period 1964 to 1973 suggests that there was no statistical significance between these two variables.

Another approach was to slash prices, especially by the Government-owned chain of hotels. As hotel occupancies fell in

TABLE 3

PROMOTIONAL EXPENDITURE PER VISITOR IN 1978/79

Country	Expenditure (US$)
Jamaica	26.98
Curacao	18.19
Venezuela	15.31
Dominican Republic	13.42
Bahamas	11.48
Barbados	7.29
US Virgin Islands	5.27
Puerto Rico	4.58

Source: "European Tourism Demand Study", op.cit.

Jamaica, many hotels, especially the Government-owned National Hotel and Properties, sharply reduced rates in an effort to attract visitors. The established arrangements with wholesalers for discounts (of about 20 per cent) on rack rates became relatively insignificant as tour operators took advantage of the situation to negotiate low net rates (about 30-40 per cent of rack rates but non-commissionable). In certain instances, similar rooms in the same hotel were being rented at substantially different prices even to the same tour operator.

Such price cutting proved ineffective in increasing occupancies, and confirms the findings of Hines that "the demand for rooms with respect to prices (is such that) a ten per cent increase in price results in a three per cent reduction in bed nights sold". It was found that higher occupancies (excluding non-economic factors) were explained more by incomes in the United States and lower air fares. With respect to incomes, "a ten per cent increase in US median income results in an eight per cent increase in bed nights sold in winter and a 14 per cent increase in summer". With regard to air fares, "a one per cent change in the New York/Jamaica fare differential leads on average to a 4.4 per cent change in bed nights sold in winter and a 3.6 per cent change in summer".

On the question of air fares, a deliberate strategy of stimulating demand by promotional air fares was used through the establishment of a Government-owned company (JAMVAC).

JAMVAC was established specifically to encourage charter flights to Jamaica. It attempted to do so by: (a) risk underwriting for tour-operator-owned charter flights by guaranteeing a minimum load factor to avoid cancellation; and (b) operating its own charters. Such charters would be on the basis of one of the following types of lease:

'Dry' lease   - cost of the aircraft plus all other charges;

'Wet' lease   - inclusive of all operational costs except passenger services (e.g. catering and

passenger insurance) with the cost based on
the number of hours flown;

'Inclusive wet' lease -   direct seat arrangements on charters based
on pre-arranged prices.

In operating its own charter flights JAMVAC mounted its own
advertising campaign but utilised the services of a 'consolidator'
(who was responsible for co-ordinating ground services and flight
arrangements) paid on a flat fee per passenger plus a percentage
for administration. JAMVAC's own operated charters did not prove
to be financially viable but its risk underwriting programme was
more successful in terms of the cost per visitor.

The programmes mounted to increase visitor arrivals and to
minimise the instability of the industry could be regarded as
adequate. But in spite of these programmes the number of arrivals
fell. It is suggested that there were two main causes for this
decline. First, the industry suffered from over-expansion and an
inability to cope - especially with leases being terminated by
transnationals. In this context the industry experienced diseconomies
of scale arising from the fact that local management was inadequate
to manage the doubling in hotel rooms over a relatively short
period. Secondly, during the depressed 1977-78 period Jamaica was
involved in an intense political debate on democratic socialism
versus a more capitalist-oriented economy. Political violence was on
the upsurge and the perception of Jamaica by the trade and the
media, especially in North America, was that it was not a desirable
vacation spot and was not safe for visitors. Thus, despite the
appropriateness of various programmes to increase visitor arrivals,
the intangible factors offset any positive impact which the
promotional programmes might have had.

THE SIGNIFICANCE OF TRANSNATIONALS

Transnationals play two major roles in tourism: as
owner/operators of hotels and as marketing outlets. With respect to
the first role, in the case of Jamaica, the contribution of
transnationals fell short of what was expected. The Government had
embarked on a major building programme of convention-type hotels
based on signed lease agreements with transnationals to provide
working capital and to operate these hotels. In four out of six
hotels the lease agreements were terminated on a 'force majeure'
clause due to the Government's declaring a State of Emergency
when political violence was at a peak. Such cancellation took place
even prior to the completion of the hotels, and the Government had
to step in and operate them even though it had neither the
management capability nor the financial resources to capitalise and
operate the hotels properly.

Another experience in Jamaica with transnationals was in the
area of loan guarantees. Guaranteed loans for convention hotels up
to 1979 were about $65.2 million for six hotels with a total of

2,328 rooms. These guarantees did not stipulate any performance conditions and the Government was obliged to pay principal and interest if the companies were unable to meet their loan repayments. In every case where a guarantee had been given, the Government has had to meet the payments due.

The second key area in which transnationals serve is as marketing outlets. The industry has become increasingly dependent on overseas tour operators whose marketing efforts can make or break an economy dependent on tourism. These tour operators construct vacation packages based on promotional air fares and frequently including room and ground facilities. The larger operators operate charters on a back-to-back basis with packaged tours.

Because of their strategic marketing position, the destiny of a country's tourism development programme rests heavily in the hands of overseas tour operators. This dependence is a major weakness in the development of tourism, since these transnational tour operators could create instability in a small economy however sound the Government's policies.

The Jamaican experience has demonstrated that small economies with a fairly sound tourism industry should expect some disruption and change in the character of the industry if they undertake any massive expansion programme over a very short period. Local management may not be able to cope and small economies should be wary of relying on lease agreements with transnationals as a reliable basis for undertaking any major hotel expansion programme. They should also recognise that transnationals are less inclined to commit resources in either fixed assets or working capital in many developing economies and especially those which attempt to introduce socialist philosophies. The preference of transnationals is more towards licensing arrangements where a rent is charged but there is no risk in terms of investment capital.

CONFLICT BETWEEN NATIONAL CARRIERS AND CHARTERS

Promotional air fares and charters are becoming increasingly more important in tourism development. Many small countries have, however, established national carriers with scheduled flights using IATA rates. Such carriers, as in the case of Jamaica, are inclined to rely more on scheduled flights than on charters to generate revenues.

There has always been a conflict in objectives between the national carrier (Air Jamaica) and the national company to promote charters (JAMVAC). Air Jamaica maintained the position that it is a scheduled carrier with its fortunes largely dependent on travellers willing to pay business and excursion fares. JAMVAC managed to operate profitably for a few years but has been losing money heavily in recent years, with losses at US$20 million in 1980. It is being reorganised in 1981 and has trimmed its fleet from ten planes in 1979 to seven in 1981. Cuts in staff and in the number of gateways have also been implemented.

In developing the market for charter flights to Jamaica, JAMVAC operated two programmes. First, it acted as a carrier operator by leasing and operating regular scheduled charter services by using a consolidator in the United States. The intention was to provide additional seats at lower fares to be competitive with a country like the Bahamas.

Secondly, it acted as an underwriter of risks for tour operators leasing aeroplanes. Under such an arrangement, a break-even load factor (say 85 per cent) is negotiated with tour operators, with JAMVAC agreeing, at no expense to the tour operators, to pay the difference between a minimum load factor (say 65 per cent) and the break-even load factor if enough seats are not sold. This aimed to encourage charters by tour operators and to minimise the risk of cancellations in the event that enough seats were not sold on a charter flight. Various arrangements were also made regarding the tour operators' participation in profits for load factors over the break-even figure.

Like the national carrier, JAMVAC also operated at a loss but this was defended on the ground that it was designed as a high-risk company to open up new routes in order to broaden the tourism market. Notwithstanding losses by both the national carrier and JAMVAC, the Jamaican experience has shown that there is an inherent conflict between national airlines and charter carriers. A clear policy on the role of airlines in developing tourism is vital.

Even with national airlines or charters the development of tourism will be hampered unless there are international airports capable of receiving flights from the tourists' home country. But the problem of high cost infrastructure to develop such airports is one with which small economies must grapple. Conventional appraisal criteria and funding might not be appropriate in examining this problem.

ECONOMIC IMPACT OF TOURISM

Tourism is often criticised on the ground that it has a high import content with minimum local value-added contribution. This is more likely to be the case in small economies where the industry is controlled by non-residents and most inputs are imported.

According to a recent study (Chen-Young, 1979), the import content (payment for goods and services) of tourism in Jamaica was approximately 37 per cent, which is in keeping with earlier studies. Such an import content would not be appreciably higher than in the manufacturing sector. But tourism's contribution to foreign exchange earnings is substantially higher, with earnings in 1979/80 representing 25.2 per cent of total foreign exchange earnings or 125 per cent more than earnings of non-traditional exports (mainly manufacturing). The import substitution contribution of manufacturing is recognised. But if the strategic thrust for development is on exports, tourism is a more significant contributing sector. This is in fact recognised under the recently agreed IMF programme with Jamaica where the projected earnings from tourism are expected to increase by US$172 million by 1983/84, as against US$70 million for non-traditional exports, even though capacity utilisation in both sectors is now approximately the same, at 45-50 per cent.

In terms of the contribution to the Jamaican economy from each dollar spent by tourists, the Chen-Young study found that the income multiplier[1] was 0.77. Based on expenditure of US$198 million, the estimated contribution to Gross Domestic Product would be US$153 million or about 4 per cent of the total. The income multiplier estimate of 0.77 is not out of line with that of the Tripartite Economic Survey (1967) (0.873), or that of Bryden and Faber (1969) (0.88).

As to the employment effect of tourism, the Chen-Young study estimated multipliers of 0.000089 per dollar for direct employment creation and 0.00010 for indirect employment creation. With expenditure of US$198 million in 1977, direct employment created would be 17,622 and indirect employment would be 19,800, giving a total of 37,422. The total employment multiplier estimate would be considerably lower than the 0.00051 estimate by Curry (1971). The estimate of direct employment created, however, is higher than the 9,141 estimated from a sample survey, possibly because of the very low room occupancy in 1977. The employment estimate must therefore be viewed with caution.

With respect to whether the industry is a burden on the budget, the Jamaican experience suggests that at low occupancies the tax intake is less than promotional and other expenditure, including revenue concessions on imports. However, at about a 45 per cent occupancy rate, the industry would begin to pay for itself with a positive overall tax contribution.

In concluding this section, the Jamaican experience suggests that tourism is no more dependent on imported inputs than manufacturing and that it generates more foreign exchange at comparable capacity utilisation levels. The industry accounts for about four per cent of Gross Domestic Product and about six per cent of total employment.

SOCIO-CULTURAL-ENVIRONMENTAL IMPACT OF TOURISM

Critics of tourism have been vocal on its adverse effects on the culture of small economies. Among the major criticisms are that tourism: (a) causes land prices to rise, with foreigners acquiring the best sites and pre-empting residents from enjoying the natural beauty and attractions of their own country; (b) superimposes an alien culture; and (c) bids away labour from the agricultural sector. These points are valid in the case of Jamaica and the manner in which the problem has been tackled includes zoning of lands, rigid approval requirements, including right of access to the public beaches, and public education on tourism.

CONCLUSIONS

The main conclusions of the paper are as follows:

(i) Despite its instability, tourism is a major earner of foreign exchange. One means of minimising instability is an orderly development programme instead of rapid expansion, given the management and labour force limitation. The Jamaican experience revealed that, even with good programmes to promote tourism, internal political unrest and unfavourable overseas publicity have a tremendous effect on the success of tourism.

(ii) The marketing of tourism is controlled by transnationals in the form of overseas tour operators. They can make or break a destination and this is a serious deficiency in using tourism as a strategy for development. Unlike the past, when transnationals were investing in tourism enterprises (usually by constructing hotels or by providing working capital to operate hotels), there appears now to be a tendency for transnationals to concentrate more on franchise agreements where a rent is paid but no risk taken in the form of providing investment capital. Even where agreements have been signed with transnationals to operate hotels, governments could find themselves having to manage hotels due to the termination of contracts by transnationals, especially where the economic picture in a country is clouded.

(iii) Charter flights and promotional fares play a key role in attracting visitors. Conflicts of objective can arise between national carriers, with scheduled flights, and charter flights. It is therefore important that government policy be clear on the role of national airlines in developing tourism and the orientation needed to do so. The infrastructure costs of developing airports are high and small economies might find it unmanageable to finance such costs. Special financing criteria and sources of funds are needed to assist small countries develop the infrastructure to accommodate international flights.

(iv) The smaller the country, the greater the leakage in foreign exchange for imports used in tourism is likely to be. In Jamaica's case the import propensity was 0.37 and it does not appear that this figure is any greater than in manufacturing. However, it appears that tourism can earn more foreign exchange at any given level of capacity utilisation. Tourism accounts for about four per cent of Gross Domestic Product and six per cent of total employment. At occupancy levels of about 45 per cent, tourism is a net contributor to the budget.

(v) The adverse cultural effects of tourism are inescapable, since large numbers of visitors in a small country must have an impact on the society. Nevertheless, with proper zoning, careful approval procedures, limitation to ownership of certain national assets, and public education programmes, it is possible to minimise the adverse cultural impact of tourism.

(vi) Given the limited internal markets of small economies and the absence of high-value natural resources in most cases, with good transportation, tourism offers one of the most realistic possibilities for economic development, notwithstanding its shortcomings as discussed.

NOTE

1.   For specification of the model, see Archer, Brian (1973).

REFERENCES

Archer, Brian, 1973, 'The Anglesey Tourist Income Model'. In "Bangor Occasional Papers in Economics", No. 2, Cardiff: University of Wales Press.

Bryden, J.M. and Faber, M.L.O., 1969, 'Multiplying the Tourist Multiplier'. In "Social and Economic Studies", Vol. 18, Institute of Social and Economic Research, University of West Indies, Jamaica.

Chen-Young & Associates, Paul, 1979, "A Study on the Economic Impact of Tourism"; for the Ministry of Foreign Affairs, Jamaica.

Curry, C.R., 1971, "Tourist Expenditure Survey", Central Planning Unit, Jamaica.

Hines, A.G., 1975, "National Tourism Plan: Analysis and Proposals"; for the Ministry of Foreign Affairs, Jamaica.

Steigenberger Consulting, Gmbh and Caribbean Tourism Research and Development Centre, 1980,"European Tourism Demand Study"; Barbados.

"Tripartite Economic Survey", 1967, Report of HMSO.

13. Project Appraisal for Small Economies

Andrew Coulson

The UNIDO[1] and OECD[2] (or 'Little-Mirrlees') systems of shadow pricing have been widely disseminated and discussed for more than ten years; and yet not a single country uses either method systematically, not even for directly productive projects.

I suspect that there are three main reasons for this apparent lack of confidence: the first is that the systems appear complex and mystifying, especially to policy-makers not trained in economics; the second is that use of these systems as currently prescribed requires a considerable allocation of skilled manpower (both to calculate and update 'national parameters' and to calculate individual shadow prices that are important in particular projects); the third is that the potential benefits from this complex and time-consuming activity have often been far from clear. This paper, written with special reference to the position of small economies, is an attempt to remedy some of these deficiencies by suggesting procedures which are not unduly time-consuming, can be justified in language that makes sense to non-economist policy-makers, and produce reasonably reliable single figures (one for each project) by which projects can be compared.

There are certainly some technical difficulties in the shadow pricing systems which tend to be played down in manuals for practitioners. For example, many professional economists have found difficulties in accepting all the arguments put forward for the use of world prices in both the UNIDO and the OECD systems[3]. Also it has often not been clear whether (and if so, how) certain objectives which are important to politicians can be given weight in project appraisals. Examples are: the wage employment generated by a project (which is not accounted for directly by the use of a shadow wage[4]); the aim of self-reliance (most politicians prefer to produce a good locally if they can[5]); and the additional value to be given to benefits which reduce the degree of inequality in a country[6]. In my view, if assigning weights to these objectives presents conceptual or theoretical difficulties, the appropriate remedy is not to attempt to cover every aspect, but rather to fall back to territory that can be defended unambiguously in simple terms.

The implications of appraising projects using shadow prices are not always spelt out. Such an appraisal is an attempt to produce a single figure (an internal rate of return, or net present value) by which the project can be accepted, rejected, or compared with other projects[7]. This is done through the use of prices in the appraisal which differ from the market prices that will be used if and when the project is implemented. Such prices can only be calculated if the importance to be given to various objectives is agreed between the politicians in power, the planners in the Ministry of Finance or Planning, the officials or companies who will implement the projects if they are approved, and any external financing agencies who may be involved. Disagreement between any two of these could lead to different rankings of projects[8]. Moreover, the implication of using shadow prices in project appraisals is that a government will frequently approve projects which are not the most profitable at market prices (were this not so there would be little point in spending much effort shadow pricing). If such projects are accepted, governments and financial agencies either have to accept greater financial costs (they may have to subsidise the projects directly), or they must be prepared to accept lower (market price) profit levels (which may well result in less re-investment out of profits). Finally, the governments concerned must be strong enough to ensure that the policies implicit in their choice of projects are carried out[9]; thus if an import-substitution project is rejected on the grounds that it would be better to develop export markets for some other products, then the government must ensure that export markets are in fact developed. If the government is not willing or able to offer subsidies, or accept lower profit rates at market prices, there is not much point in its spending time and energy on shadow pricing[10].

Finally, it has not always been clear whether the systems were intended for large or for small economies[11]. The UNIDO and OECD writers seem to have had India and Pakistan particularly in mind. On the other hand many of the case studies of shadow pricing have been carried out in much smaller economies - such as Malaysia, Chile, Ivory Coast or Kenya[12]. A case can certainly be made to the effect that these systems are much more appropriate to small economies, where trade is relatively more important than in large countries like India. It is to this that we now turn.

SMALL ECONOMIES

This is not the place to attempt a formal definition of smallness[13]; however, it seems reasonable to assume that the economies under consideration will possess some or all of the following properties:

(i)   high import dependence - and hence the need for a high ratio of exports to gross domestic product;

(ii)   an export sector largely dependent on agriculture, agricultural processing, and tourism;

(iii) a number of import-substitution industries, but a relatively small resource base and internal market, so that a strategy of self-reliance (import-substitution) cannot be more than partial, at least in the medium-term;

(iv)   flourishing small-scale and informal sectors;

(v)   quantities of goods traded too small to affect world prices of either imported or exported goods;

(vi)   a high proportion of government revenue raised from tariffs on imports, leading to considerable differences between world and domestic prices (and in many instances high rates of effective protection); and

(vii) frequent foreign exchange shortages, caused by pressure to raise both consumption and investment (government and private) faster than it is possible to raise the value of exports. This implies an urgent need to find investments that make a net contribution to foreign exchange earnings.

To these could be added, in the majority of cases:

(viii) a large part of the investment budget financed from government-to-government credits at low or zero rates of interest (i.e. foreign 'aid'), tied to particular projects, and so requiring some kind of project planning;

(ix)   the possibility that the economy is (or could be) dominated by a few projects whose expenditures are large in relation to GDP or which affect other sectors by using a large fraction of the available resources of unskilled labour, skilled labour, experienced managers, good quality land, or available investment funds;

(x)   the likelihood that linkages may be particularly important, because if value-added is to be retained locally, projects will have to be inter-related (thus an expansion of processing may require an expansion of agricultural production; or if a plant to produce PVC pipes is to be successful, the pipes must be used in all the the irrigation projects in the economy, and the irrigation itself must be economically justified from the agricultural point of view);

(xi)   conversely, if high-cost investments are undertaken, then these same linkages may mean that many parts of the economy are adversely affected. Thus an inefficient fertiliser factory can discourage innovation in agriculture, while high-cost vehicle assembly can make transport expensive, and so raise costs in almost every other sector; and

(xii) a shortage of experienced staff with technical and managerial skills (including project appraisal).

A SYSTEM OF SHADOW PRICING FOR SMALL ECONOMIES

The system of shadow pricing which follows is designed to be as appropriate as possible to an economy with the above properties. It concentrates on the international competitiveness of the proposed investments, and the basic appraisals are carried out using world prices. This is because such an economy, if it is to raise its living standards, cannot afford too many projects that are not competitive at world prices (since these will require subsidies in one form or another, and so divert resources that could be used for other forms of consumption or investment)[14]. Equally, it cannot afford to ignore projects which are competitive at world prices (especially export-oriented projects, since these are the means of earning foreign exchange). Local prices (greatly affected by duties on imports) differ greatly from world prices, so that many projects may appear profitable at local prices while not being profitable when appraised at world prices. The system also stresses, as far as possible, the need to quantify the important linkage effects, since these will be particularly important in small economies, especially when relatively large projects are under consideration. It is not suggested that this will always be easy, but it may well be that an estimate of the order of magnitude of the linkage effects (and whether they assist the project or detract from it) may be sufficient. However, even when taking account of linkage effects, many proposed projects may not appear to be competitive internationally. In such cases a number of adjustments can be made, all of which will favour the project, and all of which have a clear rationale in terms of government objectives. Some of them will require subsidies from government, or a willingness to forego commercial profit, and if this is not likely to be forthcoming, there is no point in proceeding to more appraisal.

ADJUSTMENTS IN MARKET PRICES

In financial analysis, the market price of an item in the cash flow is a sufficient indication of its cost.[15] It is the money value the project will have to pay for buying, or can expect to receive from selling, the goods and services involved. On the other hand, from the government point of view, market prices do not always reflect the values of these goods and services. The most important situations in which there may be a divergence between market prices and government valuations are summarised below.

If a country imposes import duties, either to raise revenue or to give protection to certain local industries, then the domestic prices for imported goods will be higher than their import prices (i.e. international prices in foreign exchange, plus transport costs, multiplied by the official exchange rate) by approximately the amount of the duties. The local prices could be higher still if there were monopoly producers or importers, and/or if imports were limited by quota arrangements. In the same way, if there are taxes on exports, the local earnings by the exporters will be less than the foreign exchange realisation from selling the goods, multiplied by the official exchange rate. If a government is concerned that its projects should be able to compete internationally in export markets, and its policy is to produce locally only when it is possible to do so more cheaply than importing, then it must take account of these international prices. In order to tell whether the project is competitive, it should use a valuation based directly on the international price - that is, for a good that can be exported, the realisation in foreign exchange (f.o.b. - i.e. deducting the cost of shipping) multiplied by the official exchange rate, and for a good that will be imported, the cost of landing the item (c.i.f. - i.e. including the cost of shipping and insurance). If a domestic good will substitute for an imported good, then its valuation would be the saving in foreign exchange - in other words the foreign exchange (c.i.f. cost) that would have been spent importing the good if the local product had not been made, again multiplied by the official exchange rate.

To many, to ask that projects be able to compete internationally without protection will seem a severe test, especially for industrial projects in countries at an early stage of industrialisation. If, however, sufficient projects that do pass the test can be found, there is much to be said in favour of using the test. There are, in fact, several reasons why projects may be competitive internationally. Wage rates may be low, and this will enable some projects producing goods for export to compete. If cheaper sources of supply are distant, and transport costs are high, then some import-substitution industries will be competitive, especially if they use local labour and material inputs. Other competitive projects may be associated with tourism, mineral extraction, export-oriented agriculture, or food production for the local market. If there is a free trade area, or a trade agreement with neighbouring countries, then more economies of scale can be realised and a wider range of enterprises may be competitive.

Most developing countries have balance of payments problems. The availability of foreign exchange to potential users is rigidly controlled by the government, and the rate of exchange between foreign and local currency is fixed at an 'official rate' which does not reflect the scarcity value of foreign currency. If a government feels that foreign currency is not sufficiently highly valued in terms of local currency, then in calculations which involve goods that are imported or exported, it can use a 'shadow exchange rate' - i.e. a rate of exchange that credits to or debits from each unit of foreign currency earned or spent, more local currency than is implied by the official exchange rate.

An alternative procedure is to convert foreign exchange costs into their local currency equivalents at the official exchange rate, but to lower local costs (i.e. all expenditures which do not affect imports or exports[16]) by multiplying them by a 'standard conversion factor' of less than 1.0. This has similar effects to the use of a shadow exchange rate, but the advantage of making it clear that its use implies a commitment by the government to provide a subsidy to the project, if one is required to make it acceptable to its sponsors.

If, however, very few projects pass this test, there are a number of ways in which the government can relax the conditions without giving special favours to one project rather than another:

(i)   it can remove the taxation element;

(ii)   it can use a shadow exchange rate if it feels that foreign exchange is not sufficiently valued by the official exchange rate; alternatively, it can arrive at a similar result by reducing the valuations of local products used in production. This would be done by multiplying the local costs by a standard conversion factor of less than 1.0;

(iii)   it could use a 'shadow wage rate', or a valuation of the costs of unskilled labour less than the wages employers would actually have to pay; and

(iv)   it could use a discount rate lower than the borrowing rate for long-term commercial loans.

The arguments for (i) and (ii) above have already been discussed. The paragraphs which follow deal with (iii) and (iv).

There are a number of reasons for using (in the appraisal of a project) wage rates below those which would be paid if and when the project came to be implemented. One argument is that a part of the wage may be paid in tax, and come directly back to the government. It would, therefore, be a transfer payment, and should be excluded. Another, quite different, argument is based on opportunity cost in the short-run: it is argued that, from the point of view of the economy, the cost of employing a person is merely the loss of production to the economy in the activity he would otherwise have performed. If he would have been unemployed, and produced nothing, the cost of employing him (according to this argument) would be nothing. If he would have produced in agriculture, his contribution to production would have been that of a marginal producer in agriculture. If he would have worked in the urban 'informal' sector, the cost of employing him would be the contribution to production that he would have made in that sector, etc.

There are at least three kinds of difficulty which have to be faced by anybody using a shadow wage:

(i)   difficulties in calculating the loss of production;

(ii)   difficulties in valuing that loss of production; and

(iii)   the implications in the long-term of using very low shadow wages.

The production lost by employing an underemployed unskilled worker is obviously difficult to calculate. For example, if he is a married man, production by his wife and family may be lost, as well as his own production. Or transferring him from the urban 'informal' sector to 'formal' wage employment may encourage others to leave agriculture and move to the town, so the loss of production may in fact be felt in agriculture.

The problems of valuation are strictly statistical problems. It is notoriously difficult to value production in 'subsistence' agriculture and even more so in the urban 'informal' sector. There are also difficulties relating to such matters as the differences in prices between urban and rural areas, and the different conditions of life (in the rural areas a man builds his own house, and does not need a bus to travel to work; if he earns the same income as his urban-based cousin he is actually better off).

The problems of the long-term implications of using very low shadow wages are also clear; if there is a choice of technique it will tend to favour labour-intensive alternatives which are not the cheapest at market prices. The use of the low shadow wage will therefore lower profits or imply increased costs at market prices; investors may even require a subsidy if they are to be persuaded to adopt labour-intensive techniques. This is particularly a problem if the production lost by employing the workers is worth very little, for then the implied shadow wage would be very low. No government would be prepared to use a shadow wage rate close to zero in its project appraisals, if it would then have to pay a much higher wage to employ the workforce when the project went ahead. It would inevitably - and correctly - take into account the real cost to the economy which has to be paid in the form of wages to employ the large workforce.

In practice, the complications alluded to above mean that calculation of a precise shadow wage for unskilled labour (i) is a major research undertaking, and even so (ii) differs from individual to individual and (iii) in the last resort depends on value judgements, such as the relative importance of profit and wage employment to the economy. For practical planning purposes a shadow wage of zero is unacceptable. We suggest, therefore, for an economy with severe short-term probems of employment (where expanding 'formal' wage employment immediately is more important than considerations of long-term growth), the use of a shadow wage for unskilled labour equal to half the market wage. For an economy with less severe short-term problems, concerned to raise the rate of investment, we suggest a shadow wage of around four-fifths of the market wage. For an economy not concerned about present consequences, but determined to bring about structural transformation of its economy as quickly as possible, we recommend a shadow wage equal to the market wage - i.e. to the cost that has to be borne by the employer when he employs his workforce.[17]

The discount rate is another important parameter. The lower the rate used, the more projects will be categorised as acceptable. On the one hand, if money can be borrowed cheaply from financial institutions, then there is a case for using a low rate of discount. On the other hand, if there is a shortage of investment funds, then a higher rate of discount should be used. If there is no shortage of low interest funds for foreign exchange costs, but a shortage of local funds to finance recurrent or operating costs, then a high rate of discount should again be used (so that less investment will take place, thereby lessening the local funds constraint). If, however, inflation is reducing the real cost of borrowing, then this would suggest a lower rate. And if there is a feeling among members of the government that the rate of investment is too low, and especially if they feel that sufficient long-term projects are not being implemented, then again there is a case for using discount rates substantially lower than the costs of commercial borrowing.[18]

To cut through all these complications, and make practical recommendations that will be useful to small economies, the following is suggested: if most of the country's borrowing is on commercial terms, and there are sufficient projects that are viable on commercial terms to exhaust the investment budget, then the figure recommended would be slightly below the commercial interest rate (for example, the current World Bank borrowing rate); if, however, there is a strong feeling that insufficient is likely to be invested if all projects have to earn a commercial return, and especially if concessionary finance is available for the majority of projects, then a cut-off rate of discount equal to about half the commercial rate could be used.

To sum up, it is proposed that four types of adjustment be made to improve the net present value of the majority of projects. These are: the removal of taxation from the calculations, a decrease in the valuation given to local expenditure on a project designed to earn or save foreign exchange, a lower valuation in the calculation of wages paid to certain types of labour, and the use of a discount rate which is lower than commercial borrowing rates.

Clearly such revaluations must be used in a consistent way, and not haphazardly as suits individual appraisers (which would be a sure way of ensuring that virtually every project was presented in a way which made it appear acceptable!) However, for a variety of reasons, detailed calculations of the parameters involved are not recommended. Clearly this could be a major research undertaking, and could delay the approval of projects. Moreover, many of the parameters would become out of date very quickly, especially if there were changes in government fiscal or tariff policy, or if inflation was rapid. Not least, such parameters are value judgements, and it may be more important that they be seen as value judgements (with good sense behind them) than that very detailed research is undertaken to put precise figures to them. A precise set of procedures, and a decision-chart, are discussed in a later section of this paper, after we have considered some of the issues raised by 'indirect effects'.

INDIRECT EFFECTS

When a government looks at a project an effort should also be made to evaluate its indirect effects on other parts of the economy (sometimes called 'spill-over effects', 'external effects', or 'externalities'). These are costs and benefits which arise because of the project, but which accrue to other sectors or enterprises in the economy, rather than to the project itself. In a small economy, these indirect effects may be particularly important, and it is very necessary to take them into account. This will certainly be the case if the project is large relative to the economy as a whole (as will often be the case in small countries), or uses a large proportion of the available resources of finance or skilled labour. The most important types of indirect costs and benefits are as follows.

A new project may:
- pollute the water, air or land, and thus affect fishing, drinking water supplies, tourism, other industries, and/or the living conditions of the people;
- reduce the profits from other activities. For example, handicraft shoe production could be destroyed by a new shoe factory, or the profits of an existing producer of soft drinks could be threatened by a new factory. An important special case of this is when the use of good agricultural land for one crop (sugar cane, perhaps) reduces the profits that could be made from other crops grown on the same land (e.g. rice or bananas);
- raise the price of its product (and hence the costs of industries that use the product) if the investment has to be protected. For example, a new fertiliser factory could raise fertiliser prices, and lower agricultural incomes;
- benefit others indirectly, through the facilities it provides. For example, a new dam may allow touristic uses such as fishing, even though its prime purpose is water supply and electricity generation. (It may also destroy fishing industries and agriculture downstream - examples of indirect <u>costs</u>.) A road built for a factory may benefit other users. The training given by a project may benefit other industries, etc;
- create extra profits in the industries which supply it (linkage effects). For example, a supplying factory may have surplus capacity which is used by the project. A special case of this is when the project increases the incomes of local shopkeepers and suppliers, through what are called 'multiplier effects'; and
- be more efficient than its predecessor, and lower the prices of what it produces, thereby lowering the costs of production of other producers (another example of the importance of linkages) or increasing the real income of consumers.

A large project in a small economy may have many complex indirect effects. It may, for example, employ a large proportion of the surplus labour force, and so force up wages generally; in such a situation profits in every sector of the economy are affected. It may consume a sizeable proportion of the investment funds available, and so cause many other projects to be delayed. It is, of course, not inevitable that a large project has these effects: for example, it could be financed independently of the government budget (say by a foreign company), employ few local people, and yet bring in foreign exchange. But even in such a case the large project will have a social impact (which may well be a social cost), although it may be difficult to quantify the impact.

The simplest means of taking account of indirect effects is to extend the scope and definition of the project being appraised so that the indirect effects become direct effects. For example, the project and its supplying industry can be considered together, and appraised with one cash flow built up in two sections, one for the original investment and the other for the supplying industry. This procedure can often be followed in cases where the indirect effects have an impact on only a small number of enterprises outside the immediate investment, and where the relevant data are available. On the other hand, if this procedure is used, care must be taken to ensure that the full costs of increased production from the supplying industry (including capital costs) are included.

An important principle should, however, be borne in mind when considering whether to 'internalise the externalities' in this way. This is that profits which would have been made even if the particular project had not gone ahead should not be included. Thus, for example, if it is reasonable to assume that if one investment had not gone ahead another investment would have been made elsewhere in the economy, then one way or another, multiplier effects would have been created; for that reason it is usual to omit such effects unless there are good grounds for thinking that if that particular investment had not taken place no other investment would have substituted for it. If a factory could have exported its production, but now diverts it to the new project, then it is only the gain in profit to the factory that should be considered, and this could well be small or insignificant.

In order to include indirect effects in project cash flows, they must be quantified, and in some cases this is not a simple matter. The three types of indirect effect are considered below:
- costs (e.g. from pollution) and benefits (e.g. from other uses of facilities provided) that affect others must be converted to money values. This usually involves constructing separate cash flows for the 'before' and 'after' situations for every enterprise affected. The difference between these cash flows is a measure of the indirect effect of the project on each enterprise affected. The main difficulty in practice is to gain access to the relevant data;
- gains or losses of profit in other sectors (caused by linkages or increased competition) can be evaluated in the same way; but before they can be included, care must be taken to ensure that there was no other way by which those gains in profit could have been realised (e.g. by exporting, instead of supplying the new project, or by bringing new land into production instead of reducing production of the crop previously grown); and
- consequential changes in other prices can be valued as the change in price multiplied by the average of the quantity sold at the higher price and the quantity sold at the lower price.

If, however, the indirect effects are far-reaching (such as a general rise in wages, or a project that necessitates a complete reorganisation of the capital spending programmes of the government for the following five years), then appraising the project may well

240

lie outside the scope of project appraisal alone. In such a case, approving the project is essentially the same as committing the government to a medium-term (say five-year) investment plan, and the decision whether to have it or not becomes a political one. A project appraisal that quantifies the direct benefits and costs of the investment can still be carried out, but the indirect effects are too complex to calculate. The same may also be true of a project with few economic costs to the economy, but which may be felt to have high social costs (for example, in 'undermining national culture', or increasing inequality); again the decision as to whether to go ahead is essentially political, although the decision-makers should be made aware of any potential loss of direct profit if they decide not to proceed.

A PRACTICAL PROCEDURE FOR ECONOMIC ANALYSIS

The recommended procedure is summarised in the decision chart reproduced in Figure 1. The notes here amplify what is summarised in the boxes, and give brief explanations of what is happening at each stage in the analysis.

Box 1:   The starting point is financial analysis. This involves the preparation of cash flows for each year of the project's expected life, showing the inflows or outflows for each type of expenditure, including the financing of the project from a combination of loan and equity finance.

Box 2:   From these cash flows, it is possible to calculate the after-tax rate of return to the total capital invested in the project. This will be based on the inflows and outflows for the purchases or sales of goods and services, as well as outflows which must be paid in the form of taxes if the project goes ahead.

Box 3:   It is also possible to calculate the rate of return to the equity-holders. This will be based, on the one hand, on the investment of equity capital in the project and, on the other, on the returns to that capital after tax has been paid and after loans have been repaid (together with any interest on those loans). If the return to the equity-holders is not sufficiently attractive, they will not invest. They may also, at that stage, wish to do some 'sensitivity analysis', to see how the return might vary with changes in some of the project variables; if they expect the project to be risky, then no doubt they would require a higher rate of return from the investment.

Box 4:   If the return is insufficiently attractive to the equity-holders, then it may be possible to reorganise the project to make it more attractive. It may be possible to alter the physical design, in order to reduce the investment cost; or

241

Figure 1: Decision Chart for the Economic Analysis of a Project

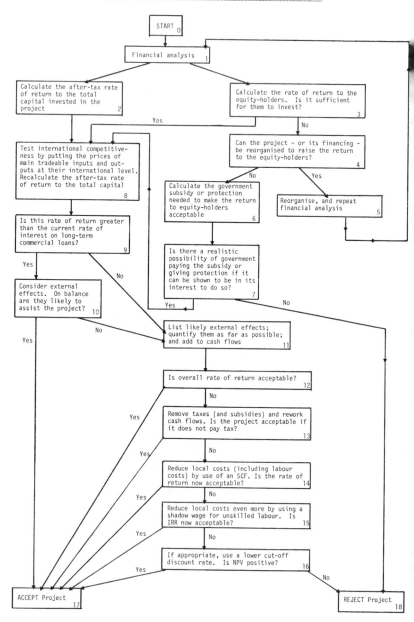

to phase the project, or to establish it more slowly. Alternatively, it may be possible to reorganise the financing of the project. For example, if more of the project can be financed by loan capital, then this may increase the return to the equity-holders.

Box 5: If it is possible to reorganise the project in some way, then it will almost always be necessary to rework the financial analysis, and start the appraisal again from the beginning.

Box 6: If it is not possible to raise the return to the satisfaction of the equity-holders, then the project can only go ahead if the government is prepared to give some sort of assistance. This might take the form of a direct financial susbsidy; or it might involve protection from competition, either in the form of a quota or a tariff on competing imports of the goods or services which the project will produce. At this stage it will be relatively straightforward to compute the order of magnitude of the subsidy needed to keep the project in business.

Box 7: If there is no realistic possibility of the government being prepared to pay such a subsidy (or offer sufficient protection), then the project should be rejected immediately, without the need for further calculation. If, however, the government might be prepared to pay, then the analysis can proceed. The remaining steps will involve preparation of the strongest possible case to the government in order to persuade it to subsidise the project.

Box 8: The first step is to test whether the project is internationally competitive, by revaluing the main inputs and outputs at their international prices. The new rate of return will probably be lower than the rate of return at market prices, but it is not inevitable that this will be so; for example, if there is an export tax on the product the rate of return could rise, as it could if the inputs into the projects had to pay very high duties (e.g. oil or oil products). If for any reason it is not possible to place an international price on an important input or output, then at this stage the local price of that commodity should be left unchanged.

Box 9: It is worthwhile checking if this rate of return is above the rate of interest on long-term commercial loans (if it is not, then the project may not generate sufficient income to pay off borrowed capital plus interest).

Box 10: If the rate of return is acceptable without consideration of any external effects, and if it is likely that on balance any external effects would increase the project's rate of return, then the project can safely be accepted, without further calculation.

Box 11: If, however, the rate of return to the project (with or without consideration of external effects) is below the cost of borrowing, then it is essential to consider external effects in as much detail as possible. As far as can be done with the data available, they need to be quantified and the resulting cash flows added to the cash flows for the project itself. There is no point in quantifying these external effects as market prices; so at this stage the important tradeable inputs and outputs of the external effects need to be put into international prices.

Box 12: If the overall rate of return is now acceptable, then a strong case can be made for the government to support the project, even if it requires subsidy or protection.

Box 13: If it is still not acceptable, all taxation elements are removed. (This is equivalent to asking whether the project would be viable if it did not have to pay tax.) If it is viable in this situation, again there is a good case to make to the government.

Box 14: If, however, it is still not viable, local costs (including unskilled labour costs) can be reduced by using a 'standard conversion factor' (SCF) of less than 1.0 (0.8 is a figure commonly used). This is an alternative to increasing the valuation of net foreign exchange incomes by use of a shadow exchange rate. Textbooks give a variety of formulae for the SCF, but it is probably best to think of it simply as a value judgement: an SCF of 0.8 is the same as a shadow exchange rate of 1.25, and involves a judgement that the official price of foreign exchange undervalues it by about 25 per cent.[19]

Box 15: If the project is still not acceptable, local costs can be reduced still more by using a shadow wage. We do not regard it as realistic to recommend a shadow wage of less than 50 per cent of the market wage, and if the country concerned has a strong commitment to maximising the rate of profit and/or the rate of investment, then even this figure is too low and 80 or 90 per cent of the market wage would be appropriate.[20] If the economy regards investment as more urgent than provision of 'formal' wage employment (for any reason), then it is inappropriate to use a shadow wage, and this step can be omitted.

Box 16: Costs have now been reduced as much as possible, and it remains only to consider whether the resulting rate of return is acceptable. The choice of cut-off discount rate is partly a matter of experience - if only a few projects are found to be acceptable at a commercial rate then it may be necessary to use a lower rate. It is also partly a matter of policy, since lower rates favour the slower-yielding, long-term investments. If the government is committed to long-term structural change, there is a stronger case for using a low cut-off discount rate than if its main strategy is to make profits and rotate its capital as quickly as possible. In any event, it is unlikely that a rate below five per cent would be acceptable to many donors or investors.

Box 17: If the project can be shown to be acceptable after any of the stages set out above, then there is a case in favour of whatever protection or subsidy arrangements are necessary for it to go ahead.

Box 18: If the project sponsors cannot persuade the relevant authorities to give protection or subsidy, or if the project cannot under any circumstances achieve a minimal rate of return, then there is no alternative but to reject it.   .

MISCELLANEOUS ADDITIONAL CONSIDERATIONS

Described above is a procedure for appraising a project. The steps could also be used for comparing different versions of a project, or different means of implementing a project. It will be the case in general that the version that is most profitable at market prices is not the most profitable at shadow prices. It is therefore very important that when preparing projects, or carrying out pre-feasibility studies, versions of the project that might be attractive at shadow prices are not discarded. In particular, labour-intensive technologies, methods using local rather than imported resources, and projects with research and development components, may be rejected if market prices are used, but may have the highest net present values at shadow prices.

Another test is worth considering; that is to check whether the project contributes 'value-added' to the economy. The 'value-added' by a project or an enterprise is the value of the goods it produces less the value of the material inputs used to produce them - i.e. costs less payments to wages, salaries, profits, interest, depreciation and tax. The value added in each year of a project's life can be calculated at box five above, by eliminating all payments to labour (i.e. using a shadow wage of zero). If the 'value-added' proves to be negative, there is no case for accepting the project, since it would be possible to import the manufactured products of the project using less foreign exchange than it would cost to import just the components to make those products. (This is a fairly common situation with automobiles in small economies: it is possible to import assembled vehicles using less foreign exchange than is needed to import just the components for local assembly.)

In practice, a common use of economic analysis is to question

245

or reject projects which appear financially profitable, but where this profitability depends on protection or hidden subsidy. It is to remove such protection that international prices are used.

In using a shadow wage, one is attempting to assess the costs of employing different types of labour in terms of a number of competing objectives (loss of production elsewhere; loss of investible funds; benefits to those employed; additional value to the government if those employed are among the poorest in the country, etc). The value judgements are often hard to make, but it is worth recognising that if a shadow wage for unskilled labour of (say) 80 per cent of the market wage is used, this is equivalent to asserting that the government values employment to the extent that it is prepared, if necessary, to offer an employer a subsidy equal to 20 per cent of his unskilled labour costs, in order to encourage him to use labour-intensive techniques.

The valuation of land can be very complex. It is of course a non-traded good (internationally). But since land used for one purpose cannot be used for another, it is often necessary to consider the indirect effects of using land for a project - e.g. the loss of profits from crops that otherwise would have been grown. Often, however, this calculation will become equivalent to carrying out a completely separate project appraisal for the alternative crop, and comparing two 'mutually exclusive projects' for the different land uses. For non-agricultural projects it may often be sufficient simply to value payments for the use of land at their commercial value, and to treat these along with the other local costs of the project.

There are also situations where it may be necessary to calculate special conversion factors for certain types of expenditure. This may happen if there are reasons for thinking that their local prices are particularly different from the international price equivalents (a possible example is transport, where oil and oil products often pay very high import or excise duties).[21] Sometimes there is no meaningful international price (e.g. for construction activities), in which case individual conversion factors can be calculated; readers who wish to follow this further are referred to the standard textbooks on social cost-benefit analysis.

CONCLUSION

Economic analysis is a means by which a government can decide whether it should accept a project that appears to be profitable financially, or subsidise or protect a project that appears not to be profitable financially. The basic criterion is the profitability of the project at international prices, although this can be modified by use of shadow exchange rates (or conversion factors applied to non-traded goods), shadow wages, and reduced cut-off discount rates. All of these - to say nothing of the basic importance of profitability at international prices - involve value judgements, and imply a consensus among those running the country and those implementing and financing the projects about the relative importance of the various considerations. At the same time, it should not be forgotten that any use of shadow prices implies that the projects chosen will not usually be the most profitable in financial terms at market prices, and that the implementors will therefore require either financial incentives (subsidies or protection) or direct government intervention (refusal of licences for projects that are financially profitable, but not justified according to economic analysis) if they are to implement the projects with the best returns according to their economic analysis.

NOTES

1. UNIDO (1972) (work by Dasgupta, Marglin and Sen). A recent attempt to make this method operational is contained in the work by Hansen, published as UNIDO (1978). This variant of the method has been used by John Weiss to calculate shadow prices for Pakistan, in UNIDO (1980).

2. Little and Mirrlees (1969), revised and improved in Little and Mirrlees (1974), and further adapted in Squire and Van der Tak (1975), and Bruce (1976). The 1972 Symposium (Oxford University Institute of Economics and Statistics (1972)) is still worth reading. Irvin (1978) discusses both the UNIDO and the OECD methods, while preferring the OECD. For a case study using the OECD method, see Scott, MacArthur and Newbery (1976).

3. For example, see J.A. Bottomley's review of Little and Mirrlees' 1974 book in "The Economic Journal", March 1975.

4. Those who wish to promote the 'informal sector' can be excused for wondering whether transferring workers from it to regular wage employment is really such an important objective, given the numbers that will continue to be employed in the 'informal sector'. But there are still those who wish to make regular wage employment an objective, and it could be given an explicit weight (or shadow price) in an appraisal. This is not customarily done, presumably because of the difficulty of putting a money value on this weight (i.e. valuing the benefit of extra employment in money terms). Note that the procedure that is commonly followed (i.e. of using a shadow price of labour based on the marginal product in the likely alternative occupation of those employed) is not the same as putting a money value on additional employment.

5. The argument, put explicitly in Little and Mirrlees (1974), is that, rather than aiming for self-reliance, a country should attempt to maximise the gains from trade. This will involve rejecting uncompetitive import-substitution industries in favour of expanding export-oriented industries, which may generate the foreign exchange to pay for the imports. But most

politicians and their industrialists are reluctant to forego local production on this ground. They do not see resources as a constraint, and would like both to expand their export-oriented industries and substitute for imports. They may also have an understandable distrust of the stability of prices in foreign markets. It is significant that the original book by Little and Mirrlees (1969) was published as part of the same OECD programme which produced the volume by Little, Scitovsky and Scott (1970); the latter advocated policies of removing protection and competing in export markets, and took as its successful models the newly industrialising countries of South East Asia.

6. Mirrlees himself stresses the problems of using income distribution weighting, advocated (among others) by Squire and Van der Tak (1975). In his 1978 paper he concludes that "if one is using a tool designed for a different purpose, one should not expect it to be simple - or safe - to use".

7. Another point of view suggests that what is wanted is not a single figure for each project, but rather a set of figures conveying information, such as the project's contribution to foreign exchange earnings, employment, government revenue, reinvestment, etc., and its capital and recurrent costs (compare the 'effects' method - see Scitovsky (1976) and Cherval and Le Gall (1978)). But an array of figures can be very confusing, and easily lead to special cases being made for particular projects on the grounds of their contribution to one particular variable. For 'accept/reject' decisions, and for project rankings, it seems highly desirable to have a single figure.

8. There are situations in which a transfer from one agent to another (for example a subsidy paid by a government to a company) can satisfy all parties, even if they do not have the same objectives.

9. As stressed, for example, by Amartya Sen (1972).

10. Sen (1972, p.490) makes a slightly different point. He suggests that those who recommend the use of world prices are either extremely powerful (and can impose the necessary trade and investment policies on all parties) or they are extremely stupid (his word) and unwilling to take account of the complexities of the real world situation as it affects individual commodities. He makes a similar point about the shadow price of labour: if, for example, a government could raise savings by increasing taxation, but chooses not to do so, then its shadow pricing should not give additional valuation to savings (ibid., p.494).

11. Most of the writing is not country-specific (for a recent example, take Irvin (1978)). But it does not seem reasonable

that precisely similar procedures should be followed by (say) India and Barbados.

12. Little and Tipping (1972), Anand (1975), Guerrero et al. (1977), Linn (1977), Little and Scott (eds.) (1976).

13. See, for example, Dommen (ed.) (1980) and Selwyn (1978).

14. One should consider competitiveness in the long-run, accepting the infant-industry argument for protection in the short-run (for a careful statement of this see Corden (1980)). On the other hand, even non-competitiveness in the short-run should not be ignored, since it has a cost to the non-competitive economy.

15. One must distinguish between the return to the total sum invested (which may be financed from several sources, including various types of loan) and the return to the equity component (if any) of the project.

16. The calculations can be very complex if indirect effects on the balance of trade are taken into account - for example, the effects on imports of extra money paid as wages. In practice it is usually sufficient to treat the main imported and exported items as 'foreign' and everything else as 'local'.

17. Books and very lengthy papers have been written calculating the shadow wage in different situations. But in the end the decision reduces to a value judgement about the importance of wage employment and the effect of high wages on profits. Almost everyone would agree that the shadow wage should be less than 1.0, and anyone who thinks about the implications should realise that consistent use of a shadow wage of less than 0.5 would involve the government in massive wage subsidies. Moreover, the marginal products calculated have usually been around half the urban 'formal-sector' wage, so this puts a lower bound to the shadow wage. However, for economies taking a long-term view and concerned to maximise investment by any possible means, there is a strong case for not using a shadow wage. (Anyone unconvinced by this reasoning might ask himself why developed countries are so reluctant to use a shadow wage even when they have unemployment; it is surely because they are determined to count the cost of employment and its effect on profits.)

18. If one accepts that governments are as responsible for the children of the present population as they are for that population itself, then there is a case for very low discount rates (more precisely, for discount rates equal to the expected growth rate of the economy). Otherwise it is very hard to justify investment in forestry and heavy industry - or much

agricultural improvement. On the other hand, there is not much to be said in favour of projects which never recover their costs (i.e. with rates of return below zero). But a government with limited investment opportunities, but a long-term view, which measures the costs and benefits of its projects at international prices, can make a case for accepting projects with very low (but positive) rates of return (at international prices). Note that even a zero return will imply a positive return to value-added (since we have not put a zero price to labour.)

19. We suggest a standard conversion factor of 0.8 or 0.7. If, at the official exchange rate, foreign exchange is undervalued by 25 per cent, then the standard conversion factor should be 0.8. If it is undervalued by 50 per cent, the correct figure would be 0.67; but we doubt if such a great undervaluation could last for long. A figure of 0.7 corresponds to an undervaluation of about 40 per cent. Note that these figures will be very sensitive to changes in relative rates of inflation, and to changes in government trade, tariff and exchange rate policy.

20. Note that in box 14 we have already reduced unskilled labour costs by the standard conversion factor (say 0.8). If we now use a shadow wage equivalent to 50 per cent of the market wage, then the total wage adjustment (boxes 14 and 15 together) is equivalent to a shadow wage equivalent to 40 per cent (50 per cent of 0.8) of the market wage.

21. There are, however, also reasons for not using a very low shadow price for oil - for example if the country has a policy of energy conservation, or wishes to use local sources of power (such as hydro-electric, or even nuclear) in preference to fossil fuel.

REFERENCES

Anand, S., 1975, "Appraisal of a Highway Project in Malaysia: Use of the Little-Mirrlees Procedures". In IBRD Staff Working Paper No. 213.

Bottomley, J.A., 1975, review of I. Little and J. Mirrlees "Project Appraisal and Planning for Developing Countries". In "The Economic Journal", Vol. 85, No.1.

Bruce, C., 1976, "Social Cost-Benefit Analysis: A Guide for Country and Project Economists to the Derivation and Application of Economic and Social Accounting Prices". In IBRD Staff Working Paper No. 239.

Cherval, M. and Le Gall, M., 1978, "The Methodology of Planning: Manual of Economic Evaluation of Projects: The Effects Method", Paris: Ministere de la Cooperation.

Corden, W.M., 1980, 'Trade Policies'. In Cody, J., Hughes, H.

and Wall D., eds., "Policies for Industrial Progress in
Developing Countries", Oxford: Oxford University Press.
Dommen, E., ed., 1980, 'Islands'. In "World Development", a
special issue, Vol. 8, No.12.
Guerrero, P., Howard, E., Lal, D. and Powers, T., 1977, "Pilot
Study on National Accounting Parameters: Their
Estimation and Use in Chile, Costa Rica and Jamaica",
Washington, D.C: Inter-American Development Bank.
Hansen, J.R., 1978, "Guide to Practical Project Appraisal:
Social Cost-Benefit Analysis in Developing Countries",
New York: United Nations.
Irvin, G., 1978, "Modern Cost-Benefit Methods: An Introduction to
Financial, Economic and Social Appraisal of Development
Projects", London: Macmillan.
Linn, J.F., 1977, "Economic and Social Analysis of Projects: A
Case Study of Ivory Coast". In IBRD Staff Working Paper
No. 253.
Little, I.M.D. and Mirrlees, J.A., 1969, "Manual of Industrial
Project Analysis in Developing Countries", Volume 2:
"Social Cost-Benefit Analysis", Paris: OECD.
Little, I.M.D. and Mirrlees, J.A., 1974, "Project Appraisal and
Planning for Developing Countries", London: Heinemann.
Little, I.M.D. and Scott, M. Fg., eds., 1976, "Using Shadow
Prices", London: Heinemann.
Little, I.M.D., Scitovsky, T. and Scott, M. Fg., 1970,
"Industry and Trade in Some Developing Countries: A
Comparative Study", Oxford: Oxford University Press.
Little, I.M.D. and Tipping, D., 1972, "A Social Cost-Benefit
Analysis of the Kulai Oil Palm Estate, West Malaysia",
Paris: OECD.
Oxford University Institute of Economics and Statistics, 1972,
'Symposium on the Little-Mirrlees Manual of Industrial
Project Analysis in Developing Countries'. In "Oxford
University Institute of Economics and Statistics
Bulletin", Vol. 34, No.1.
Scott, M. Fg., MacArthur, J.D. and Newbery, D.M.G., 1976,
"Project Appraisal in Practice: the Little-Mirrlees
Method Applied in Kenya", London: Heinemann.
Selwyn, P., 1978, "Small Poor and Remote: Islands at a
Geographical Disadvantage", Brighton: Institute of
Development Studies, Discussion Paper No. 123.
Sen, A.K., 1972, 'Control Areas and Accounting Prices: An
Approach to Economic Evaluation'. In "The Economic
Journal", Vol. 82. Reprinted in Layard, R., ed., 1972,
"Cost-Benefit Analysis", London: Penguin.
Squire, L. and Van der Tak, H., 1975, "Economic Analysis of
Projects", Baltimore: Johns Hopkins University Press.
United Nations Industrial Development Organization, 1972,
"Guidelines for Project Evaluation" ('The UNIDO
Guidelines') (authors Partha Dasgupta, Amartya Sen and
Stephen Marglin), New York: United Nations.

251

14. Regression Analysis of Growth Patterns in Small Economies

Biswajit Banerjee[*]

One of the major interests of development economists has been the study of the patterns of economic development. The development patterns of countries are generally seen as the outcome of the effects of (a) 'universal' factors, such as those related to the level of income, (b) 'general' factors, such as resource endowment and market size, over which the government has little or no control, and (c) government policies. A major objective of research has been to separate the effects of 'universal' factors from those of the other two types. A common method of doing so has been to estimate regression equations utilising data for a number of countries at a particular point in time.[1]

In this paper, I have estimated regression equations to describe variations in the importance of the manufacturing sector, in trade patterns, and in sources of growth among countries with populations in 1978 of five million or less. Data were sought for a sample of forty countries, but the effective sample size varied from one equation to another because countries were dropped from the estimation if data for any of the variables included in the equation were missing.[2]

SHARE OF THE MANUFACTURING SECTOR IN GDP

The 'universal' factors in the regression equations are usually proxied by per capita income. This variable represents the effects of changes in the composition of demand and in factor proportions that are associated with rising income. It is generally assumed that a consistent pattern of change in resource allocation will be produced as the level of per capita income rises. With rising income, demand shifts away from food and other primary products, and relatively more physical capital and skilled manpower become available; hence the share of manufacturing in total output is expected to rise.

The share of manufacturing output is also affected by market size, usually proxied by the population of a country. An increase in market size may permit the exploitation of economies of scale, and may make the substitution of imports by domestic production

*I am grateful to Sanjaya Lall for helpful discussions and for comments on an earlier draft. I am alone responsible for all errors and omissions.

worthwhile. However, economies of scale are not equally important in all branches of manufacturing, and it is not certain how strong their influence will be in small economies.

The effects of 'universal' factors may be offset or supplemented by resource endowment and government policies. In previous studies these two factors have been proxied by trade patterns. Countries endowed with natural resources are likely to turn to manufacturing at a later stage of development as the changing composition of domestic demand can be met more easily by exporting primary products and importing manufactured goods. Countries can overcome the constraint of inadequate domestic demand - represented jointly by income level and market size - on the size of the manufacturing sector if the output can be exported.

In addition to the variables discussed so far, Chenery and Taylor (1968) included the share of gross fixed capital formation in GNP in their regression equations. When domestic savings, skills and technology are constraints, the manufacturing sector can also be promoted by encouraging an inflow of foreign capital. However, the effect of this last variable has not been considered in previous regression analyses.[3]

There is no uniformity in the specification of the regression equations in previous studies. Chenery (1960) estimated a double-log equation in which income and population were the only variables and were entered linearly. Chenery and Taylor (1968) estimated double-log equations with and without the trade and capital formation variables, and income was entered in a quadratic form. Chenery and Syrquin (1975) estimated semi-log equations in which both income and population were entered in quadratic log form.

In this study equations have been estimated with both semi-log and double-log functional forms. For each formation, equations have been estimated with and without the trade and capital formation variables, and income and population have been expressed in linear and quadratic log forms. Such an exercise gives an idea of the sensitivity of the results to alternative specifications. However, tests required to decide which functional form is more suitable have not been carried out.

The regression equations describing the variations in the share of the manufacturing sector in GDP are presented in Table 1 for the semi-log formulation and in Table 2 for the double-log formulation. The estimates in the semi-log formulation contained in columns 1-3 of Table 1 suggest that, for the present sample, income and population ought to be specified in linear rather than in quadratic form. When per capita income and population are the only explanatory variables and are entered in linear form (column 1), both are significant determinants of the share of the manufacturing sector. But when squared terms are added to the equation (columns 2 and 3), not only is there a reduction in $\bar{R}^2$, but also the coefficients of the respective variables cease to be significantly different from zero.

When squared terms in income and population are introduced in the double-log formulation, the behaviour of the coefficients and of $\bar{R}^2$ is somewhat different from that observed for the semi-log formulation. As columns 1-3 of Table 2 show, there is no reduction in $\bar{R}^2$ in the successive specifications, and only population loses its significance when entered in quadratic form. Per capita income remains significant throughout. However, any conclusion on whether the income elasticity of the manufacturing share tends to decline as income rises, as indicated by the statistical significance of the squared income term, is affected by how the population variable is specified. The coefficient for the squared income term is not significantly different from zero when population is entered in linear form (column 2), but becomes significantly different when it is entered in quadratic form (column 3).

The findings on the squared income term, however, appear to be sensitive to sample fluctuations. When the exercise is repeated for a smaller sample of 34 observations, the coefficient for the squared income term is statistically significant irrespective of how the population variable is specified.[4]

The specification for which estimates are presented in column 4 of Tables 1 and 2 contains the same proxies for resource endowment and government policy as those used by Chenery and Taylor (1968). However, in sharp contrast to the results obtained in their study, these two factors do not appear to be important in either functional form in explaining the share of manufacturing among the present sample of countries. The coefficients for the shares of primary exports, manufactured exports and gross domestic investment in GDP are not significantly different from zero.[5]

Column 5 of Tables 1 and 2 contains the estimates of the specification in which foreign investment has been substituted for gross domestic investment in the list of explanatory variables. This variable was measured by the percentage share in GNP of repatriated earnings from direct foreign investment in the reporting country, because this measure is likely to be less erratic than values of actual capital inflows. The coefficient for foreign investment has the predicted positive sign in the double-log formulation but an unexpected negative sign in the semi-log one; however, in neither formulation is it significantly different from zero. The overall fit of this specification is not as good as that obtained when gross domestic investment was included in the equation: $\bar{R}^2$ is lower in column 5 than in column 4 in both Tables.

In one specification (not reported here) the effect of location on the share of manufacturing was examined. Location was represented by three variables: a dummy variable for islands, a dummy variable for land-locked countries, and distance from the nearest OECD country. However, the addition of these variables to the regression equation did not add to its explanatory power. There was a reduction in $\bar{R}^2$ and all three coefficients were not significantly different from zero. Perhaps it would have been better to sub-divide the sample into regional groups and test for differences between them. In the present exercise this would have involved a small number of observations in each group, and the estimates obtained might not have been reliable.

A notable difference between the semi-log and double-log functional forms is that in the presence of trade and capital formation variables (columns 4 and 5 of Tables 1 and 2), the coefficient for population is significant in the latter but not in the former. In the semi-log functional form the best fit is obtained when income and population are the only variables and are entered in linear form (column 1). This specification does not have the highest $\bar{R}^2$ in the double-log formulation. However, given that the trade and capital variables are not significant and that unexpected results are obtained when squared terms are entered in the equation, it can perhaps be claimed that the simple specification in column 1 is also satisfactory for the double-log formulation. How do the estimates of the two functional forms compare? The elasticities are lower in the semi-log formulation than in the double-log one: the income and size elasticities at the mean values implied by the estimated coefficients in the semi-log formulation are 0.37 and 0.17 respectively, compared to 0.40 and 0.23 respectively obtained in the double-log formulation (and shown directly by the coefficients). We cannot discriminate between the two sets of estimates until tests have been carried out on the suitability of alternative functional forms; this is beyond the scope of the present paper. A comparison of R^2 or $\bar{R}^2$ is not adequate for this purpose because the independent variables are explaining different things in the two formulations.[6]

The estimates of income elasticity of the share of the manufacturing sector in GDP obtained in this study are similar to, and the estimates of size elasticity are higher than, those obtained by Chenery and Taylor (1968) for the share of industry in GDP in their sample of countries with populations of 15 million or less. Fifteen of the 35 such countries had a population of less than five million. The income and size elasticities obtained by Chenery and Taylor were 0.37 and 0.05 respectively.[7] Chenery and Taylor, however, obtained a better overall fit of the regression equation. They obtained an R^2 of 0.62 compared to 0.32 obtained in the present study.

VARIATIONS IN TRADE PATTERNS

In the previous section the shares of primary and manufactured exports in GDP were treated as exogenous variables. However, it can be argued that comparative advantage changes as capital and human skills grow with rising income, and this facilitates the growth of manufactured exports. Manufactured exports are, however, likely to fall in importance as the size of the domestic market increases, since output will be diverted away from exports to meet domestic needs.

The regression equation for the double-log formulation, presented in column 3 of Table 3, confirms the hypothesis of a positive relationship between per capita income and the share of manufactured exports in GDP, but does not indicate any tendency for manufactured exports to decline in importance with an increase in population. The coefficient for population is not significantly different from zero. The income elasticity of manufactured exports in GDP is close to unity.

In the regression equation presented in column 4 of Table 3 an attempt has been made to accommodate the effects of foreign capital inflow and government trade policy. The latter variable was proxied by taxes on international trade and transactions as a percentage of total current revenue. Although the share depends on both the tax rate and the volume of trade, a lower share can crudely be interpreted as evidence of a liberal trade policy and a negative relationship postulated between this variable and manufactured exports. However, neither of the two variables appears to have any significant effect on the importance of manufactured exports, and their presence reduces the value of $\bar{R}^2$.

In the semi-log formulation (columns 1 and 2 of Table 3), the R^2 for the first specification is significant at the five per cent level but none of the explanatory variables is significant. This result is in sharp contrast to the pattern observed in the previous section: there it was found that, in the simplest specification, variables which were significant in the double-log formulation were also significant in the semi-log one.

An equation (not reported in Table 3) was also estimated to explain the share of primary exports in GDP. It is noteworthy that in both functional forms the coefficients for per capita income and population - the only explanatory variables included in the equation - and the overall fit of the equation indicated by R^2 were not significant even at the ten per cent level.

SOURCES OF GROWTH

The mean value of the average rate of growth of GDP experienced by the countries in the sample during the period 1970-77 was 4.2 per cent. At the one extreme was Jamaica which experienced no growth at all, and at the other was Malta which recorded an average annual growth of 11.4 per cent. A regression equation was estimated to identify the important determinants of growth. A similar exercise has been carried out by Blazic-Metzner and Hughes[8] (referred to as BH hereafter), but their study differs from this one in three respects:

(i) In the equation in the present study, the rates of growth of GDP and the explanatory variables (except for the secondary school enrolment ratio) are for the period 1970-77. The growth rates in the BH study are for 1965-78.

(ii) The proxies for the development of human resources and the inflow of foreign capital have been measured differently, and the list of explanatory variables in the present study does not include the growth of gross domestic savings. In this study the increase in the secondary school enrolment ratio (as measured by the difference between the ratio in 1977, or most recent estimate, and in 1960, or the nearest year thereto) has been included as a proxy for the development of human resources, instead of the level of the adult literacy rate as used by BH. Also, in this study one variable has been used to represent the foreign capital inflow while

BH use three.

(iii) The sample size in the present study is smaller than that used by BH. Because of missing variables, the regression equation was based on observations for 32 countries. BH's equation for countries with populations of five million or less is based on 39 observations, and six of the countries in their sample (viz. Bahrain, Cape Verde, Guinea-Bissau, Sao Tome and Principe, Israel and Libya) do not appear in the present study.

The regression estimates for the growth of GDP are presented in Table 4. They confirm the findings of BH that the growth of exports was closely associated with the rate of economic growth of small countries, that inflation has a significant negative relationship with the growth of GDP, and that growth of manufacturing and population growth are not significant, though their coefficients have the expected signs. The findings on the growth of agriculture, development of human resources, and inflow of foreign capital, however, differ from those obtained by BH. In the estimated equation in the present study, the coefficient for the growth of agriculture is significant at the one per cent level. Indeed, it ranked second to the growth of exports in the explanation of the variance in growth of GDP[9]. As might be expected, the coefficient for the increase in the secondary school enrolment ratio is positive and significant at the five per cent level. In the BH equation, their proxy for the development of human resources was not statistically significant and had the 'wrong' sign.

A surprising finding of the present study is that foreign investment has a significant negative relationship with the growth of GDP. This perhaps suggests that slowly growing countries are also beginning to receive foreign investment. It is interesting to note that though the three foreign capital inflow variables in the BH study were not significant, two of them also had negative signs.

Most of the differences in the findings between the two studies can probably be attributed to the differences in the reference period and in the sample size.

CONCLUSIONS

This paper has described the variations in the share of the manufacturing sector in GDP, in trade patterns and in sources of growth for a sample of countries with populations in 1978 of five million or less by estimating regression equations. The principal findings are as follows:

(i) Per capita income and population are important determinants of the share of the manufacturing sector in GDP, but factors such as resource endowment and location, which are specific to individual countries, are not. This lends support to the hypothesis that there is a similar pattern of change in the structure of production as development takes place, and indicates that economies of scale are important even in small countries.

(ii) The composition of exports shifts towards manufactured

goods as incomes rise. Per capita income is the only significant variable in explaining variations in the share of manufactured exports in GDP.

(iii) The growth of exports and of agriculture are the two most important variables in the explanation of the variations in the growth of GDP. The rate of growth of GDP is related positively to an increase in the secondary school enrolment ratio and negatively to the rate of inflation. Surprisingly, there is a negative relationship between the growth of GDP and that of foreign investment, and the influence of the growth of manufacturing is not significant.

The results obtained in the regression equations are, however, sensitive to the choice of the functional form of the equation, to the form in which the explanatory variables are specified and to sample fluctuations. This should lead to caution in making generalisations about growth patterns from cross-country evidence. A large number of small countries which were eligible for inclusion in the sample had to be excluded because of missing variables. It is quite possible that their inclusion would have altered the size and significance of the coefficients for the explanatory variables.

NOTES

1. See, for example, Chenery (1960), Chenery and Taylor (1968), Chenery and Syrquin (1975).

2. The countries in the sample were: Barbados, Belize, Benin, Botswana, Burundi, Central African Republic, Chad, Congo, Costa Rica, Cyprus, El Salvador, Fiji, Gabon, The Gambia, Guinea, Guyana, Haiti, Honduras, Hong Kong, Jamaica, Jordan, Lesotho, Liberia, Malta, Mauritania, Mauritius, Nicaragua, Niger, Panama, Papua New Guinea, Paraguay, Rwanda, Sierra Leone, Singapore, Somalia, Surinam, Swaziland, Togo, Trinidad and Tobago and Uruguay.

3. Chenery and Syrquin (1975) included 'net resource inflow' as an explanatory variable in their equation. This variable represents the joint effects of exports, imports, savings and investment.

4. The estimates presented in columns 4 and 5 of Tables 1 and 2 are based on 34 observations. Observations for Belize, Burundi, Guinea, Hong Kong, Lesotho and Liberia had to be dropped because information on the export variables was missing. The regression equation based on 34 observations for the double-log specification in column 2 of Table 2 is:

$$-9.3631 + 2.6825 \text{ PCGNP} - 0.1784 \text{ (PCGNP)}^2 + 0.2855 \text{ POP}$$
$$(4.1217)** \quad (1.2352)** \qquad (0.0947)*** \qquad (0.1077)**$$

$$R^2 = 0.3717, \quad \bar{R}^2 = 0.3089, \quad F = 5.9162*$$

where PCGNP is the per capita GNP and POP is the population.

5. The coefficient for manufactured exports just fails to be significant at the ten per cent level in both the functional forms.

6. See Goldberger (1964), p.217.

7. See Chenery and Taylor (1968), equation C for industry in Table 3, p.396.

8. See paper by Blazic-Metzner and Hughes in this volume.

9. This is indicated by the beta coefficients which are not reported here. (Beta coefficients are the regression coefficients when the variables are defined in terms of standard deviation units.)

REFERENCES

Chenery, H.B., 1960, 'Patterns of Industrial Growth.' In "American Economic Review", Vol. 50, No. 4.
_____ and Syrquin, M., 1975, "Patterns of Development, 1950-1970", London: Oxford University Press.
_____ and Taylor, L., 1968, 'Development Patterns: Among Countries and Over Time'. In "The Review of Economics and Statistics," Vol. 50, No. 4.
Goldberger, A.S., 1964, "Econometric Theory", New York: John Wiley & Sons, Inc.
The World Bank, 1980, "World Development Report", Washington, D.C.
_____, 1980, "World Tables", Washington, D.C.
United Nations Conference on Trade and Development, 1979, "Handbook of International Trade and Development Statistics", New York: United Nations.

TABLE 1

REGRESSION RESULTS OF THE SEMI-LOG FORMULATION: MANUFACTURING OUTPUT
(DEPENDENT VARIABLE: SHARE OF MANUFACTURED OUTPUT IN GDP)

Independent Variables	Coefficients (1)	Coefficients (2)	Coefficients (3)	Coefficients (4)	Coefficients (5)
Constant	-35.2170 (13.4377)**	-84.0684 (51.3154)	-51.2626 (64.8390)	-16.1457 (18.4867)	-26.3987 (17.4524)
GNP per Capita a/	4.9081 (1.1071)*	19.6630 (14.9988)	22.3860 (15.4128)	4.1263 (1.5261)**	3.5831 (1.5182)
(GNP per Capita)^2	..	-1.1281 (1.1436)	-1.3232 (1.1721)	..	..
Population b/	2.2520 (1.1463)***	2.4767 (1.1691)**	-9.8509 (14.8329)	2.3382 1.4134	2.4930 (1.5759)
(Population)^2	..	..	0.8835 (1.0597)	..	..
Primary Exports c/	..	..	..	-0.8415 (1.6489)	-0.9798 (1.8411)
Manufactured Exports d/	..	..	..	1.1526 (0.6940)	1.1295 (0.7242)
Gross Domestic Investment e/	..	..	..	-4.1714 (3.2081)	..
Foreign Investment f/	..	..	..	..	-0.0299 (0.9366)
R^2	0.3471	0.3643	0.3767	0.4004	0.3642
$\bar{R}^2$	0.3118	0.3113	0.3054	0.2933	0.2506
F	9.8347*	6.8760*	5.2871*	3.7387*	3.2073**
N	40	40	40	34	34

.. Not included in the particular equation.

Notes: Standard errors are given in parentheses.
* Significant at the 1 per cent level. ** Significant at the 5 per cent level.
*** Significant at the 10 per cent level.

For sources see the following page.

Definitions and Sources:

a/ GNP per capita figures used are at market prices and in US dollars. The reference period is 1978 in most cases and 1977 in some cases (World Bank, 1980).

b/ Population figures are in thousands and are for the year 1978 (World Bank, 1980).

c/ Primary exports as a per cent of GDP in 1977 or 1978. This was calculated as follows: ((100 - percentage share of manufactured goods in total merchandise exports) x merchandise share of exports of goods and services, in per cent x total exports as a per cent of GDP) divided by 10,000 (World Bank, 1980 and UNCTAD, 1979).

d/ Manufactured exports as a per cent of GDP in 1977 or 1978. This was calculated as follows: (total exports as a per cent of GDP x percentage share of manufactured exports in total merchandise exports x merchandise share of exports of goods and services, in per cent) divided by 10,000 (World Bank, 1980 and UNCTAD, 1979).

e/ Gross domestic investment as a percentage of GDP, during the period 1970-77 (World Bank, 1980).

f/ Direct foreign investment income (in 1977 or most recent estimate) as a percentage of GNP. Direct foreign investment income is a debit item in the balance of payments table and consists largely of repatriated earnings from direct foreign investment in the reporting country. When running the regressions the negative sign was omitted (UNCTAD, 1979).

g/ Taxes on international trade and transactions as a percentage of total current revenue in 1977 (World Bank, 1980 and UNCTAD, 1979).

TABLE 2

REGRESSION RESULTS OF THE DOUBLE-LOG FORMULATION: MANUFACTURING OUTPUT
(DEPENDENT VARIABLE: SHARE OF MANUFACTURED OUTPUT IN GDP)

Independent Variables	Coefficients (1)	Coefficients (2)	Coefficients (3)	Coefficients (4)	Coefficients (5)
Constant	-1.9168 (1.1790)	-8.4325 (4.4219)	-4.1699 (5.5161)	-0.8587 (1.4248)	-1.5618 (1.3307)
GNP per Capita a/	0.4042 (0.0971)*	2.3721 (1.2925)***	2.7259 (1.3112)**	0.3280 (0.1176)*	0.2966 (0.1158)**
(GNP per Capita)^2	..	-0.1505 (0.0985)	-0.1758 (0.0997)***	..	..
Population b/	0.2321 (0.1006)**	0.2621 (0.1007)**	-1.3397 (1.2619)	0.2809 (0.1089)**	0.3030 (0.1202)**
(Population)^2	..	..	0.1148 (0.0902)	..	..
Primary Exports c/	..	..	..	-0.0489 (0.1271)	-0.0721 (0.1404)
Manufactured Exports d/	..	..	..	0.0892 (0.0535)	0.0853 (0.0552)
Gross Domestic Investment e/	..	..	..	-0.2611 (0.2473)	..
Foreign Investment f/	..	..	..	..	0.0169 (0.0714)
R^2	0.3029	0.3622	0.3905	0.4135	0.3914
$\bar{R}^2$	0.2842	0.3091	0.3208	0.3088	0.2827
F	8.7424*	6.8150*	5.6048*	3.9482*	3.6009**
N	40	40	40	34	34

.. Not included in the particular equation.

Notes: Standard errors are given in parentheses.
For definitions and sources, see Table 1.
* Significant at the 1 per cent level. ** Significant at the 5 per cent
level. *** Significant at the 10 per cent level.

TABLE 3

REGRESSION RESULTS: DETERMINANTS OF MANUFACTURED EXPORTS
(DEPENDENT VARIABLE: SHARE OF MANUFACTURED EXPORTS IN GDP)

Independent Variables	Semi-Log Formulation		Double-Log Formulation	
	Coefficients (1)	Coefficients (2)	Coefficients (3)	Coefficients (4)
Constant	25.4600 (38.5486)	16.4483 (75.2085)	-5.1199 (4.9409)	-8.8296 (9.3838)
GNP per Capita a/	2.9296 (2.9789)	3.3660 (4.8017)	0.9818 (0.3821)**	1.1684 (0.5991)***
Population b/	-4.7473 (3.2787)	-3.2405 (4.4878)	-0.0247 (0.4174)	0.2429 (0.5599)
Foreign Investment f/	..	2.6366 (2.3750)	..	0.5121 (0.2963)
Taxes g/	..	-1.1014 (6.3092)	..	0.1561 (0.7872)
R^2	0.1765	0.2439	0.2443	0.2605
$\bar{R}^2$	0.1223	0.1277	0.1956	0.1468
F	3.3215**	2.0978	5.0122**	2.2901***
N	34	31	34	31

..   Not included in the particular equation.

Notes: Standard errors are given in parentheses.
For definitions and sources, see Table 1.
* Significant at the 1 per cent level. ** Significant at the 5 per cent level. *** Significant at 10 per cent level.

TABLE 4

REGRESSION RESULTS: DETERMINANTS OF GROWTH
(DEPENDENT VARIABLE: GROWTH OF GDP)

Independent Variables	Coefficients
Constant	3.0937 (1.2731)**
Growth of Exports	0.2417 (0.0430)*
Foreign Investment	-0.0106 (0.0055)***
Growth of Manufacturing	0.1228 (0.0756)
Growth of Agriculture	0.3662 (0.0720)*
Increase in Consumer Price Index	-0.0794 (0.0255)*
Increase in Secondary School Enrolment Ratio	0.0451 (0.0215)**
Growth of Population	-0.3918 (0.4290)
Area	0.00002 (0.00008)
R^2	0.8737
$\bar{R}^2$	0.8298
F	19.8920*
N	32

..   Not included in the particular equation.

Notes: Standard errors are given in parentheses.
 * Significant at the 1 per cent level. ** Significant
 at the 5 per cent level. *** Significant at the 10 per
 cent level.

Sources: The basic data are from the World Bank (1980) and
 UNCTAD (1979).

Participants at the
Conference on Small Economies

Marlborough House, London,
2-5 June 1981

Mr. Alister McIntyre (Chairman),
Acting Deputy Secretary-General, UNCTAD, Geneva.

Prof. Esra Bennathan, Professor of Political Economy,
University of Bristol.

Prof. Amit Bhaduri, Professor of Economics,
Jawaharlal Nehru University, New Delhi.

Mr. Edward Dommen, Special Programme for Least Developed, Land-
locked and Island Developing Countries, UNCTAD, Geneva.

Prof. David Edwards, Director,
Project Planning Centre for Developing Countries, University of
Bradford.

Prof. Maxwell J. Fry, Professor of Economics,
University of California, Irvine, U.S.A.

Mr. S.M. Funna, Lecturer in Economics,
University of Sierra Leone, Freetown.

Prof. Gerry Helleiner, Professor of Economics,
University of Toronto, Canada.

Ms. Helen Hughes, Director, Economic Analysis and Projections
Department, The World Bank, Washington, D.C.

Mr. Tony Hughes, Permanent Secretary,
Ministry of Finance, Solomon Islands.

Dr. Sanjaya Lall, Senior Research Officer,
Institute of Economics and Statistics, University of Oxford.

Dr. Vaughan Lewis, Visiting Fellow,
Yale University, New Haven, U.S.A.

266

Prof. Peter Lloyd, Professorial Fellow,
The Research School of Pacific Studies,
The Australian National University, Canberra.

Mr. Kenneth Matambo, Director of Economic Affairs,
Ministry of Finance and Development Planning, Botswana.

Mr. F.A.R. Mullings, Director, Economics and Programming
Department, Caribbean Development Bank, Barbados.

Mr. John Samy, Director of Economic Planning,
Suva, Fiji.

Mr. Percy Selwyn, Fellow,
Institute of Development Studies, University of Sussex.

Prof. Amartya Sen, Drummond Professor of Political Economy,
University of Oxford.

Prof. R.M. Sundrum, Professorial Fellow,
The Research School of Pacific Studies,
The Australian National University, Canberra.

Prof. M.L. Treadgold, Professor of Economics,
University of New England, Armidale, Australia.

Dr. Paul Chen-Young, Consultant,
Kingston, Jamaica.

Commonwealth Secretariat

Mr. C.J. Small, Deputy Secretary-General.
Dr. Bimal Jalan, Director, Economic Affairs.
Dr. B. Persaud, Assistant Director, Economic Affairs.
Mr. Q.S. Siddiqi, Assistant Director, Economic Affairs.
Mr. I.R. Thomas, Chief Economics Officer.
Mr. D.I. Huntley, Chief Economics Officer.
Dr. M.V.D.J. Karunasekera, Senior Economics Officer.

Index

271

272